DATE DUE

DEMCO 38-296

William Schuman

William Schuman. Photo courtesy of the Library of Congress with the permission of Anthony W. Schuman.

William Schuman

A Bio-Bibliography

K. GARY ADAMS

Bio-Bibliographies in Music, Number 67
Donald L. Hixon, *Series Adviser*

Greenwood Press
Westport, Connecticut • London

Library of Congress Cataloging-in-Publication Data

Adams, K. Gary.
    William Schuman : a bio-bibliography / K. Gary Adams.
        p.   cm.—(Bio-bibliographies in music, ISSN 0742–6968 ; no.
67)
    Includes bibliographical references (p.   ) and indexes.
    Discography
    ISBN 0–313–27359–6 (alk. paper)
    1. Schuman, William, 1910—Bibliography.   2. Schuman, William,
1910—Discography.   I. Title.   II. Series.
    ML134.S3986A33   1998
    780'.92—dc21   98–13564
    [b]   MN

British Library Cataloguing in Publication Data is available.

Library of Congress Catalog Card Number: 98–13564
ISBN: 0–313–27359–6
ISSN: 0742–6968

First published in 1998

Greenwood Press, 88 Post Road West, Westport, CT 06881
An imprint of Greenwood Publishing Group, Inc.

Printed in the United States of America

The paper used in this book complies with the
Permanent Paper Standard issued by the National
Information Standards Organization (Z39.48–1984).

10 9 8 7 6 5 4 3 2 1

Contents

Acknowledgments

As is always the case, the preparation of a volume such as this requires assistance from a great many persons. I should like to thank the library staffs of the following institutions for their valuable help: The Library of Congress, The New York Public Library at Lincoln Center, The Juilliard School, University of Virginia, University of North Texas, and Rice University. Special thanks is reserved for the librarians at Bridgewater College, particularly to Thelma Hall, who, without fail, pursued my interlibrary loan requests cheerfully and professionally, and to Audrey Moats, who was extremely helpful in locating certain bibliographical information. Substantial computer assistance was provided by Aaron Klein and Karen Anderson of the Bridgewater College Computing Center and by Cami Aleshevich, a Bridgewater College student.

Several other individuals contributed greatly to the completion of this work. I should like to thank three of my colleagues at Bridgewater College for their help: Edward W. Huffstetler, Jeffrey H. Pierson, and, most especially, Philip F. O'Mara, who diligently read the entire manuscript and offered several helpful suggestions throughout the evolution of the project. Karl F. Miller, the director of the Historic Recordings Collection at the University of Texas at Austin, deserves special mention. His knowledge of Schuman was invaluable in the compilation of the discography and the works and performances list. I am greatly indebted to Tony Schuman and Andrea Schuman for their valuable suggestions regarding the biography. My gratitude also goes to Don Hixon, series adviser, and to Marilyn Brownstein, Alicia Merritt, and Pamela St. Clair of Greenwood Press, for their advice and, above all, their great patience with me as I prepared this volume for publication. I should also like to express sincere thanks to Bridgewater College for a sabbatical in the spring of 1991, which allowed me to begin my research for this book.

Finally, I should like to offer my greatest thanks to Bob Evans for his generous computer help, and to my wife, Mary Kay, for her expertise in proofreading and indexing, as well as for their support and encouragement throughout this entire project.

Preface

William Howard Schuman has, for over fifty years, been recognized as one of the most celebrated figures in twentieth-century music. His multifarious career, in which he successfully combined the occupations of composer, educator, and arts administrator, is unparalleled. The music of Schuman has been the object of extensive study, research, and performance since the late 1930s and early 1940s, when opinions about his compositions were made public by such eminent writers and musicians as Leonard Bernstein, Aaron Copland, Paul Rosenfeld, and Nathan Broder. In 1954, Flora Rheta Schreiber and Vincent Persichetti published their landmark monograph, still recognized as a seminal contribution to Schuman literature. My purpose in compiling this volume is to present a brief introduction to the composer's life and career and to provide a guide to the breadth and quality of writing about Schuman published through 1994. It is my hope that this bio-bibliography will prove to be a useful research tool for further investigation of the composer: a reexamination of Schuman's works is called for; a reassessment of his contribution to modern American culture, especially related to his guidance of the Juilliard School and Lincoln Center, is long overdue; and the definitive biography of the composer is yet to be written.

This book is divided into five main sections: Biography, Works and Performances, Discography, Bibliography, and Bibliography of Writings by Schuman. Section I, Biography, traces Schuman's life and career, with a decided emphasis on providing a record of the composer's compositional activity. Section II, Works and Performances, presents a chronological catalog (organized alphabetically within each year) of the composer's works, each preceded by the mnemonic "W." The following information, when known, is included with the title: date of composition, publisher, duration, performers, movements, and, if appropriate, authors of texts. I have also supplied facts about the premiere performance of most compositions and, for the more significant works, added a listing of other selected performances. Section III, Discography, contains an alphabetical listing organized by composition of commercial recordings of Schuman's music, each preceded by the mnemonic "D." Each entry is then listed, in chronological order if the date is known, by recording label and number and gives the performers, conductor, and, when possible, selections by other composers on the recording. Though the compilation of any discography is fraught with problems, I have attempted to present a clear and accurate catalog of Schuman recordings, whether or not currently available. Section IV, Bibliography, is an annotated bibliography, subdivided into three parts, each arranged alphabetically by author: Part I, Bibliographies,

Catalogs, and Discographies; Part II, Biographical Studies, General Stylistic Studies, and General References to Schuman; and Part III, Works, divides Schuman's compositions into seven categories by genre. Each citation is preceded by the mnemonic "B." Section V, Writings by Schuman, contains an annotated bibliography of writings by William Schuman in chronological order. Each entry is preceded by the mnemonic "S." The book concludes with an author index, an index of compositions, and a general index of proper names.

Since the literature about Schuman is vast, the bibliography that comprises the heart of this volume is selective rather than comprehensive. While I have attempted to include the most significant literature about Schuman issued in scholarly books, articles, and dissertations, I have also found it necessary to consider selected newspaper articles and representative concert and recording reviews. Additionally, brief notices and announcements from several sources determined to be helpful in documenting Schuman's career have been included. Articles and reviews from *The New York Times* are particularly important since that newspaper provides a complete chronicle of Schuman's activities from his days as a young composer to his death in 1992. With some notable exceptions, encyclopedia and dictionary articles, record jacket notes, reviews of books, and writings of a popular or introductory character have been excluded. One article, Alfred W. Cochran's review of *Dances* (*Notes*, June 1989), was inadvertently omitted from the bibliography, and two dissertations, both completed at Indiana University, were discovered too late for inclusion in the bibliography: Stephen Dombek's 1994 D.Mus. dissertation entitled *A Critical Assessment of Selected Symphonies of William Schuman for the Conductor* and Julie Schnepel's 1995 Ph.D. dissertation entitled *The Critical Pursuit of the Great American Symphony, 1893-1950*.

I have personally perused, with some few exceptions, all of the items contained in the bibliography. For a few unpublished dissertations not available through interlibrary loan, annotations were based on abstracts located in *Dissertation Abstracts International*. Some items that I was not able to examine personally are listed without annotation if they seemed appropriate for this research guide.

William Schuman

Biography

THE EARLY YEARS: 1910-1935

William Howard Schuman, one of America's most distinguished composers, was born in New York City on 4 August 1910. His parents, Samuel and Rachel Schuman, named their son in honor of William Howard Taft, then president of the United States. The Schumans were of German descent, tracing their family ancestors back to Munich and to a small village near Eisenach. Samuel Schuman anglicized the family surname from Schuhmann to Schuman.

From all accounts, William Schuman enjoyed a typical middle-class upbringing during his formative years in New York. Music making was a favorite entertainment in the Schuman household, a focus which, no doubt, played a strategic role in the future composer's outlook on music during his school days and beyond. Bill, as he was known to his family, even studied violin privately with Blanche Schwarz, although he did not prove to be an assiduous student of the instrument. However, Schreiber, one of Schuman's biographers, recounts a recital at Wurlitzer Auditorium when "Bill, now fourteen, played MacDowell's *To a Wild Rose* and a Serenade by Pierné. . . . He also was one of a quartet playing Handel's Largo" (Schreiber and Persichetti 3. See: B328). She goes on to mention a concert the following year when Schuman performed several compositions at Chickering Hall.

Schuman commenced his formal education at Manhattan's P.S. 165, although he was later identified as a gifted student and, as a result, was moved to Speyer Experimental Junior High School for Boys. At Speyer he demonstrated an exceptional fascination with drama, even to the point of writing and producing his own play, *College Chums*. During the summer of 1925 between junior and senior high school, Schuman received a stipend from the French government to spend his vacation in France. Upon returning to the United States, he matriculated at New York City's George Washington High School, where he soon organized a jazz band known as "Billy Schuman and his Alamo Society Orchestra." Schuman later recalled: "I sang with the band and played in it —and also acted as business manager. We played at weddings, bar mitzvahs, proms, and were really quite successful. . . . During the summers, at camp, I wrote musical shows and songs. Several of the songs were even published" (qtd. in Keats, "William Schuman" 69. See: B199). All of those popular songs were written in collaboration with Edward B. Marks, Jr. Subsequently, Schuman would compose popular songs set to the lyrics of other writers, most notably Frank Loesser.

In his youth Schuman's summers, other than the summer vacation in France, were spent at Maine's Camp Cobbossee, where he was an enthusiastic participant in the camp's programs, especially in his favorite sport, baseball. Camp Cobbossee was also the site of his maiden musical composition, the tango entitled *Fate*, written by the young tyro at the age of sixteen (Rouse, *Documentary* 2. See: B39). Schreiber reports that one of Schuman's noteworthy successes at camp was the production of his musical comedy *It's Up to Pa*, a collaboration with Marks, which was the source of two published songs.

Following graduation from George Washington High School, Schuman enrolled in the School of Commerce at New York University in February of 1928. A business career seemed preferable at this point in his life. Pragmatic experience in the business world was gained while he was a student through a part-time position at the Paramount Advertising Agency (Rouse, *Documentary* 2. See: B39). During this time, however, music, particularly the popular music of New York's Tin Pan Alley, continued to engage his attention. This preoccupation reached its apogee with approximately forty songs composed in collaboration with Frank Loesser.

At the age of nineteen, Schuman, on the evening of 4 April 1930, experienced an event which transformed his life. Urged by his sister to accompany her to a concert at Carnegie Hall, he heard an orchestral concert for the first time. Arturo Toscanini led the New York Philharmonic Orchestra in a performance of Zoltán Kodály's *Summer Evening*, Richard Wagner's "Funeral Music" from *Götterdämmerung*, and Robert Schumann's Third Symphony (*Rhenish*). "It was not the music *per se* that affected him most profoundly; it was the combined visual and aural stimulus of a large orchestra and the incredible variety of colors and nuances such a body of men could create" (Rouse, *Documentary* 4. See: B39).

Inspired by what he had heard, Schuman made the decision to leave New York University the day after the concert in order to pursue a career in music. He later remembered the events of that day as follows:

> 'I've got to be a musician,' I thought. 'My life has to be in music.' All those sounds were still going 'round and 'round in my head. As I passed 78th Street and West End Avenue, I noticed a sign on a private house: Malkin Conservatory of Music. I walked in and said: 'I want to be a composer. What should I do?' The woman at the desk said promptly: 'Take harmony lessons.' So I signed up to study harmony with Max Persin (qtd. in Keats, "William Schuman" 69. See: B199).

Schuman's introduction to and subsequent study with Persin proved to be a propitious experience for the young beginner. Indeed, Persin's rather unorthodox approach to the study of harmony may have subliminally laid the groundwork for Schuman's later formulation of the Literature and Materials of Music curriculum, for Persin was one of those rare teachers who preferred the study of musical scores over textbook exercises. Schuman's intense and lengthy sessions with Persin were enhanced by Schuman's immersion in New York's concert life.

By 1931 he had enrolled for counterpoint lessons under Charles Haubiel, a knowledgeable though pedantic teacher. Remarkably, at the end of his year of study with Haubiel, Schuman was composing contrapuntal exercises employing up to fourteen voices (Schreiber and Persichetti 9. See: B328). Other musical study by the composer during the early thirties involved summer study (1932 and 1933) at the Juilliard School with Bernard

Wagenaar and Adolf Schmid; study in Europe at Salzburg's Mozarteum in 1935, where he studied conducting; and receiving his bachelor's degree in music education at Columbia University Teachers College, which he completed in 1935 after only two academic years. Two years later, in 1937, he finished his master's degree at Columbia.

THE SARAH LAWRENCE YEARS: 1935-1945

The decade from 1935 to 1945 was pivotal in Schuman's career. Not only did he assume his first professional teaching position in music at Sarah Lawrence College, but he also studied with the older composer who became his mentor, Roy Harris; received the attention of several musicians and writers such as Elliott Carter, Leonard Bernstein, Paul Rosenfeld, Alfred Frankenstein, and Nathan Broder; was awarded several prestigious awards, such as the Pulitzer Prize, a Guggenheim Fellowship, and the New York Music Critics Circle Award; achieved success with many new compositions; and, perhaps most significant of all, married Frances Prince on 27 March 1936. Mrs. Schuman, who was herself an active proponent of the arts, supported her husband in all his endeavors. Their two children, Anthony William and Andrea Frances, were born in 1943 and 1949 respectively.

When Schuman graduated from Columbia in 1935, he, characteristically, had already initiated a search for a college teaching position. He perused innumerable college catalogs in the hope of finding an institution which matched his own innovative concepts of education, concepts which had been doubtless shaped by Schuman's experience at Columbia with, in his opinion, traditional and outmoded educational techniques. Attracted to the statement of purpose published in the catalog of Sarah Lawrence College, he inquired there about the possibility of an appointment for the following fall, and, though at first unsuccessful, his persistence was rewarded after a few months. According to Schreiber and Persichetti, because of his first interview with the president of Sarah Lawrence, Schuman was recommended for a music post at the Brooklyn Ethical Culture School. In informing the young musician of his failure to win the job, the school's principal told him, "Male teachers are not good for a school of this kind. The children try to imitate the man's voice and sing an octave lower" (qtd. in Schreiber and Persichetti 12. See: B328). Then, shortly after this interview, Schuman was offered and accepted a position on the faculty of Sarah Lawrence College at Bronxville, New York.

The summer of 1935 was an eventful one for the new college graduate. He spent those months in Salzburg, Austria, where he studied conducting and came into contact with such luminaries in the world of music as Felix Weingartner, Bruno Walter, and Arturo Toscanini. In addition, his First Symphony, scored for chamber orchestra, was taking shape during those months in Europe.

After returning to the United States in September, Schuman began his fruitful ten-year association with Sarah Lawrence College, employment which provided the foundation for most of his innovative ideas about music education, eventually culminating in the Literature and Materials of Music curriculum implemented by Schuman at the Juilliard School. Many years later he recalled the following about his teaching at Sarah Lawrence in an interview with Sheila Keats:

I was asked to give a course in the performing arts, although we didn't use the term then. How do you bring people to the arts? How do you teach them? Start right with the materials. The first assignment I gave in music was: listen to ten hours of music before next week's class, and try to hear at least twenty pieces. The idea was to plunge right in, get the sounds in their heads ("William Schuman" 70. See: B199).

Over the entire span of his career as a music educator and administrator, Schuman wrote copiously about his own theories of music education. Perhaps the most important early article by the composer on this subject was published in 1938 in the journal *Modern Music*. Entitled "Unconventional Case History," Schuman traces the progress of a Sarah Lawrence student involved in a nontraditional approach to the study of music composition. He relates the fundamental concepts of his unorthodox approach as follows:

The study of composition is by nature a highly integrated one. Here the procedures followed were in exact opposition to the conventional set-up, where one takes up first theory, then harmony, counterpoint, orchestration and finally composition. This development proceeded on all fronts as the need for the material arose. . . . The result of such a complete, integrated picture of composition is a clear understanding of the possibilities which the art holds for the individual student. The language of music no longer remains a mystery; it can be mastered like any other. What she may eventually say in this medium will be determined by the quality of her whole personality (227. See: S2).

Although Schuman had composed his first work, other than juvenilia, in 1932, the *Potpourri* for orchestra (which was never published and was later withdrawn by the composer), the Sarah Lawrence years marked the rise of the young college professor as a noteworthy American composer. However, his initial efforts were not particularly successful. In 1932-33 he finished the *Chorale Canons* and in 1934 brought several chamber works (which he later withdrew) to fruition: the *Two Pastorales*, the *Canon and Fugue*, and the *Choreographic Poem*. After completing his First Symphony in 1935, he entered it into the competition for the Bearns Prize at Columbia University in 1936, an award he had been denied a year earlier with his *Chorale Canons*. Failing to win the prize for a second time and discouraged by the negative assessment of the work offered by Daniel Gregory Mason, the distinguished chairman of Columbia's music department, Schuman decided to pursue further study with a composer whom he greatly admired, Roy Harris.

In the summer of 1936 Schuman enrolled in three of Harris's courses at the Juilliard School. Beginning in the following fall, he regularly traveled for lessons to Harris's home at Princeton, New Jersey, where Harris taught at Westminster Choir College. For two years, from 1936 to 1938, Schuman honed his compositional skills under the guidance of the older composer.

Through Harris, Schuman became interested in early music, in medieval modes. In his own works Harris had applied the principles of this early music and he now explained the principles to Schuman. In Harris's early works Schuman heard sounds he had never before heard in music and the influence was strong. So, too, was the influence of Harris's ideas on polyharmony (Schreiber and Persichetti 15. See: B328).

Schuman, with Harris accompanying him, eventually heard a performance of his symphony presented on 21 October 1936 under the auspices of the Composers Forum Laboratory of the Works Progress Administration. At that concert the Gotham Symphony Orchestra under Jules Werner offered a lackluster rendition of the symphony. Two other compositions by the composer were presented that evening, the *Chorale Canons* and the First String Quartet. Schuman soon withdrew both the symphony and the string quartet.

1937 was a productive year in composition for Schuman, a year which saw the completion of the *Prelude and Fugue* for Orchestra, the Second String Quartet, the Second Symphony, and two choral works, *Pioneers* and the *Choral Etude*. However, none of these works received performances until the next year. 1938 proved to be a year in which Schuman was to garner a great deal of recognition as a composer.

Schuman's Second Symphony brought Schuman to the attention of another young composer who was to remain his advocate and friend for life, Aaron Copland. Copland had served as a judge for the composition contest sponsored by the Musicians Committee to aid Spanish Democracy. Schuman's symphony won the first prize and, according to the notice which appeared in the 17 April 1938 *New York Times* ("Notes of Musicians" section 10, p. 6. See: B267), was to receive both a performance and publication, neither of which occurred. However, two performances of the symphony soon followed. The premiere performance of the work occurred on 25 May 1938 when it was played by the WPA Greenwich Village Orchestra under the baton of Edgar Schenkman. Almost immediately the symphony received another reading by the CBS Orchestra, conducted by Howard Barlow. According to Schreiber, Aaron Copland was present at both concerts.

Meanwhile, *Pioneers*, which received its premiere performance on 23 May 1938 by the Westminster Festival Chorus conducted by Henry Switten, further enhanced Copland's opinion of Schuman. Writing in the May-June 1938 publication of *Modern Music*, Copland, in reviewing the newly published edition of *Pioneers* by J&W Chester, prophesied that "Schuman is, so far as I am concerned, the musical find of the year. There is nothing puny or miniature about this young man's talent. If he fails he will fail on a grand scale. . . . From the testimony of this piece alone, it seems to me that Schuman is a composer who is going places" ("Scores and Records" 245-46. See: B751).

Schuman's first big break came when Copland brought the symphony to the attention of Serge Koussevitzky, the eminent conductor of the Boston Symphony Orchestra. Koussevitzky scheduled the symphony for a Boston concert in February of 1939. Except for the review by the music critic of the *Boston Transcript*, Moses Smith (who wrote that "The young composer clearly knew what he wanted to say and how to say it. Furthermore—and this is more obviously a matter of opinion—what he had to say was worth saying" [qtd. in Pettis, "WPA" 110] See: B282), the response to the composition was generally negative. Over forty years later, Schuman recalled: "When my Second Symphony was played in Boston, it was practically hissed off the stage—not because it was avant-garde but because it wasn't terribly good; it didn't really know how to make its points" (qtd. in Hitchcock, "All-American" 14. See: B173). Despite the generally negative reception in Boston, the symphony drew favorable responses from two men who would do much to promote Schuman's career: the young Harvard musician Leonard Bernstein and the esteemed music critic Paul Rosenfeld. Bernstein, reporting on American compositions played by Koussevitzky and the Boston Symphony, observed in the journal *Modern Music* that the work "was for the most part a joy to hear. A first impression is one of formidable structure, direct, clear, unified, and innocent of padding" ("Boston" 183. See: B428). The *Musical Quarterly* article written by Paul Rosenfeld clearly helped to establish Schuman as a major American composer, if only because the review linked Schuman with Copland and Harris. In discussing the Second Symphony, the *Prologue* for orchestra and chorus, and the Second String Quartet, Rosenfeld noted that the middle movement of the quartet "is a piece of beautifully sustained song pervaded by a sensuousness not invariably to be found in modern music," and declared the Second Symphony to be music of "energy and grandeur" ("Copland-Harris-Schuman" 380. See: B631). By the summer of 1939 the Second Symphony had also received a hearing on CBS Radio. A review of that broadcast was published in *Modern Music* by Goddard Lieberson, who remarked, "There is much to be said for the work of . . . William Schuman, though his Symphony is not my conception of a composition in that form" ("Over the Air" 67. See: B568). Lieberson then goes on to speculate that Schuman probably borrowed certain stylistic elements from the music of Roy Harris and to criticize the composition's "lack of development and breadth" (67. See: B568). Also in 1939 Schuman composed the *Quartettino for Four Bassoons*, the aforementioned *Prologue* for chorus and orchestra, the *American Festival Overture*, a revision of *Prelude* for women's chorus, and, in December, the Third String Quartet. The premiere at Carnegie Hall of the *Prologue*, presented by the Federal Symphony Orchestra of New York and conducted by Alexander Richter, was highly praised by Nicolas Slonimsky. His *New York Times* review the following day declared that "Mr. Schuman is forging to the front among native composers of the day" ("Composers' Forum" 20. See: B780).

It was a performance of the *American Festival Overture* on 6 October 1939 by Koussevitzky and the Boston Symphony Orchestra that marked Schuman's greatest success to that time. Written for one of Koussevitzky's Festival of American Music concerts and completed with the approval of Roy Harris, who, according to Schreiber, had actually convinced the conductor to program the work for the festival, the overture was, for the most part, a triumph. After the concert, Koussevitzky offered Schuman the following advice, telling him, "Now you must begin to hate Roy Harris" (qtd. in Schreiber and Persichetti 19. See: B328). Subsequent concerts in New York of the overture by Koussevitzky and the Boston Symphony were also well received. For these New York performances Schuman had revised the ending of the work. Elliott Carter, reviewing these concerts in *Modern Music*, proclaimed that the overture "has vitality and conviction behind it" and concluded that "Schuman's gift is undeniable, though so far his musical material has shown a tendency to be slight" ("New York Scene" 96. See: B451). Much has been written about this watershed piece and its impact upon the composer's career and compositions. Karl Miller has correctly observed that "The extroverted optimism of the *American Festival Overture* set the tone for much of Schuman's work" ("Schuman at 75" 30. See: B246).

The 10 November 1939 edition of *The New York Times* published an article which revealed that Schuman had received a commission from Town Hall and the League of Composers to compose a work, either for a chamber group or a solo performer, for a subsequent recital at Town Hall. The distinguished panel making the selection of Schuman consisted of Aaron Copland, Mrs. Theodore Steinway, Olga Samaroff, Leopold Stokowski, and Randall Thompson. When Schuman delivered his Third String Quartet, which received its promised performance at Town Hall on 27 February 1940, success was again Schuman's.

After the Third String Quartet Schuman completed the secular cantata *This Is Our Time*. Alexander Smallens led the combined forces of the People's Philharmonic Choral Society and the New York Philharmonic Orchestra in a grand Independence Day concert at Lewisohn Stadium on 4 July. The most reliable description of this work was provided by the composer himself in a 30 June 1940 *New York Times* article written in anticipation of the impending performance of the cantata. Schuman, in the conclusion of the article, seems to have embraced *Gebrauchsmusik*, when he wrote:

> the composers whose music is performed by our leading symphonic organizations must devote a portion of their energies to music for amateurs. This music must be in addition to, not at the expense of, other works. Furthermore the composer writing for

the amateur must make his compromise in technical matters and never in the emotional or intellectual validity of his offering ("Amateurs and Pros" section 9, p. 5. See: S6).

By the beginning of 1941 Schuman had completed his Third Symphony, a work now acknowledged by many musicians and scholars as a masterpiece. After a triumphant performance by Koussevitzky and the Boston Symphony Orchestra in the fall of that year on 17 October, the New York premiere followed almost immediately; acclaim for the work was widespread. The eminent music critic Olin Downes referred to the symphony as "brilliant and audacious" ("Mr. Schuman's Third" See: B479). Leonard Bernstein was inspired to write: "Almost as exciting as hearing the music itself is to observe how Schuman's progress is manifested in the *Third Symphony*—a progress alive, radiant, optimistic. It is, in fact, all one piece—his development and his music—a pattern of health and youth, and work, and hope" ("Young American" 99. See: B429). Further recognition came to the composer when the Third Symphony won the first Music Critics Circle Award. Now established as a major figure in American music, Schuman's confidence as a composer resulted in a steady flow of works from his pen over the next five decades. H. Wiley Hitchcock has written of the Third Symphony: "This is *positive* music, music that never wheedles, that asserts rather than implies, that lets you know where it stands, that says, 'Take me or leave me'" ("All-American" 15. See: B173).

Even before the first performance of the Third Symphony Schuman finished work on his Fourth Symphony in August of 1941. On 22 January 1942 the Fourth Symphony was first played by the Cleveland Orchestra conducted by Artur Rodzinski. Shortly thereafter the symphony was presented in Philadelphia and New York by Eugene Ormandy and the Philadelphia Orchestra. Unfortunately, the critical reception was far less enthusiastic than for the composer's previous symphony. Both Olin Downes and Virgil Thompson wrote uncomplimentary reviews. Christopher Rouse, in his important *William Schuman Documentary*, has observed that the Fourth Symphony "lacked the monolithic monumentality and heroic grandeur—not to mention the fascinating structural cohesiveness—of its predecessor, and it remains to this day less popular" (10. See: B39). By the end of 1941 Schuman had created his first score for band, *Newsreel*, completed on 16 November.

Four compositions occupied Schuman in 1942, though only one of them was performed in that year. *Requiescat*, for women's chorus, was premiered in April by the Sarah Lawrence College chorus with the composer conducting. Another choral setting, the *Holiday Song*, was completed in May and received its first performance by Robert Shaw the following January. Schuman's next project was the revision of the Concerto for Piano and Orchestra, which, though finished in July of 1942, did not have its premiere until 13 January 1943 by Rosalyn Tureck and the Saidenberg Sinfonietta on an all-Schuman concert. On 16 October 1942 Schuman concluded work on another composition destined to further enhance his reputation as a composer. His cantata for chorus and orchestra, *A Free Song*, was awarded the first Pulitzer Prize for music and had its premiere the following March in Boston. That performance was directed by Koussevitzky, who conducted the combined forces of the Harvard Glee Club, the Radcliffe Choral Society, and the Boston Symphony Orchestra.

Moved by the events of World War II, Schuman's first opus of the following year was *Prayer 1943*, which was later renamed *Prayer in Time of War* by the composer. The debut of this inspirational war composition was given by Fritz Reiner and the Pittsburgh Symphony Orchestra on 13 February 1943. By June Schuman had brought to fruition his first solo piano piece, *Three-Score Set*, dedicated to Carl Engel in honor of his sixtieth birthday. Late in the year Schuman finished the *William Billings Overture*, which, though ultimately withdrawn by the composer, was later reworked into the *New England Triptych* in the mid 1950s.

During this year Schuman, still only in his early thirties, attained yet another huge success with the *Symphony for Strings* (Symphony No. 5), a work Rouse believes "did the most to solidify Schuman's acceptance" (*Documentary* 10. See: B39). The result of a commission awarded by the Koussevitzky Music Foundation, the symphony was first heard on a 12 November 1943 concert played by the Boston Symphony with Koussevitzky conducting. The review published in the *Boston Herald* stated that Schuman was "well on his way to becoming the foremost American composer of the day" (qtd. in Schreiber and Persichetti 21. See: B328). Several other performances soon followed the Boston premiere. "As taut and concise as the Symphony No. 3 is expansive and majestic, the Fifth Symphony remains one of Schuman's most popular works, representing at its best his early dynamically affirmative style" (Rouse, *Documentary* 10. See: B39).

Early in 1944 Schuman completed the score for the film "Steeltown," composed for the Office of War Information. In the same month, February, he finished his contribution to the *Variations on a Theme by Eugene Goossens*, which received its first performance in April of the following year with Goossens conducting the Cincinnati Symphony Orchestra. His next work, *Side Show*, written in collaboration with Billy Rose for Rose's Broadway revue "The Seven Lively Arts," was completed in July, but, unfortunately, it was never staged as intended. However, Schuman revised the score for orchestra and gave it a new name, *Circus Overture*. By August, Schuman had produced two more pieces, the song *Orpheus With His Lute* and an a cappella setting of *Te Deum*, which were originally intended to be part of the incidental music to Shakespeare's *Henry VIII*, but the dramatic production was never staged.

The only composition written by the composer during his final year at Sarah Lawrence was the ballet *Undertow*, finished on 22 February 1945. Commissioned by the choreographer Antony Tudor, the premiere performance occurred in April of that year in New York City and another presentation of the work in Los Angeles soon followed in the fall. Without question, this initial stage work marked a new direction for the composer. Writing in 1974, Sheila Keats described *Undertow* as a score "full of tension: rhythms here produce apprehension, climaxes are sharp and brutal, and the short, contrasting sections appear in stark succession, often without benefit of transition" ("William Schuman" 72. See: B199). Christopher Rouse's assessment written six years later is even more perceptive:

> But many in the audience were equally unprepared for the expansion and expressivity—the darkness and tragedy of the new score. Tudor's portrait of depravity and violence called forth a more brooding language from the composer, and if the compositions that preceded the ballet might be termed 'affirmative,' the scores that succeed *Undertow* might well be called 'expressionistic' (*Documentary* 12. See: B39).

As Schuman's decade of teaching at Sarah Lawrence College was coming to a close, two articles appeared which seemed to solidify his position as a major American composer. The most scholarly examination of Schuman's music up to 1945 was published by Nathan Broder in the January 1945 issue of *The Musical Quarterly*. Broder's essay concluded with the statement that Schuman "must already be considered worthy of a high place in the ranks of contemporary composers" ("William Schuman" 26. See: B63). Only a month earlier, in December of 1944, Alfred Frankenstein's article on Schuman in *Modern Music* commenced with the following memorable pronouncement: "The evidence is accumulating on all sides and the conclusion is inevitable: William Schuman has caught the boat" ("American Composers" 23. See: B139).

Since 1938, Schuman had enjoyed a productive association with the publishing firm of G. Schirmer, largely through the friendship of its director of publication, Carl Engel. After Engel's death on 6 May 1944, Schuman, who had received a strong recommendation from Koussevitzky, was offered the position as director of publication and immediately accepted. Because he was obligated to Sarah Lawrence until June of 1945, he arranged to work at Schirmer in his spare time while continuing to fulfill his final year's contract with the college. Schuman formally assumed his new position on 1 June 1945; however, exactly two months later, it was made public that he had been persuaded to leave his post at G. Schirmer to become the new director of the Juilliard School of Music. Yet even after going to Juilliard, Schuman maintained an association with G. Schirmer as publications adviser, a relationship which was not dissolved until the end of 1951.

THE JUILLIARD YEARS: 1945-1962

On 1 October 1945 Schuman succeeded Ernest Hutcheson as the president of the Juilliard School of Music in New York City. The appointment, which was confirmed by an election of the Juilliard board of directors on July 31, was announced the following day by *The New York Times* ("Schuman to Head" 15. See: B346). Reaction to the announcement of Juilliard's new president was generally favorable, though it was considered remarkable for such a young man to assume such a prestigious position. *Newsweek*, in an August 13 article entitled "Maestro in Play Clothes," printed the following description: "Unlike his distinguished and dignified predecessors, John Erskine and Ernest Hutcheson, he is addicted to loud sports jackets and other Esquire-ish attire. . . . He is both infectiously enthusiastic and practical, a type usually not associated with the austerity of academic music" (100. See: B235).

Shortly after beginning his new post, Schuman launched plans to revitalize the school. By the following January, he divulged his intention to merge the separate Juilliard Graduate School and the Institute of Musical Art into the new Juilliard School of Music ("Single Unit" 19. See: B197). At the same time Schuman filled key administrative positions at the newly unified institution. Norman Lloyd, a colleague of Schuman's from Sarah Lawrence, was named to the staff in charge of student activities; Mark Schubart, an employee of *The New York Times*, was selected to supervise public activities; and George Wedge, who had been the Institute of Musical Art's dean, was chosen for a position in the administration and to be the director of the summer session. Announced, too, at this time, were the appointments of several outstanding musicians to the faculty, among them Robert Shaw and William Bergsma (19. See: B197). In May of that year Schuman disclosed the formation of a resident string quartet, which would promote quartet literature through virtuoso performances, serve student composers in performances of their compositions, and coach chamber music groups ("Adds 28" 17. See: B194). In addition, this May announcement revealed the hiring of twenty-eight new faculty and staff members, including such prominent performers as the pianist Beveridge Webster, the violinist Joseph Fuchs, the cellist Leonard Rose, and the violist Milton Katims; the conductor Thor Johnson to direct the orchestra; and Edgar Schenkman as head of the opera department.

One year later, on 13 May 1947, *The New York Times* printed an article which proclaimed Schuman's intention to eliminate Juilliard's tradition-laden theory department and replace it with a new concept in music education to be known as the "Literature and Materials of Music" ("Literature" 30. See: B196). Without question, the Literature and Materials of Music program was one of the most important changes made by Schuman at Juilliard. Indeed, this innovative renovation of Juilliard's curriculum by Schuman has had a wide-ranging effect on music education as a whole and must be considered one of the composer's greatest accomplishments. Schuman's idea, in general, was to replace the compartmentalized approach to music theory with one in which the music itself would serve as the basis for a comprehensive system. Also reported in this article were the appointments of several distinguished composers to teach the Literature and Materials of Music curriculum: Vincent Persichetti, Robert Goeb, Robert Ward, Peter Mennin, and Richard Franko Goldman. Six years later, in his trenchant introduction to *The Juilliard Report on Teaching the Literature and Materials of Music*, Schuman traced the history of the Literature and Materials of Music program at Juilliard, revealed that his teaching experience at Sarah Lawrence prompted him to question conventional teaching techniques, recalled that this new curriculum was formulated in collaboration with Norman Lloyd, and described the organization of the program (7-24. See: S24). In an earlier article published in *The Musical Quarterly*, Schuman thoroughly explained the premise of the newly implemented music curriculum:

> It is our belief that the primary goal of education in music theory is to achieve a meaningful transfer of theoretical knowledge into practical performance. This premise granted, it must follow that conventional courses in music theory have been far from successful. . . . You will, perhaps, also agree that most of our professional musicians who have been trained in 'systems' of harmony are rather ill-informed about the compositional techniques of the music they perform. It is obvious that there must be an understanding of the composer's art if music is to be performed, in terms of the technical and esthetic demands of its style. Gifted performers often understand these matters in more or less intuitive fashion, if they have not learned from teachers or from their own study. But this cannot be said of the average professional musician ("On Teaching" 156. See: S16).

Though too numerous to discuss here, several other substantial developments at Juilliard occurred during Schuman's tenure. Among the most important were the revitalization of the opera department, the creation of the Division of Dance, the implementation of the Bachelor of Science degree, and the promotion of contemporary music.

The responsibilities of heading The Juilliard School did not impede Schuman's activities as a composer. *Truth Shall Deliver*, the first work completed by the composer after moving to Juilliard, was an a cappella choral work for male voices, which received its premiere performance by the Yale Glee Club on 7 December 1946. By the spring of 1947, Schuman had finished the first of his three ballets written in collaboration with Martha Graham. *Night Journey*, a watershed score which was first performed at Harvard University in May for that university's Symposium on Music Criticism, was commissioned by the Elizabeth Sprague Coolidge Foundation. Described as a "somber score" (Hall, "Bio-Discography" 18. See: B21) and as a composition in which "the new Schuman burst forth fully" (Rouse, *Documentary* 15. See: B39), *Night Journey* remains a masterpiece in twentieth-century American ballet literature. Upon the request of Samuel Dushkin, the eminent violinist, Schuman wrote a violin concerto that, though completed in its original version in July of 1947, did not attain its final form until 1959. The 1947 score was first presented by Isaac Stern and the Boston Symphony Orchestra nearly three years later on 10 February 1950. Six years later, on 26 February 1956, Stern performed the second version of the score. The final version received its initial performance on 9 August 1959 at the Aspen Music Festival, with violinist Roman Totenberg.

Schuman's highest achievement as a symphonist was accomplished during the late forties. On 14 May 1948, *The New York Times* published a brief announcement that William Schuman had been awarded a one thousand dollar commission by the Dallas Symphony Society to compose a composition for the Dallas Symphony Orchestra ("Dallas Award" 28. See: B331). Schuman fulfilled his commission by writing his Sixth Symphony, a work regarded by many as his masterpiece. Completed on 31 December 1948, this one-movement symphony was premiered by Antal Dorati and the Dallas Symphony Orchestra on 27 February 1949. Two years later, at a public rehearsal the day before the first New York performance, the conductor, Eugene Ormandy, "told the audience that the new score was 'one of the most wonderful and difficult' he had ever played" (qtd. in Persichetti, "Philadelphia" See: B604). David Hall has remarked:

> In terms of stylistic range, extremes of dynamics and color, contrapuntal and rhythmic virtuosity, and general demands made on the executant capacities of the orchestra, there is nothing quite like this work in the annals of mainstream American symphonism. . . . The dramatic impact of the piece can be described only as shattering ("Bio-Discography" 2: 18. See: B21).

Following close on the heels of the Sixth Symphony, Schuman finished his second ballet for Martha Graham late in the summer of 1949. Billed as a choreographic poem for orchestra, *Judith* was given its premiere performance by the Louisville Orchestra on 4 January 1950, with Robert Whitney conducting. Received enthusiastically, the ballet was soon presented to receptive audiences in New York City as well. A review of the Louisville performance maintained:

> *Judith* was the first dance ever commissioned by a symphony orchestra for presentation on a concert program, and Mr. Schuman's score was the first ever commissioned for such a work. The music is not as frenzied as that of *Night Journey*, but it is perhaps even more potent dramatically. It is music in blacks and greys, music of understatement and tremendous restrained power (Sabin, "Martha Graham" 67. See: B821).

William Bergsma, in a review of the 1950 study score published by G. Schirmer, wrote, "With such works as *Judith* . . . William Schuman has entered a new perspective. . . . *Judith* stands among the best scores of today" ("Review" 564. See: B795). However, Hans Redlich, reviewing the work only two months later, was less enamored with Schuman's ballet, contending that the composition "is too self-assured and thematically too little distinguished to capture the imagination of the more sophisticated listener" ("Review" 241. See: B819). Richard Franko Goldman, though, proclaimed that "*Judith* has the virtues of Schuman at his best. The obvious fact about Schuman is that he is a big composer, vehement, self-confident, and emphatically positive. He is, in a sense, a musical Walt Whitman" ("Current Chronicle" 258. See: B801). *Judith* won a New York Music Critics Circle Award in the category of dance for works presented in New York during the 1950 and 1951 seasons ("Circle Award" 23. See: B371).

As Schuman neared the end of his first five years at Juilliard, he composed his engaging score for band, *George Washington Bridge*, a work which, among others by the composer, "could never have been conceived by anyone but an American" (Hitchcock, "All-American" 15. See: B173). But the most substantial piece produced by Schuman in 1950 was the Fourth String Quartet, which surely stands among the composer's most distinguished works in the area of chamber music. Written to celebrate the 150th anniversary of the Library of Congress, this piece was sponsored by the Elizabeth Sprague Coolidge Foundation and received its premiere performance at the Library of Congress in October. The oft-quoted evaluation of the quartet by Aaron Copland published in the July 1951 *Musical Quarterly* bears repeating here: "A composition like the Fourth String Quartet makes one understand why Schuman is generally ranked among the top men in American music. . . . This is music written with true urgency: compact in form, ingenious in its instrumental technique, quite experimental as to harmony" ("Current Chronicle" 394. See: B716). Three years later, Vincent Persichetti wrote: "String Quartet No. 4 is mature Schuman, exciting, fresh, and ingenious. It is a landmark both in his musical development and in contemporary chamber literature. This is Schuman of a wider harmonic palette and unfailing urgency" ("Modern American" 474. See: B735).

From 1951 until 1953 Schuman labored to complete his first opera, *The Mighty Casey*. Set to a libretto by Jeremy Gury, this music drama, despite the composer's love of baseball, has proven to be one of his least successful compositions. Opening to modest success in Hartford, Connecticut, at the Hartt College of Music on 4 May 1953, one reviewer argued that "despite some clever scoring and a few interesting harmonic and rhythmic ideas *The Mighty Casey* never really came to life until the game—and the opera —were nearly over" (RePass, "New American Opera" 227. See: B836). Perhaps the high-water mark for this opera was reached when it was produced on the television show "Omnibus." Soon after finishing *The Mighty Casey* Schuman composed his first major work for solo piano, *Voyage*. Though intended as a cycle of five pieces, *Voyage* actually received its initial performance on 17 May 1953 in a version for chamber orchestra and choreography arranged for Martha Graham. The original piano score was first played by Lillian Steuber three months later on 18 August at a Sigma Alpha Iota concert in Chicago. In 1972, the composer prepared yet a third version of *Voyage* for the Eastman Philharmonic Orchestra.

During the mid-1950s Schuman created two of his most successful orchestral works: *Credendum* and *New England Triptych*. The genesis of *Credendum* was unprecedented—the first musical composition to be commissioned by a governmental agency, the State Department's U.S. National Committee for UNESCO. When the fifth National Conference of the agency was held in Cincinnati, Thor Johnson led the Cincinnati Symphony Orchestra in a concert on 4 November 1955 that presented *Credendum* for the first time. New York City first heard *Credendum* on 13 March, presented by Eugene Ormandy and the Philadelphia Orchestra. Writing for *The Musical Times* soon after these performances, Denis Stevens offered the following evaluation: "The signs of weakness often inherent in a commissioned work are reassuringly absent here. It is as if Schuman had warmed spontaneously to his task, creating a deeply felt work of original cast and powerful design" ("Notes" 268. See: B674). However, not all opinions of *Credendum* have been positive. Peter Davis decried in 1964 that "William Schuman's 'Credendum' is perhaps the worst piece of music I have ever heard" ("New York Philharmonic" 31. See: B467).

Perhaps *New England Triptych* ranks as the composer's most popular and accessible work. Like *Credendum*, *New England Triptych* was initially heard in a venue other than New York. André Kostelanetz, who commissioned the work, conducted the Miami University Symphony in the premiere on 28 October 1956; the first New York performance came less than two weeks later, on 8 November, at a concert of the New York Philharmonic.

The origin of *New England Triptych* actually dates back to the *William Billings Overture* of 1943, a composition in which Schuman used three hymn tunes by the eighteenth-century American composer: "Be Glad Then, America"; "When Jesus Wept"; and "Chester." Dissatisfied with the overture, Schuman subsequently revamped the work into the multi-movement *New England Triptych*. With the publication of the revision, the composer withdrew the earlier Billings-inspired composition. Due to the enormous popularity of *New England Triptych*, Schuman later made arrangements of each of the movements for concert band. In a 1958 review of the orchestral score published by Merion Music, Robert Sabin submitted an apt comparison of the two composers, concluding that "Like Billings, Schuman is a bold thinker . . . he keeps the salt and sting of life itself in his art"("Tribute to Billings" 212. See: B637).

It was also during this period that Schuman composed two smaller works: "The Lord Has a Child," a solo song set to a text by Langston Hughes, and *Four Rounds on Famous Words*, an unaccompanied choral piece. Thirteen years later the composer added an additional movement to the original four rounds.

Christopher Rouse effectively argues that 1958 must be considered a turning point in Schuman's stylistic evolution as a composer, referring to the scores produced by the composer in 1958 and after as "rhetorical."

> These more recent scores, which I call 'rhetorical' in the best sense of the word, are more stoic, almost ritualized in their sense of tragedy. I say 'tragedy' rather than 'gloom' because Schuman's music, however serious, is never morbid; his music speaks more of resignation than of surrender . . . but now the language is more dissonant still than in an earlier piece such as the Third Symphony, and the grandeur is more often tempered by a contemplation of other concerns ("Schuman and His Generation" 74. See: B312).

Though two compositions, *Three Piano Moods* and *Carols of Death* for a cappella chorus, date from this year, it is the latter work, set to texts by Walt Whitman, which clearly signals the inception of Schuman's new style. The three *Carols of Death* are generally regarded as the finest of the composer's choral works.

After a hiatus of a dozen years from the writing of a symphony, Schuman opened the decade of the 1960s with his Seventh Symphony, which was composed to celebrate the seventy-fifth anniversary of the Boston Symphony Orchestra on a commission from the Koussevitzky Music Foundation of the Library of Congress. The premiere of this symphony was given by the Boston Symphony Orchestra under Charles Munch on 21 October 1960. Approximately a month later, the Boston Symphony presented the work at Carnegie Hall. Material extracted from two of Schuman's earlier compositions was incorporated into the new symphony: the second movement of *Three Piano Moods* and music from the documentary film *The Earth is Born*. The review, which appeared in the *Musical Courier* a little more than a month after the first performance of the work, depicted the score as follows: "The music is both lean and lusty, altogether 'American' in its dynamism and brass component. But Schuman clearly understands that volume must serve rhetoric, and he handles his forces convincingly" (Frias, "Boston Symphony" 27. See: B507). Winthrop Sargeant's review of the first New York performance was far less enthusiastic:

> Nobody, as far as I could make out, approached the other night's performance expecting it to slake a deep thirst for emotional experience, and nobody left the hall with his heart aflame or with his brain set tingling by intellectual stimulation. The

new symphony, like many of its kind, was not so much a work of art as what is nowadays called a status symbol ("The Inside Track" 231. See: B642).

In 1961, Schuman wrote only a single composition, the very beautiful Fantasy for Cello and Orchestra entitled *A Song of Orpheus*. Based on the composer's song with the same title of 1944 composed as incidental music for a production of Shakespeare's *Henry VIII*, this score was commissioned for the cellist Leonard Rose by the Ford Foundation. The premiere performance took place on 17 February 1962 in Indianapolis, with Leonard Rose and the Indianapolis Symphony Orchestra under the direction of Izler Solomon. An account of the concert noted, "The audience . . . warmly welcomed the impressive inaugural given the score . . . critical response matched audience reception" (Gwiasda, "Indianapolis" 27. See: B516).

Meanwhile, in New York, a press release dated 13 September 1961 announced the election of the composer to the presidency of the Lincoln Center for the Performing Arts, effective 1 January 1962 ("Elected President" 3-4. See: B401). *The New York Times* observed, "The development is a healthy one for our cultural life" (" Lincoln Center" 44. See: B349). Part of Schuman's letter to Juilliard's faculty advising them of his decision envisioned the following: "I believe that the Center can provide leadership in bringing large numbers of Americans to a new interest in music, drama and the dance . . . Lincoln Center can be and must be a dynamic constructive force" ("Elected President" 4. See: B401).

Ten days after the public announcement of Schuman's new position, the Juilliard School published its intention to honor the composer with the title of President Emeritus at the end of the year ("New Title" 17. See: B260). In December the Juilliard faculty made public its decision to donate an endowed seat in Schuman's name at Lincoln Center's new Juilliard Theater ("Faculty Honors Schuman" 3. See: B131).

THE LINCOLN CENTER YEARS: 1962-1968

When Schuman assumed the presidency of Lincoln Center at the beginning of 1962, he immediately encountered, in his usual energetic and optimistic manner, a plethora of difficulties associated with the developing arts center. The physical plant itself was still in the planning stages except for Philharmonic Hall, which was then under construction. The Lincoln Center for the Performing Arts officially opened nine months later on 23 September 1962, when Leonard Bernstein conducted the New York Philharmonic Orchestra in an inaugural concert at Philharmonic Hall (later renamed Avery Fisher Hall). Also presented during the Center's first official week were a series of programs, some of which included works commissioned for the festivities by Aaron Copland, Walter Piston, and Samuel Barber. Henry Cowell, Vincent Persichetti, and Virgil Thomson were charged with composing new works for the dedication, scheduled the same week, of the new organ in Philharmonic Hall; however, due to delays in completing the instrument, this recital was postponed until December. Within a few weeks of the initial performances in the new auditorium a controversy arose concerning the quality of the hall's acoustics. Schuman countered rumors about the acoustics by reporting that the conductors associated with the opening concerts were questioned about the hall's acoustics, and he indicated that, though the opinions of the conductors were mixed, any acoustical problems would be corrected (Ericson, "Philharmonic Hall Acoustics" 46. See: B113).

Controversy also surrounded the negotiations between Lincoln Center and City Center. An agreement between the two institutions was reached on 28 March 1963 when the Lincoln Center confirmed that the New York City Ballet would appear in the New·York State Theatre for several weeks during the seasons of 1964-65 and 1965-66 (Palatsky, "Center Situation" 36. See: B274). Eventually both the New York City Ballet and the New York City Opera became constituent members of Lincoln Center. The Metropolitan Opera was one of the original institutions associated with the Center.

From the outset, Schuman, who had negotiated that Juilliard would be a member of the Center as early as 1957, had expressed tremendous interest in having Lincoln Center take an active and prominent role in arts education. One of his first decisions was to hire his former colleague Mark Schubart, then dean at Juilliard, to direct the Center's education program. *The New York Times* article that reported Schubart's appointment of 13 June 1962 made reference to his role in making the arts available to public school children through the Lincoln Center Student Program organization (Gelb, "Mark Schubart" 25. See: B148). One of the significant components of the education arm planned by Schuman was the Teachers Institute. Schuman first disclosed his plans for this project on 17 March 1962 in Chicago, where he gave a speech to a Music Education Conference. Eric Salzman, in writing about Schuman's long-range plan for the institute, declared: "The underlying idea is to produce stimulating teachers who can be cultural leaders in their communities" ("Aid Teachers" 85. See: B318). Though the first institute was scheduled to occur in 1966, the enterprise did not actually get under way until the middle 1970s, some years after Schuman's retirement from Lincoln Center.

Among other imaginative artistic organizations envisioned by Schuman for the Center were the Lincoln Center Film Society, the Chamber Music Society of Lincoln Center, the Music Theater of Lincoln Center, and the Great Performers series. He officially announced his desire to include films, both American and foreign, as part of the Center's cultural offerings in March of 1962 (Archer, "Movies" 34. See: B50). However, even though four New York Film Festivals took place at Lincoln Center prior to 1968, it was not until May 1969, several months after Schuman's resignation from the Center, that the Film Society of Lincoln Center became an official member of the institution. Schuman encouraged the practice of chamber music at Lincoln Center from the outset. In 1966 he appointed Charles Wadsworth to work with him in organizing chamber ensembles and concerts for Lincoln Center. Eventually, the generosity of Alice Tully led to the construction of the chamber music hall which bears her name. Yet it was not until early in 1969 that the Chamber Music Society of Lincoln Center received recognition as an authorized member of Lincoln Center. In September of that year the debut of the Chamber Music Society marked the official unveiling of the new Alice Tully Hall. Another art form, uniquely American, brought to Lincoln Center through the efforts of Schuman was music theater. Schuman joined forces with Richard Rodgers, who supervised the organizational details, to establish the Music Theater of Lincoln Center in 1963, which presented its first offering, *The King and I*, in the summer of 1964. Concerned with the lack of solo recitals at Lincoln Center, Schuman persuaded the Center to inaugurate the Great Performers series in 1968.

Several other projects desired by Schuman were realized while he was at Lincoln Center. As early as 1962 he had expressed an interest in the Center sponsoring spring and summer concerts and festivals. To that end André Kostelanetz was engaged to direct the New York Philharmonic Orchestra in a series of Promenade concerts in the spring which proved to be enormously popular. More importantly, in the summers of 1967 and 1968 the Center sponsored large and elaborate festivals which, though extremely successful, were not continued because they proved to be too costly. It was also during this period that the Haydn-Mozart concerts were established, a very popular series of concerts which eventually led to the acclaimed Mostly Mozart series. Without question, Schuman's great achievement at Lincoln Center was in the area of artistic programming.

Even the responsibilities associated with heading Lincoln Center did not curtail Schuman's creative activities. Less than a month after beginning his new duties, the 25 January 1962 issue of *The New York Times* published an article which announced that ten composers, including Schuman, were awarded commissions by the New York Philharmonic to produce compositions for the opening season of Lincoln Center's Philharmonic Hall ("Ten Works" 24. See: B374). This commission resulted in Schuman's initial work of his Lincoln Center years, the Eighth Symphony. Presented on 4 October 1962 by the New York Philharmonic under the baton of Leonard Bernstein, this three-movement symphony, which employed material from Schuman's Fourth String Quartet in the last two movements, attained immediate success. A *Time* article, in discussing the rehearsals for the approaching premiere of the symphony, asserted that the score "was a typically Schuman-crafted product: powerful, impetuous, rhythmically complex and grindingly dissonant—a work more notable for its vigor and blaring momentum than for charm or lyric effect" ("The Two Schumans" 54. See: B386). Later commentators have referred to the score as "an orchestral *tour de force*" (Miller, "William Schuman at 75" 31. See: B246), "A tight and sure work" (Keats, "William Schuman" 75. See: B199), and "one of Schuman's most intense and uncompromising works, fresh in its steely sonorities" (Rouse, *Documentary* 23. See: B39). Further acclaim came to Schuman when, in a review of the first recording of the symphony, Jay S. Harrison hailed the composer as "America's greatest symphonist" ("Philharmonic Commission" 61. See: B525).

Three works were composed by Schuman in 1963, his second year at Lincoln Center: the appealing arrangement for orchestra of Charles Ives's *Variations on "America,"* the choral composition *Deo Ac Veritati*, and *The Orchestra Song*. The orchestral version of Ives's *Variations on "America"* for organ was written by Schuman on commission from Broadcast Music, Inc. in celebration of that organization's twentieth anniversary. According to Sheila Keats, "Schuman must have had real fun with it; Ives' renegade humor obviously appealed to him. . . . The piece, whose brilliance and humor are irresistible, has proved enormously popular" ("William Schuman" 77. See: B199). Not all critics, though, have been so enamored with Schuman's arrangement. Bruce Archibald, writing in a review for *Notes*, concluded unsympathetically that "While remaining faithful to the notes, William Schuman's orchestration removes the work from the plane of wry New England humor to that of commercial comedy" ("Review" 157. See: B416). Nevertheless, this work has attained immense popularity. For the ceremonies in April surrounding the installation of Colgate University's new president, Schuman submitted *Deo Ac Veritati*, a choral work for male chorus. *The Orchestra Song*, arranged later by Schuman as *The Band Song*, was based on the composer's own 1939 choral setting of an Austrian folk song with the same title. One of the rare reviews of this work has pessimistically called it "a mild amusement" (Archibald, "Review" 157. See: B416).

The following year witnessed the completion of only a single composition, the *Amaryllis Variations* for string trio. Commissioned for an anniversary celebration by the Elizabeth Sprague Coolidge Foundation of the Library of Congress, this chamber work consists of a set of contrapuntal variations on a seventeenth-century English song composed by John Hilton. According to the score, which calls for three women's voices ad lib in addition to the strings, "the words are given to enable the performer to project the melody with the clarity of a singer." When Schuman delivered his composition for the 31 October premiere at the Library of Congress, it was met with mixed criticism. One commentator argued that, for string trios, *Amaryllis* would serve as "a companion piece for the Mozart Divertimento in E flat" (Thorpe, "Coolidge Festival" 64. See: B746). Another critic, however, faulted the composition for "the juxtaposition of tonal and nontonal materials," yet applauded "the seriousness of the piece and the brilliance of the string writing" (Evett, "Current Chronicle" 408. See: B725). Inspired by the initial New York performance of *Amaryllis*, Ralph Lewando evaluated the work as an "admirable piece" ("Schuman's Amarylis [*sic*]" 88. See: B731).

Schuman's final ballet for Martha Graham, *The Witch of Endor*, was the sole composition brought to fruition in 1965. Apparently one of the few performances of this work was the 2 November 1965 premiere conducted by Robert Irving. Later withdrawn by the composer, this ballet did not achieve the success of Schuman's earlier scores in that genre. A 1966 review of the production declared that Schuman's music "moved relentlessly along in a narrow dynamic range, desperately avoiding anything resembling a melodic line" (Krokover, "Martha Graham—Indomitable" 142. See: B810).

Because the leadership of Lincoln Center made increasing demands on his time, three years passed before Schuman finished another composition. By 1968, armed with a commission to produce a work in memory of Alexander Hilsberg, Schuman completed his Ninth Symphony, subtitled "Le Fosse Ardeatine." In the previous year Schuman had visited Italy, where he toured the Ardeatine Caves near Rome, the site of the 1944 massacre of 335 Italians by German soldiers to avenge the deaths of thirty-two of their comrades killed by Italian resistance forces. Moved deeply by this experience, Schuman based the program of his new symphony on this World War II atrocity. When Eugene Ormandy and the Philadelphia Orchestra gave the initial performance of this three-movement symphony on 10 January 1969 in New York's Philharmonic Hall, Edmund Haines, reviewing the concert for *High Fidelity and Musical America*, wrote, "Schuman's Symphony represents an advance in his own idiomatic development . . . the total impact is compelling, the intent communicative" ("Philadelphia Orchestra" MA-22. See: B518). This powerful, intense, and tragic composition has continued to receive accolades since that first performance. A 1972 record review asserts that the work displays "a conception of musical time that is unique to Schuman, expressively powerful, and . . . utterly American" (Trimble, "Two Ninths" 70-71. See: B680); and a 1984 review calls the Ninth "a masterpiece of economy and craftsmanship" (Blois, "Review" 43. See: B431).

By the summer of 1968, Schuman had finished a score for concert band entitled *Dedication Fanfare*, which was chartered by the New Music Circle of St. Louis for the 4 July 1968 celebration surrounding the inauguration of the new Gateway to the West Arch in St. Louis.

Later in 1968 Schuman produced his final composition while at Lincoln Center, *To Thee Old Cause*, described by Karl Miller as "perhaps Schuman's most moving work" ("William Schuman at 75" 161. See: B246). Written for the 125th anniversary of the New York Philharmonic Orchestra, this seventeen-minute score, subtitled "Evocation for Oboe, Brass, Timpani, Piano, and Strings," is a work inspired by stirring lines selected from Walt Whitman's *Leaves of Grass* and was written in remembrance of two recently assassinated political figures, Robert Kennedy and Martin Luther King. Leonard Bernstein conducted the New York Philharmonic in the 3 October 1968 premiere of *To Thee Old Cause*, with Harold

Gomberg as oboe soloist. Also presented on the concert was Schuman's Third Symphony.
Subsequent reviews of Schuman's new opus were generally favorable. On October 19, Irving
Kolodin declared in *Saturday Review* that "Throughout, one is aware of a majesty of means,
an absolute certainty of purpose which distributes emphasis (and the absence of it) exactly to
the advancement of the composer's esthetic intent" ("Music to My Ears" 56. See: B552).

Despite the fact that so much was accomplished by Schuman during these years at
Lincoln Center, by 1967 the strain of heading the institution was, more and more, beginning
to take its toll. Throughout his tenure Schuman was embroiled with the art center's financial
problems and, at times, with personnel difficulties. It is not surprising, then, that Schuman
was finding less time to compose as the demands of the job intensified. The decisive event
which ultimately led him to tender his resignation, effective 31 December 1968, was an April
1968 heart attack, which, though relatively mild, created the need for him to greatly reduce
his activities.

THE POST LINCOLN CENTER YEARS: 1969-1992

Retirement did not greatly reduce the flow of compositions from Schuman's pen. For
the first time in his professional career, he had the freedom to devote himself to composition
fully, with occasional diversions given to lecturing, writing, and other activities. Shortly
after his resignation from Lincoln Center, Schuman, moved by the death of the great
American artist Ben Shahn and commissioned by the artist's friends to write a memorial
tribute, composed one of his finest scores, *In Praise of Shahn: Canticle for Orchestra*.
Completed in 1969, the world premiere of this three-part composition occurred on 29 January
1970, with Leonard Bernstein conducting the New York Philharmonic Orchestra. The
immediate critical reception of the composer's first work after leaving Lincoln Center was, at
best, mixed. Miles Kastendieck wrote that Schuman's piece "reconfirms his compositional
skill without further enhancing his reputation" ("Back to Back" See: B542), while Irving
Kolodin, reviewing the first performance for *Saturday Review*, found that its "appeal is a
strong one" ("Music to My Ears" 58. See: B553). Later writers have lauded *In Praise of
Shahn* as "life-celebrating" and "splendidly effective" (Hall, "Bio-Discography" 21. See:
B21), "noble and deeply moving" (Miller, "William Schuman at 75" 161. See: B246), and
"among Schuman's most immediate and satisfying scores" (Rouse, *Documentary* 24. See:
B39). Rouse has aptly compared the work to *Credendum*, referring to both as "articles of
faith" (*Documentary* 24. See: B39).

As the seventies began, Schuman's productivity declined somewhat. His first pieces
of this decade, two choral scores, both written on commission, appeared in 1971. *Mail Order
Madrigals*, set to texts taken from an 1897 Sears Roebuck Catalogue, was originally
performed by the Iowa State University Singers on 12 March 1972, and *Declaration
Chorale*, a choral setting of texts by Walt Whitman, received its premiere performance on 30
April 1972 by the International Choral Festival Choruses led by Robert Shaw. Then
followed in 1972 the orchestral version of his earlier ballet *Voyage*, written on a commission
from the Eastman School of Music. When he received an invitation from the Ford
Foundation in 1973 to compose a large-scale work for the violist Donald McInnes, Schuman
again created a masterpiece, the *Concerto on Old English Rounds*. It is not surprising that

Schuman returned to previously used material for inspiration, the song "Amaryllis," employed almost a decade earlier as the basis of his 1964 *Amaryllis*, a set of variations for string trio. This unorthodox five-movement concerto is not cast in traditional form. Instead, the scoring for solo viola, women's chorus, and orchestra allows the composer to weave the "Amaryllis" tune and three other rounds ("Great Tom is Cast," "Who'll Buy Mi Roses," and "Come Follow Me") into a mellifluous fabric that "blends Jacobean and twentieth-century harmonic textures and rhythms into a wholly intriguing tonal web and tapestry" (Hall, "Bio-Discography" 22. See: B21). Michael Tilson Thomas conducted the Boston Symphony Orchestra, the Radcliffe Choral Society, and soloist Donald McInnes in the first performance of *Concerto on Old English Rounds* on 29 November 1974. Almost four years later, Eric Domville was inspired to reflect that "This is a work of rare beauty and imagination" ("Rare Beauty" 54. See: B475). Meanwhile Schuman was not averse to employing these four rounds again in his 1973 choral fantasy for unaccompanied women's chorus entitled *To Thy Love*. For the unveiling of the Smithsonian's Hirshhorn Museum and Sculpture Garden, Schuman delivered his only score of 1974, a brass and percussion ensemble piece called *Prelude for a Great Occasion*, premiered by instrumentalists from the National Symphony Orchestra on 1 October 1974.

Schuman's stature was further enhanced in his sixty-fifth year, 1975, with the completion of his tenth and final symphony, subtitled "American Muse." It is one of two Schuman compositions commissioned specifically for the 1976 Bicentennial celebration by the National Symphony Orchestra. The world premiere for both of these works and for his cantata *Casey at the Bat* took place in Washington on 6 April 1976, with Antal Dorati conducting the National Symphony Orchestra. There can be no question of the fact that in this final symphonic essay Schuman achieved a synthesis of the nobility and strength of style characteristic of his finest works. Though arguably not his best symphony, it, nevertheless, is a fitting testament to his artistic maturity and skill as a composer. The composer's own comments about the Tenth Symphony provide helpful insight into its *raison d'être*:

> My Symphony No. 10 is subtitled *American Muse* because it is dedicated to our country's creative artists past, present and future . . . America's creative men and women of letters, music, visual arts and all forms of theater. This work . . . is for my colleagues, with gratitude for their achievements and joy in the identification of being one of them (qtd. in Freed, Richard. Program notes to RCA Victor recording. See: D97).

An arrangement for concert band of the first movement of *New England Triptych*, "Be Glad Then, America," also appeared in 1975.

During the Bicentennial year Schuman completed a second work specifically for the 1976 celebration, *The Young Dead Soldiers*, perhaps one of the composer's least accessible scores. Fired by Archibald MacLeish's text, this setting for soprano, horn, woodwinds, and strings was premiered, together with the Tenth Symphony, at the aforementioned April concert. While critical opinion about this composition is, not unexpectedly, varied, Rouse seems to capture the essence of *The Young Dead Soldiers* in the following statement: "It is austere and unremittingly bleak . . . and may best be described as a single fifteen-minute melody over a dissonant chordal accompaniment. . . . There is an asceticism in *The Young Dead Soldiers* unusual to Schuman, and in this regard it is unique, standing apart from his other scores" (*Documentary* 25. See: B39).

That April concert also presented another Schuman composition for the first time, though it was not prepared specifically for the Bicentennial. *Casey at the Bat*, a cantata derived from *The Mighty Casey*, was commissioned by the Norlin Corporation. Joining with the National Symphony in this premiere were the Westminster Choir, Rosalind Rees, and Robert Merrill. A continuing interest in the song "Amaryllis" inspired Schuman's last creation of this year, the *Amaryllis: Variants on an Old English Round* for string orchestra.

Two years later Schuman resumed publication with *In Sweet Music*, a chamber work in which he turned for the third time to Shakespeare's poem "Orpheus With His Lute," using material from both his original song setting of 1944 and *A Song of Orpheus* of 1961. Written for the unusual instrumentation of voice, flute (doubling on piccolo and alto flute), viola, and harp, this composition was commissioned by the Chamber Music Society of Lincoln Center. That organization, which was established by Schuman, gave the premiere performance of *In Sweet Music* on 29 October 1978 at Alice Tully Hall. Certainly among the best of the composer's chamber works, one reviewer has noted that it established "for Schuman a firm position in the mainstream of twentieth-century vocal chamber music" (Dalheim, "Rosalind Rees Sings" 100. See: B719). His next work, also completed in 1978, was suggested by a proposal from the Metropolitan Opera Association to create an offering in celebration of Eleanor Robson Belmont's one hundredth birthday. The result of this new commission was *XXV Opera Snatches*, for either unaccompanied trumpet or flute.

By the end of the seventies Schuman had focused his attention on two compositions, *Three Colloquies* and *Time to the Old*, both finished in 1979. When the New York Philharmonic Orchestra invited the composer to prepare a work for its French horn soloist, Philip F. Myers, he responded with *Three Colloquies*, a three-movement score for French horn and orchestra. In this work Schuman recalls material from his eighth and ninth symphonies and from the 1947 version of his violin concerto (Hall, "Bio-Discography" 22. See: B21). Critical opinion of *Three Colloquies* has ranged from Richard Freed's assessment that "the work as a whole is powerful stuff" ("Review" 121. See: B505) to Harold Schonberg's pronouncement that the music "does not really have much nourishment" ("A New Schuman" section 3, p. 10. See: B648). *Time to the Old*, "an unrelentingly somber setting of three Archibald MacLeish poems about death and dying" (Henahan, "Gregg Smith Singers" section 3, p. 25. See: B845), stands as Schuman's sole song cycle. Rosalind Rees, soprano, and Thomas Muraco, piano, gave the debut on 19 May 1980 as part of a program which featured several other vocal and choral works by Schuman.

Following a year in which he did not publish any new compositions, Schuman, now in his eighth decade, finished two sets of variations in 1981, both of which were based on his 1956 song "The Lord Has a Child." For the festivities surrounding the centennial celebration of the St. Louis Symphony Orchestra, he was requested to compose an orchestral piece. On 24 September 1982, Leonard Slatkin led the St. Louis Symphony Orchestra in the premiere performance of *American Hymn: Orchestral Variations on an Original Melody*. An invitation from the American Bandmaster's Association and the United States Air Force Band resulted in the commission of *American Hymn: Variations on an Original Melody* for concert band. Composed in honor of the fiftieth anniversary of the American Bandmaster's Association, it was initially presented on 5 March 1981 by the United States Marine Band. This score also appears in a version for brass quintet. Another work for orchestra was also completed in 1981, the concert version of his 1947 ballet *Night Journey*, entitled *Night Journey: Choreographic Poem for Fifteen Instruments*.

Over the next two years Schuman concentrated on a pair of choral works. 1982's *Esses*, which acquired its title from the letter "s" beginning the name of each of the composition's four sections ("Suggestions," "Serenata," "Stillness," "Singaling"), was commissioned by Ithaca College and premiered there on 13 November 1982 by the Ithaca

College Choir. The following year he produced a choral cycle of eight movements for mixed chorus, *Perceptions*, commissioned for four different choral groups, the Gregg Smith Singers, the Dale Warland Singers, I Cantori, and the Philadelphia Singers, by the National Endowment for the Arts. On 9 January 1983, the Gregg Smith Singers gave the world premiere of *Perceptions* at Greenwich, Connecticut. Also published in 1983 was Samuel Adler's organ transcription of Schuman's *When Jesus Wept*, the second movement of *New England Triptych*.

By 1985 Schuman had begun to create a work for the centennial celebration of the Statue of Liberty. The genesis of the composition was rather unusual in that a consortium of musical institutions was jointly involved in commissioning the composer for this project. Among them were the Crane School of Music of Potsdam College, the New York Philharmonic Orchestra, and several other orchestras. This commission resulted in *On Freedom's Ground*, subtitled "An American Cantata," set to a text by the Pulitzer Prize winning poet Richard Wilbur. Schuman and Wilbur closely collaborated on this sizable cantata for baritone, chorus, and orchestra, which was premiered in Avery Fisher Hall on 28 October 1986, exactly one hundred years after the dedication of the statue. In a sententious performance review published in *Musical America*, Lesley Valdes praised the work of the composer, remarking that "it is honest music that the distinguished Schuman, now 75, has composed" ("New York Philharmonic" 50. See: B786). In October of 1985 Lincoln Center was the scene of a spectacular birthday gala held in honor of Schuman's seventy-fifth birthday (although his birthday was almost two months earlier). Several distinguished speakers praised the composer and the evening was capped with a concert of selected Schuman works. As a surprise gift to the birthday guests, Schuman composed a divertimento for wind quintet and percussion entitled *Dances*, which was played for the first time by the Chamber Music Society of Lincoln Center as the final selection on the evening's concert.

The next year the Houston Symphony Orchestra asked Schuman to compose an orchestral piece for the commemoration of the Texas Sesquicentennial in 1986. In September *Showcase: A Short Display for Orchestra* was introduced by Sergiu Comissiona and the Houston Symphony at a concert in the Bayou City as part of the Sesquicentennial's festivities. When the Walter W. Naumberg Foundation offered Schuman his second commission of 1986, he responded with *Awake, Thou Wintry Earth*, a duet for clarinet and violin (also arranged for flute and bassoon). An Alice Tully Hall concert showcased the clarinetist Charles Neidich and the violinist Curtis Macomber performing the composition on 10 March 1987. Writing in *The New Yorker*, Andrew Porter portrayed the chamber work as being comprised of "two slight, agreeable movements" ("Musical Events" 110. See: B736).

Two disparate chamber pieces were composed by Schuman in 1987, the very brief *Cooperstown Fanfare* for two trumpets and two trombones and the composer's last string quartet, the fifth. The former composition, only a minute in length, was written for Glimmerglass Opera's new house, the Alice Busch Theater, while the substantial string quartet, which takes approximately thirty minutes to perform, was created for the First New York International Festival of the Arts on commission from the Chase Manhattan Bank. The *Cooperstown Fanfare* was heard in Cooperstown, New York, the home of the Glimmerglass Opera, on 28 June 1987, and, nearly a year later, the Orford String Quartet presented the initial hearing of the Fifth String Quartet on 21 June 1988.

Three significant commissions were granted to Schuman in 1988. His second and last opera, *A Question of Taste*, was the first commissioned work of the Glimmerglass Opera Company. For this one-act opera, J.D. McClatchy wrote the libretto, based on Roald Dahl's story "Taste." The Glimmerglass Opera mounted the world premiere of the opera on 24 June

1989 as part of an operatic twin bill together with Schuman's other opera, *The Mighty Casey*. During the intermission between the two works, the composer offered remarks about his music (Kandell, "Glimmerglass Opera" 36. See: B830). These productions were staged in Cooperstown, New York, as part of the festivities surrounding the fiftieth anniversary of the baseball Hall of Fame. Looking ahead to a request for a composition from the Van Cliburn International Competition, Schuman produced his final piano work. For *Chester: Variations for Piano*, he once again used the well-known William Billings hymn as the foundation of a score. This set of variations, prepared for the eighth Van Cliburn competition held in Fort Worth, Texas, in 1989, was a mandatory piece for all semi-finalists. When the official celebration for Leonard Bernstein's seventieth birthday was planned, Schuman was asked by the Boston Symphony Orchestra to offer one of eight tributes in honor of Bernstein. On 28 August 1988, Seiji Ozawa led the Boston Symphony Orchestra in *Let's Hear it for Lenny*, a set of orchestral variations on "New York, New York."

From the beginning of his career Schuman displayed an affinity for choral music. It is entirely fitting then, that for his final composition, his lifelong interest in the choral medium was concluded with a reexamination of a choral work written more than thirty years earlier, the 1956 setting of the Langston Hughes text, *The Lord Has a Child*. Schuman's 1990 version of this text, arranged for mixed chorus and brass quintet, was composed for the 350th anniversary of Greenwich, Connecticut. Less than two months before his eightieth birthday, the Greenwich Choral Society introduced Schuman's work on a 16 June 1990 concert.

Even the last months of Schuman's life were filled with activity. When I interviewed him at his Park Avenue apartment in May of 1991, he told me that he was pursuing several new projects. In addition, he was vitally interested in helping me in any way possible with the preparation of this volume, and he eagerly anticipated its completion. But not long after that, a decision was made for the composer to have hip surgery. On 22 February 1992 Schuman died of heart failure at the age of 81 after an operation at Manhattan's Lenox Hill Hospital. The obituary by Bruce Lambert published in *The New York Times* the following day hailed the composer as a champion of American music ("Schuman Is Dead" 48. See: B215). Any summation of the life of this remarkable and influential man seems woefully inadequate. However, the closing statement written by Joseph Machlis to his own biography of Schuman, published a little more than thirty years ago, is still apropos:

> William Schuman won success without any compromise on his part. It is precisely because he remained faithful to his ideals that he has been able to impress his personality, both as a composer and educator, upon the American scene. In both capacities he has made a vital contribution to our musical life ("Schuman" 148. See: B231).

Works and Performances

This catalog of Schuman's compositions, listed in chronological order, does not include the popular songs of the composer. I am very grateful to Karl Miller for providing information about several important performances. Most of Schuman's autograph scores are in the Library of Congress. See: **B8, B11, B17, B36, B39**

W1   *GOD'S WORLD* (1932; E.B. Marks; 3 min.)
       For voice and piano.
       Text by Edna St. Vincent Millay.

W2   *POTPOURRI* (1932; withdrawn by composer; Ms)
       For orchestra.
       Never performed in public.

W3   *FOUR CANONIC CHORUSES* (1933; G. Schirmer; 8 min.)
       For a cappella mixed chorus.
       See: **D34**
       Movements: 1. Epitaph (Edna St. Vincent Millay)
                    2. Epitaph for Joseph Conrad (Countee Cullen)
                    3. Night Stuff (Carl Sandburg)
                    4. Come Not (Alfred Lord Tennyson)

Premiere

W3a 3 May 1935: New York; Columbia University Teachers College A Cappella Choir; Carl Gutekunst, conductor.

W4   *CANON AND FUGUE* (1934; withdrawn by composer; Ms; 8 min.)
       For piano trio.
       Never performed in public.

W5   *CHOREOGRAPHIC POEM FOR SEVEN INSTRUMENTS* (1934; withdrawn by composer; Ms)
For chamber group of seven instruments.
Never performed in public.

W6   *TWO PASTORALES* (1934; withdrawn by composer; Ms)
First Pastorale for contralto and clarinet (also for 2 violas, or violin and cello).
Second Pastorale for flute, oboe, and clarinet (also flute, violin, and clarinet).

Premiere

(First Pastorale; Second Pastorale was never performed in public)

W6a 1942: New York; broadcast for WQXR radio in honor of that station's twentieth anniversary.

W7   *SYMPHONY NO. 1* (1935; withdrawn by composer; Ms; 30 min.)
For chamber orchestra of eighteen instruments.
See: **B673**
Movements: 1. Allegro a Risoluto
                    2. Allegretto
                    3. Adagio

Premiere

W7a 21 October 1936: New York; Gotham Symphony Orchestra; Jules Werner, conductor.

W8   *STRING QUARTET NO. 1* (1936; withdrawn by composer; Ms)
Movements: 1. Adagio-Allegro con spirito
                    2. Adagio
                    3. Allegro vigoroso

Premiere

W8a 21 October 1936: New York; New String Quartet.

W9   *CHORAL ETUDE* (1937; Carl Fischer; 4 min.)
For a cappella mixed chorus.
Wordless syllabic text.
See: **D23**

Premiere

W9a 16 March 1938: New York; Madrigal Singers; Lehman Engel, conductor.

W10 *PIONEERS* (1937; G. Schirmer; 8 min.)
Originally published by J.&W. Chester.
For double a cappella mixed chorus.
Text by Walt Whitman.
See: **B751, B765**

Premiere

W10a 23 May 1938: Princeton, NJ; Westminster Festival Chorus; Henry Switten, conductor. See: **B450**

W11 *PRELUDE AND FUGUE* (1937; withdrawn by composer; Ms)
For orchestra.

W12 *STRING QUARTET NO. 2* (1937; Boosey and Hawkes; 16 min.)
Originally published by Arrow Music Press.
See: **D73, B741, B743**
Movements: 1. Sinfonia
2. Passacaglia
3. Fugue

Premiere

W12a Spring 1938: New York; Forum String Quartet.

W13 *SYMPHONY NO. 2* (1937; withdrawn by composer; Ms; 18 min.)
Symphony in one movement.
See: **B452, B673**

Premiere

W13a 25 May 1938: New York; Greenwich Orchestra; Edgar Schenkman, conductor.
See: **B450, B631**

Other Selected Performances

W13b 11 September 1938: New York; CBS Radio Broadcast; CBS Symphony; Howard Barlow, conductor. See: **B568**

W13c 17 February 1939: Boston; Boston Symphony Orchestra; Serge Koussevitzky, conductor. See: **B428**

W14 *AMERICAN FESTIVAL OVERTURE* (1939; G. Schirmer; 9 min.)
For orchestra.
Composed for ASCAP's Festival of American Music in Boston, 1939.
See: **D1, D2, D3, D4, D5, D6, B328**

Premiere

W14a 6 October 1939: Boston; Boston Symphony Orchestra; Serge Koussevitzky, conductor.

Other Selected Performances

W14b November 1941: Pittsburgh; Pittsburgh Symphony Orchestra; Fritz Reiner, conductor.

W14c 5, 6 November 1942: New York; New York Philharmonic Orchestra; Howard Barlow, conductor.

W14d 10 August 1947: Boston; Boston Symphony Orchestra; Serge Koussevitzky, conductor.

W14e 18, 19 March 1948: New York; New York Philharmonic Orchestra; Leopold Stokowski, conductor.

W14f 31 December 1948: Boston; Boston Symphony Orchestra; Serge Koussevitzky, conductor.

W14g 1 August 1955: Boston; Boston Symphony Orchestra; Richard Burgin, conductor.

W14h 2, 3, 4, 5 October 1958: New York; New York Philharmonic Orchestra; Leonard Bernstein, conductor.

W14i 7, 8, 9 June 1966: New York; New York Philharmonic Orchestra; Morton Gould, conductor.

W14j 28, 31 July; 1, 2 August 1970: New York; New York Philharmonic Orchestra; Sixten Ehrling, conductor.

W14k 24, 25 February 1986: Seattle; Seattle Symphony Orchestra; Kazuyoshi Akiyama, conductor.

W14l September 1989: Washington, DC; National Symphony Orchestra; Mstislav Rostropovich, conductor. See: **B577**

W14m 26, 27 March 1990: Fort Lauderdale, FL; Philharmonic Orchestra of Florida; John Yaffe, conductor. See: **B629, B669**

W14n 22 August 1990: Wolf Trap; New York Philharmonic Orchestra; Zubin Mehta, conductor. See: **B578**

W14o 13 September 1990: Washington, DC; National Symphony Orchestra; Mstislav Rostropovich, conductor. See: **B579**

W14p 27, 28, 29 September 1990: Atlanta; Atlanta Symphony Orchestra; Robert Shaw, conductor. See: **B419**

W14q 23 June 1991: Atlanta; Atlanta Symphony Orchestra; George Hanson, conductor. See: **B531**

W14r 13 September 1991: St. Louis; St. Louis Symphony Orchestra; Leonard Slatkin, conductor. See: **B705**

W14s 12, 13 February 1992: Miami, FL; St. Louis Symphony Orchestra; Leonard Slatkin, conductor. See: **B630**

W14t 23 February 1992: Washington, DC; St. Louis Symphony Orchestra; Leonard Slatkin, conductor. See: **B580**

W14u 11, 12 March 1993: Orlando, FL; Florida Symphony Orchestra; Andrews Sill, conductor. See: **B444**

W14v November 1993: Charlotte, NC; Charlotte Repertory Orchestra; Stephen Platte, conductor. See: **B667**

W15 *THE ORCHESTRA SONG* (1939; G. Schirmer; 3 min.)
For voices.
Text by Marion Farquhar, based on an Austrian folk song.

W16 *PRELUDE FOR VOICES* (1939; G. Schirmer; 4 min.)
For a cappella women's chorus or a cappella mixed chorus.
Text by Thomas Wolfe.
See: **D67, D68, D69, B747**

Premiere

W16a 24 April 1940: New York; Sarah Lawrence Chorus; William Schuman, conductor.

Other Selected Performance

W16b May 1986: Washington, DC; University of Maryland Chorus Chamber Singers; Paul Traver, conductor. See: **B846**

W17 *PROLOGUE* (1939; G. Schirmer; 7 min.)
For mixed chorus and orchestra.
Text by Genevieve Taggard.

Premiere

W17a 7 May 1939: New York; Federal Symphony Orchestra and the chorus of the New York City High School of Music and Art; Alexander Richter, conductor. See: **B631, B780, B783**

W18   *QUARTETTINO FOR FOUR BASSOONS* (1939; Peer; 5 min.)
Also arranged for four clarinets or four saxophones.
Also published by the Boletin Latino-Americano de Musica, 1941, Suplemento
Musical.
See: **D70, B712, B727**
Movements: 1. Ostinato
2. Nocturne
3. Waltz
4. Fughetta

Premiere

W18a The 1939 New Music Quarterly Recording. See: **D70**

W19   *STRING QUARTET NO. 3* (1939; Merion Music; 24 min.)
Originally published by G. Schirmer.
Commissioned by the League of Composers and by Town Hall.
See: **D74, D75, D76, D77, B202, B741**
Movements: 1. Introduction and Fugue
2. Intermezzo
3. Rondo Variations

Premiere

W19a 27 February 1940: New York; Coolidge Quartet. See: **B201, B722, B728**

Other Selected Performances

W19b 19 September 1986: Miami, FL; Composers Quartet. See: **B737**

W19c 17 June 1994: Harrisonburg, VA; Madison String Quartet.

W20   *THIS IS OUR TIME* (1940; Boosey and Hawkes; 30 min.)
Secular Cantata No. 1.
For mixed chorus and orchestra.
Text by Genevieve Taggard.
Movements: 1. Celebration (SATB)
2. Work (TTBB)
3. Foundation (SATB)
4. Questions (SSAA)
5. Fanfare (SATB)

Premiere

W20a 4 July 1940: New York; People's Philharmonic Choral Society and the New
York Philharmonic Orchestra; Alexander Smallens, conductor. See: **B782, S6**

W21 *NEWSREEL, IN FIVE SHOTS* (1941; G. Schirmer; 8 min.)
For concert band (also arranged for orchestra).
See: **D58, B591**
Movements: 1. Horse Race
2. Fashion Show
3. Tribal Dance
4. Monkeys at the Zoo
5. Parade

Premiere

W21a 1942: University Park, PA; Pennsylvania State College Band; George S. Howard, conductor.

W21b 14 July 1942: New York; New York Stadium Symphony Orchestra; Alexander Smallens, conductor.

W22 *SYMPHONY NO. 3* (1941; G. Schirmer; 30 min.)
See: **D80, D81, D82, B328, B575, B673**
Movements: Part I
1. Passacaglia
2. Fugue
Part II
3. Chorale
4. Toccata

Premiere

W22a 17 October 1941: Boston; Boston Symphony Orchestra; Serge Koussevitzky, conductor.

Other Selected Performances

W22b 23 November 1941: New York; Boston Symphony Orchestra; Serge Koussevitzky, conductor.

W22c 19, 20, 21, 22 October 1944: New York; New York Philharmonic Orchestra; Artur Rodzinski, conductor. See: **B477, B479**

W22d 17 October 1947: Boston; Boston Symphony Orchestra; Richard Burgin, conductor.

W22e 14 November 1947: New York; Boston Symphony Orchestra; Serge Koussevitzky, conductor.

W22f 18 April 1952: Boston; Boston Symphony Orchestra; Pierre Monteux, conductor.

W22g 8 May 1952: Paris; Boston Symphony Orchestra; Pierre Monteux, conductor. See: **B477, B480**

W22h 13, 14, 16 October 1960: New York; New York Philharmonic Orchestra; Leonard Bernstein, conductor.

W22i 29 August 1963: Hollywood, CA; New York Philharmonic Orchestra; Leonard Bernstein, conductor.

W22j 8 September 1963: Chicago; New York Philharmonic Orchestra; Leonard Bernstein, conductor.

W22k 11 September 1963: Ann Arbor, MI; New York Philharmonic Orchestra; Leonard Bernstein, conductor.

W22l 13 September 1963: Columbus, OH; New York Philharmonic Orchestra; Leonard Bernstein, conductor.

W22m 14 September 1963: Cleveland; New York Philharmonic Orchestra; Leonard Bernstein, conductor.

W22n 16 September 1963: Philadelphia; New York Philharmonic Orchestra; Leonard Bernstein, conductor.

W22o 22 September 1963: Washington, DC; New York Philharmonic Orchestra; Leonard Bernstein, conductor.

W22p 31 October; 1, 2, 3 November 1963: New York; New York Philharmonic Orchestra; Josef Krips, conductor.

W22q 30 July 1967: Chicago; Chicago Symphony Orchestra; Seiji Ozawa, conductor.

W22r 2, 3 October 1967: Houston; Houston Symphony Orchestra; André Previn, conductor.

W22s 3, 4, 5, 7 October 1968: New York; New York Philharmonic Orchestra; Leonard Bernstein, conductor. See: **B552, B646**

W22t 24 February 1969: London; London Symphony Orchestra; André Previn, conductor. See: **B464, B527**

W22u 1980: Los Angeles; Los Angeles Philharmonic Orchestra; Carlo Maria Giulini, conductor. See: **B625**

W22v 2, 3, 4, 7 October 1980: Boston; Boston Symphony Orchestra; Seiji Ozawa, conductor. See: **B232, B487**

W22w 1981: New York: New York Philharmonic Orchestra; Leonard Bernstein, conductor.

W22x 12, 13 October 1985: St. Louis; St. Louis Symphony Orchestra; Leonard Slatkin, conductor.

W22y 5, 6, 7, 10 December 1985: New York; New York Philharmonic Orchestra; Leonard Bernstein, conductor.

W22z 6, 7, 8 February 1986: Chicago; Chicago Symphony Orchestra; Leonard Slatkin, conductor. See: **B417**

W22aa 27 April 1990: Philadelphia; Philadelphia Orchestra; Leonard Slatkin, conductor. See: **B697**

W22bb 23 July 1990: Cabrillo Music Festival; Dennis Russell Davies, conductor. See: **B533**

W22cc 3, 4 August 1990: Tanglewood; Boston Symphony Orchestra; Dennis Russell Davies, conductor. See: **B492, B608, B627**

W23 *SYMPHONY NO. 4* (1941; G. Schirmer; 24 min.)
See: **D83, D84, B592, B634, B635, B673**
Movements: 1. Quarter note = circa 72
2. Tenderly, simply
3. Quarter note = 144

Premiere

W23a 22, 24 January 1942: Cleveland; Cleveland Orchestra; Artur Rodzinski, conductor. See: **B535**

Other Selected Performances

W23b 13 August 1980: Tanglewood; Berkshire Music Center Orchestra; Gunther Schuller, conductor. See: **B486**

W23c 15, 16 May 1986: Phoenix; Phoenix Symphony Orchestra; Theo Alcantara, conductor.

W24 *CONCERTO FOR PIANO AND ORCHESTRA* (1942, revised from an earlier 1938 version; G. Schirmer; 20 min.)
In three movements.
For chamber orchestra and piano.
See: **D24, B421**

Premiere

W24a 13 January 1943: New York; Saidenberg Sinfonietta; Rosalyn Tureck, piano; Daniel Saidenberg, conductor. See: **B128, B478, B504**

Other Selected Performance

W24b June 1985: New York; 92nd St. Y Chamber Symphony; Horacio Gutiérrez, piano. See: **B470**

W25   *A FREE SONG* (1942; G. Schirmer; 22 min.)
Secular Cantata No. 2.
For mixed chorus and orchestra.
Text by Walt Whitman.
See: **B765, B778**
Movements: 1. Too Long, America; Look Down, Fair Moon
                       2. Song of the Banner at Daybreak

Premiere

W25a 26 March 1943: Boston; Boston Symphony Orchestra, Harvard Glee Club, and the Radcliffe Choral Society; Serge Koussevitzky, conductor.

Other Selected Performances

W25b 3 April 1943: New York; Boston Symphony Orchestra, Harvard Glee Club, and the Radcliffe Choral Society; Serge Koussevitzky, conductor. See: **B378**

W25c 25 August 1945: London; at the Proms. See: **B149**

W25d 9 September 1971: Washington, DC; National Symphony Orchestra; Antal Dorati, conductor. See: **B773**

W25e 4 March 1984: Philadelphia; Singing City; Elaine Brown, conductor. See: **B762**

W26   *HOLIDAY SONG* (1942; G. Schirmer; 3 min.)
For voice and piano.
Also arranged for mixed chorus with piano and women's chorus with piano.
Text by Genevieve Taggard.

Premiere

W26a 13 January 1943: New York; Collegiate Chorale; Robert Shaw, conductor.

W27   *REQUIESCAT* (1942; G. Schirmer; 3 min.)
For women's chorus and piano or mixed chorus and piano.
Wordless text.

Premiere

W27a 4 April 1942: New York; Sarah Lawrence College Chorus; William Schuman, conductor.

Other Selected Performance

W27b May 1947: Nashville, TN; Fisk University. See: **B785**

W28 *PRAYER IN TIME OF WAR* (1943; G. Schirmer; 14 min.)
For orchestra.
Initially entitled *Prayer 1943*.
See: **D65, D66, B634**

Premiere

W28a 26 February 1943: Pittsburgh; Pittsburgh Symphony Orchestra; Fritz Reiner, conductor.

Other Selected Performances

W28b 25, 26, 28 March 1943: New York; New York Philharmonic Orchestra; Fritz Reiner, conductor.

W28c December 1943: New York; NBC Symphony Orchestra; Leopold Stokowski, conductor.

W28d 6 October 1944: Boston; Boston Symphony Orchestra; Serge Koussevitzky, conductor. See: **B675**

W29 *SYMPHONY NO. 5* (1943; G. Schirmer; 17 min.)
Symphony for Strings.
Commissioned by the Koussevitzky Music Foundation.
Dedicated to the memory of Mme Natalie Koussevitzky.
See: **D85, D86, D87, D88, B673**
Movements: 1. Molto agitato ed energico
2. Larghissimo
3. Presto

Premiere

W29a 12 November 1943: Boston; Boston Symphony Orchestra; Serge Koussevitzky, conductor. See: **B344, B496**

Other Selected Performances

W29b 19 December 1947: Boston; Boston Symphony Orchestra; Eleazar de Carvahlo, conductor.

W29c 1952: Pittsburgh; Pittsburgh Symphony Orchestra, William Steinberg, conductor.

W29d 5, 6, 7 November 1959: New York; New York Philharmonic Orchestra; Leonard Bernstein, conductor.

W29e 29, 30 September; 1, 2, 19 October 1966: New York; New York Philharmonic Orchestra; Leonard Bernstein, conductor.

W29f 24 October 1966: Newark, NJ; New York Philharmonic Orchestra; Leonard Bernstein, conductor.

W29g 7, 8 October 1968: Houston; New York Philharmonic Orchestra; André Previn, conductor.

W29h 23 June 1974: London; Los Angeles Chamber Orchestra; Neville Marriner, conductor. See: **B425**

W29i 1980: Aspen Music Festival.

W29j 17 November 1985: New York; American Composers Orchestra; Paul Dunkel, conductor. See: **B98, B611, B651**

W29k March 1990: Chicago; Chicago String Ensemble; Alan Heatherington, conductor. See: **B690**

W29l 9 May 1990: Minneapolis; Minnesota Orchestra; Edo de Waart, conductor. See: **B569**

W29m 19 January 1991: Seattle; Seattle Symphony Orchestra; Gerard Schwarz, conductor. See: **B582**

W29n 16 October 1992: St. Paul; St. Paul Chamber Orchestra; Hugh Wolff, conductor. See: **B503**

W30   *THREE-SCORE SET* (1943; G. Schirmer; 6 min.)
For piano.
Composed in honor of Carl Engel's sixtieth birthday.
See: **D102, D103, D104, B848**

Premiere

W30a 29 August 1943: New York; Jacques de Menasce, piano.

W31   *WILLIAM BILLINGS OVERTURE* (1943; G. Schirmer, later withdrawn by composer)
For orchestra.

Premiere

W31a 17, 18 February 1944: New York; New York Philharmonic Orchestra; Artur Rodzinski, conductor.

Other Selected Performance

W31b 2 April 1944: New York; New York Philharmonic Orchestra; Artur Rodzinski, conductor.

W32 *CIRCUS OVERTURE* (1944; G. Schirmer; 8 min.)
Originally entitled *Side Show*.
Commissioned by Billy Rose for his revue entitled *The Seven Lively Arts*.
Two versions for orchestra: full orchestra and small orchestra.
D. Owen prepared an arrangement for concert band in 1972.

Premiere

W32a 24 November 1944: Philadelphia; theater orchestra; Maurice Abranavel, conductor (small orchestra version).

W32b 17 December 1944: Pittsburgh; Pittsburgh Symphony Orchestra; Fritz Reiner, conductor (full orchestra version).

Other Selected Performances

W32c 26 February 1949: New York; New York Philharmonic Orchestra; Walter Hendl, conductor.

W32d 1953: Stuttgart, Germany; Stuttgart Symphony.

W32e 9, 10 October 1982: Houston; Houston Symphony Orchestra; C. William Harwood, conductor.

W32f 23 April 1990: San Francisco; San Francisco Conservatory of Music Orchestra; Denis de Coteau, conductor. See: **B683**

W33 *ORPHEUS WITH HIS LUTE* (1944; G. Schirmer; 3 min.)
For voice and piano.
Text by William Shakespeare.
Commissioned for a performance of Shakespeare's *Henry VIII* by Billy Rose.
See: **D61, D62**

W34 *STEELTOWN* (1944; Ms; 30 min.)
Music for a World War II film.
Commissioned by the United States Office of War Information.

W35   *TE DEUM* (1944; G. Schirmer; 4 min.)
For a cappella mixed chorus.
Latin text.
Commissioned for a performance of Shakespeare's *Henry VIII* by Billy Rose.
See: **D98, D99**

Premiere

W35a April 1945: Cambridge, MA; Sarah Lawrence Chorus and Harvard Glee Club;
G. Wallace Woodworth, conductor.

Other Selected Performance

W35b 27 March 1992: Chicago; William Ferris Chorale; William Ferris, conductor.
See: **B788**

W36   *VARIATIONS ON A THEME BY EUGENE GOOSSENS* (1944; Ms; 4 min.)
Variation V, Molto Tranquillo.
For string orchestra.
Schuman composed Variation V as part of a composite score written in honor of
Eugene Goossens and the Cincinnati Symphony Orchestra.

Premiere

W36a 23 March 1945: Cincinnati; Cincinnati Symphony Orchestra; Eugene
Goossens, conductor.

W37   *UNDERTOW* (1945; G. Schirmer; 25 min.)
Ballet and concert version (*Undertow: Choreographic Episodes for Orchestra*) of
ballet for orchestra.
Commissioned by the American Ballet Theatre.
See: **D107, D108, D109, D110, B328, B813**
Movements (concert version): 1. Prologue-Birth and Infancy
                             2. The City-Adolescence and Manhood
                             3. Epilogue-Guilt

Premiere

W37a 10 April 1945: New York; American Ballet Theatre; Antony Tudor,
choreographer; Antal Dorati, conductor.

W37b 29 November 1945: Los Angeles; Los Angeles Philharmonic Orchestra;
Alfred Wallenstein, conductor (concert version).

Other Selected Performances

W37c 29 April 1945: New York; American Ballet Theatre. See: **B823**

W37d 3, 4, 5, 6, 12 October 1946: New York; New York Philharmonic Orchestra; Artur Rodzinski, conductor.

W37e 4 December 1950: New York; NBC Symphony Orchestra; Guido Cantelli, conductor.

W37f 18, 19 January 1992: San Francisco; American Ballet Theatre; Emil De Cou, conductor. See: **B806, B824**

W38 *TRUTH SHALL DELIVER* (1946; G. Schirmer; 4 min.)
For a cappella men's chorus.
Text from Geoffrey Chaucer, adapted by Marion Farquhar.

Premiere

W38a 7 December 1946: New Haven, CT; Yale Glee Club; Marshall Bartholomew, conductor.

W39 *CONCERTO FOR VIOLIN AND ORCHESTRA* (1947, first revision in 1956, final revision in 1959; Merion Music; 30 min.)
Originally published by G. Schirmer.
Commissioned by Samuel Dushkin.
See: **D25, D26, D27, B638**
Movements: 1. Allegro risoluto-Molto tranquillo-Tempo I-Cadenza-Agitato, fervente
2. Introduzione: Adagio-Quasi cadenza-Presto leggiero- Allegretto-Adagietto-Poco a poco accelerando al Allegro vivo

Premiere

W39a 10 February 1950: Boston; Boston Symphony Orchestra; Isaac Stern, violin; Charles Munch, conductor (first version). See: **B484, B588, B708**

W39b 26 February 1956: New York; Juilliard Orchestra; Isaac Stern, violin; Jean Morel, conductor (second version). See: **B493, B511**

W39c 9 August 1959: Aspen, CO; Aspen Festival Orchestra; Roman Totenberg, violin; Izler Solomon, conductor (final version).

Other Selected Performances

W39d October 1961: Cincinnati; Cincinnati Symphony Orchestra; Joseph Fuchs, violin; Max Rudolf, conductor. See: **B534**

W39e 16 August 1985: Cabrillo Music Festival; Maryvonne Le Dizes-Richard, violin; John De Main, conductor. See: **B460**

W39f 24 November 1985: American Symphony Orchestra; Mark Peskanov, violin; Leonard Slatkin, conductor.

W39g 12 November 1992: San Francisco; San Francisco Symphony Orchestra; Robert McDuffie, violin; Libor Pisek, conductor. See: **B457, B684**

W40   *NIGHT JOURNEY* (1947; Merion Music; 30 min.)
Ballet.
Commissioned for Martha Graham by the Elizabeth Sprague Coolidge Foundation of the Library of Congress.
See: **D59, D60, B822**

Premiere

W40a 7 May 1947: Cambridge, MA; Martha Graham, choreographer; Louis Horst, conductor.

Other Selected Performance

W40b 21 January 1988: San Francisco; San Francisco Chamber Orchestra; William McGlaughlin, conductor.

W41   *SYMPHONY NO. 6* (1948; G. Schirmer; 29 min.)
Symphony in one movement for orchestra.
Commissioned by the Dallas Symphony Orchestra League.
See: **D89, D90, B452, B540, B636, B673**

Premiere

W41a 27 February 1949: Dallas; Dallas Symphony Orchestra; Antal Dorati, conductor. See: **B463**

Other Selected Performances

W41b 13 September 1951: Copenhagen, Denmark; Philadelphia Orchestra; Eugene Ormandy, conductor.

W41c 13 November 1951: New York; Philadelphia Orchestra; Eugene Ormandy, conductor.

W41d November 1951: Philadelphia; Washington, DC; Baltimore; Philadelphia Orchestra; Eugene Ormandy, conductor. See: **B604**

W41e 1953: Philadelphia; Philadelphia Orchestra; Eugene Ormandy, conductor.

W41f 17, 18, 20 April 1958: New York; New York Philharmonic Orchestra; Leonard Bernstein, conductor.

W41g 2 May 1958: Caracas, Venezuela; New York Philharmonic Orchestra; Leonard Bernstein, conductor.

W41h 13 May 1958: Lima, Peru; New York Philharmonic Orchestra; Leonard Bernstein, conductor.

W41i 18 May 1981: New York; American Composers Orchestra; Dennis Russell Davies, conductor. See: **B544**

W41j 26 September 1990: Minneapolis; Minnesota Orchestra; Edo de Waart, conductor. See: **B501**

W41k 3 April 1991: San Francisco; San Francisco Symphony Orchestra; Edo de Waart, conductor. See: **B456**

W42 *JUDITH: CHOREOGRAPHIC POEM* (1949; G. Schirmer; 24 min.)
Ballet.
Commissioned by the Louisville Orchestra for Martha Graham.
See: **D41, D42, D43, D44, B328, B792, B793, B795, B796, B812, B820, B822**

Premiere

W42a 4, 5 January 1950: Louisville, KY; Louisville Orchestra; Martha Graham, choreographer; Robert Whitney, conductor. See: **B811, B821**

Other Selected Performances

W42b 29 December 1950: New York; Louisville Orchestra; Martha Graham, choreographer; Robert Whitney, conductor. See: **B801**

W42c 10, 11, 12, 13 November 1955: New York; New York Philharmonic Orchestra; Dimitri Mitropoulos, conductor.

W42d 31 September 1993: Pittsburgh; Pittsburgh Symphony Orchestra; Lorin Maazel, conductor. See: **B798**

W43 *GEORGE WASHINGTON BRIDGE* (1950; G. Schirmer; 9 min.)
For concert band.
See: **D35, D36, D37, B438, B537, B566, B613**

Premiere

W43a 30 July 1950: Interlochen, MI; National Music Camp Band.

W44 *STRING QUARTET NO. 4* (1950; G. Schirmer; 28 min.)
Commissioned by the Elizabeth Sprague Coolidge Foundation of the Library of Congress for the 150th anniversary of the founding of the library.
See: **D78, B710, B743**
Movements: 1. Adagio
          2. Allegro con fuoco
          3. Andante
          4. Presto

W44a 28 October 1950: Washington, DC; Hungarian Quartet. See: **B720, B744**

Other Selected Performances

W44b 23 September 1951: Berlin; Berlin Philharmonic Quartet.

W44c 17 December 1951: New York; Juilliard String Quartet. See: **B716**

W44d 1 February 1960: New York; Lenox Quartet. See: **B732**

W45   *THE MIGHTY CASEY* (1953; G. Schirmer; 80 min.)
Opera in three scenes.
Libretto by Jeremy Gury (based on Ernest L. Thayer's poem "Casey at the Bat").
For soloists, mixed chorus, dancers, and orchestra.
See: **D46, D47, B75, B162, B829, B837**

Premiere

W45a 4, 5, 6 May 1953: Hartford, CT; Hartt College of Music; Elmer Nagy, stage director; Moshe Paranov, conductor. See: **B205, B825, B836, B838, B843**

Other Selected Performances

W45b 6 March 1955: CBS television. See: **B831, B839**

W45c October 1958: Washington, DC; performance by the Navy Ordinance Division.

W45d November 1958: Los Angeles; University of California at Los Angeles.

W45e 30 August 1967: New York; Theater Workshop for Students of the East River Amphitheater. See: **B828, B842**

W45f September 1976: New York; Alice Tully Hall. See: **B841**

W45g 23 July 1986: Cooperstown, NY; Glimmerglass Opera. See: **B833**

W45h 24 June 1989: Cooperstown, NY; Glimmerglass Opera. See: **B827, B830, B844**

W45i August 1991: New York; Juilliard School. See: **B826**

W46   *CHORUSES FROM "THE MIGHTY CASEY"* (1953; G. Schirmer; 14 min.)
For mixed chorus and piano four hands.
Text by Jeremy Gury.

W47 *VOYAGE: A CYCLE OF FIVE PIECES FOR PIANO* (1953; Merion Music; 24 min.)
Commissioned for the Golden Anniversary of Sigma Alpha Iota.
Also arranged for chamber orchestra.
See: **D120, D121, B853, B854**
Movements: 1. Anticipation
              2. Caprice
              3. Realization
              4. Decision
              5. Retrospection

Premiere

W47a 18 August 1953: Chicago; Lillian Steuber, pianist. See: **B384**

Other Selected Performance

W47b May 1986: Washington, DC; Gary Steigerwalt, piano. See: **B846**

W48 *VOYAGE FOR A THEATER* (1953; withdrawn by the composer; Ms; 25 min.)
Ballet.
Arrangement for chamber orchestra of the piano cycle *Voyage*.
See: **B822, B853**

Premiere

W48a 17 May 1953: New York; Martha Graham, choreographer; Simon Sadoff,
conductor.

W49 *CREDENDUM: ARTICLE OF FAITH* (1955; Merion Music; 18 min.)
For orchestra.
Commissioned by the Department of State for the U.S. Commission for UNESCO.
See: **D29, B230**
Movements: 1. Articles of Faith Declaration
              2. Chorale
              3. Finale

Premiere

W49a 4 November 1955: Cincinnati; Cincinnati Symphony Orchestra; Thor Johnson,
conductor. See: **B206, B595**

Other Selected Performances

W49b 9, 10, 12, 13 March 1956: New York; Philadelphia Orchestra; Eugene
Ormandy, conductor. See: **B461, B567, B584, B674**

W49c 20 March 1956: Baltimore; Philadelphia Orchestra; Eugene Ormandy,
conductor.

W49d 21 March 1956: Washington, DC; Philadelphia Orchestra; Eugene Ormandy, conductor.

W49e 8, 9 November 1956: New York; New York Philharmonic Orchestra; Dimitri Mitropoulos, conductor.

W49f 8, 9 November 1957: New York; New York Philharmonic Orchestra; Dimitri Mitropoulos, conductor.

W49g 1, 2, 3, 4 October 1964: New York; New York Philharmonic Orchestra; Josef Krips, conductor. See: **B467**

W49h 6 July 1985: Tanglewood; Boston Symphony Orchestra; Leonard Slatkin, conductor. See: **B616**

W49i 17, 18, 19, 20, 22, 24, 25 August 1985: New York; New York Philharmonic Orchestra; Leonard Slatkin, conductor.

W49j 17, 18, 19, 22 October 1985: Washington, DC; National Symphony Orchestra; Mstislav Rostropovich, conductor. See: **B576**

W49k 7, 8, 10 November 1985: Los Angeles; Los Angeles Philharmonic Orchestra; Leonard Slatkin, conductor.

W50 *CHESTER OVERTURE* (1956; Merion Music; 6 min.)
For concert band.
Commissioned by Pi Kappa Omicron.
Schuman's arrangement of the third movement of *New England Triptych*.
See: **D16, D17, D18, D19, D20, D21, D22, B438, B440, B537, B538, B602, B623, B709**

Premiere

W50a January 1957: Louisville, KY; University of Louisville Band. See: **B707**

Other Selected Performance

W50b 19 June 1957: New York; Goldman Band. See: **B420**

W51 *FIVE ROUNDS ON FAMOUS WORDS* (1956; Merion Music; 12 min.)
For a cappella mixed chorus or women's chorus.
The fifth round was added by the composer in 1969.
See: **D33**
Movements: 1. Health
            2. Thrift
            3. Caution
            4. Beauty
            5. Haste

Selected Performances

W51a May 1986: Washington, DC; University of Maryland Chorus Chamber Singers; Paul Traver, conductor. See: **B846**

W51b 12 May 1990: New York; New York Virtuoso Singers; Harold Rosenbaum, conductor. See: **B177**

W52 *THE LORD HAS A CHILD* (1956; Merion Music; 3 min.)
For mixed chorus and piano or women's chorus and piano.
Also arranged as a solo song with piano accompaniment.
Text by Langston Hughes.

W53 *NEW ENGLAND TRIPTYCH* (1956; Merion Music; 15 min.)
Three pieces for orchestra.
Commissioned by André Kostelanetz.
See: **D48, D49, D50, D51, D52, D53, D54, D55, D56, D57**
Movements: 1. Be Glad Then, America
2. When Jesus Wept
3. Chester

Premiere

W53a 26 October 1956: Miami, FL; University of Miami Symphony Orchestra; André Kostelanetz, conductor. See: **B682**

Other Selected Performances

W53b 3 November 1956: New York; New York Philharmonic Orchestra; André Kostelanetz, conductor. See: **B476, B571**

W53c May 1957: Cleveland; Cleveland Symphony Orchestra. See: **B702**

W53d 3 November 1957: New York; New York Philharmonic Orchestra.

W53e 15 March 1958: New York; New York Philharmonic Orchestra; André Kostelanetz, conductor.

W53f 1, 2 January 1960: Boston; Boston Symphony Orchestra; Aaron Copland, conductor.

W53g 28 December 1961: New York; New York Philharmonic Orchestra; Werner Torkanowsky, conductor.

W53h 22 January 1962: New York; New York Philharmonic Orchestra; André Kostelanetz, conductor.

W53i 29, 30 May 1964: New York; New York Philharmonic Orchestra; André Kostelanetz, conductor.

W53j 25, 26 October 1980: Houston; Houston Symphony Orchestra; C. William Harwood, conductor.

W53k 29 April 1984: Boston; Civic Symphony; Max Hobart, conductor. See: **B481**

W53l 15 November 1984: Philadelphia; Philadelphia Orchestra; Rafael Frühbeck de Burgos, conductor. See: **B693**

W53m June 1985: San Francisco; San Francisco Symphony Youth Orchestra; David Milnes, conductor. See: **B360**

W53n 15 August 1985: Saratoga Springs, NY; Philadelphia Orchestra; William Smith, conductor.

W53o 14, 15, 16, 19 November 1985: Washington, DC; National Symphony Orchestra; Rafael Frühbeck de Burgos, conductor. See: **B589**

W53p 26 November 1985: Fort Lauderdale, FL; Philharmonic Orchestra of Florida; Emerson Buckley, conductor. See: **B628**

W53q 2 April 1987: Phoenix; Phoenix Symphony Orchestra; James Sedares, conductor. See: **B427, B482**

W53r 7 July 1987: Philadelphia; Philadelphia Orchestra; Leonard Slatkin, conductor. See: **B696**

W53s March 1989: Washington, DC; combined orchestras of the Symphony Orchestra of the National Taiwan Academy of Arts and the Conservatory Orchestra of Brooklyn College; Dorothy Klotzman, conductor. See: **B626**

W53t 21 May 1989: Seattle; Seattle Youth Symphony; Rubin Gurevich, conductor. See: **B422**

W53u 12 July 1989: Great Woods; Pittsburgh Symphony Orchestra; Leonard Slatkin, conductor. See: **B489**

W53v 21 November 1989: Denver; Colorado Symphony Orchestra; Murry Sidlin, conductor. See: **B659**

W53w 3 December 1989: Washington, DC; The Juilliard Orchestra; Leonard Slatkin, conductor (first and third movements). See: **B338**

W53x 10 November 1990: Walnut Creek, CA; Marin Symphony; Gary Sheldon, conductor. See: **B454**

W53y 11 November 1990: Walnut Creek, CA; California Symphony; Barry Jekowsky, conductor. See: **B455, B510**

W53z 23, 26 January 1991: New Orleans; New Orleans Symphony; William Henry Curry, conductor. See: **B508**

W53aa 16, 17 January 1992: Phoenix; Phoenix Symphony Orchestra; James Sedares, conductor. See: **B483, B563**

W53bb 24 June 1992: Philadelphia; Philadelphia Orchestra; Andrew Litton, conductor. See: **B685**

W53cc 27 June 1992: Houston; Houston Symphony Orchestra; Stephen Stein, conductor. See: **B465**

W53dd 29 March 1993: Orlando, FL; Jacksonville Symphony Orchestra; Lawrence Leighton Smith, conductor. See: **B445**

W53ee 12 November 1993: Sacramento, CA; Sacramento Symphony Orchestra; Morton Gould, conductor. See: **B581**

W54   *CAROLS OF DEATH* (1958; Merion Music; 11 min.)
For a cappella mixed chorus.
Text by Walt Whitman.
Commissioned for the Laurentian Singers of St. Lawrence University.
See: **D10, D11, D12, D13, D14, B754, B756, B765, B775**
Movements: 1. The Last Invocation
2. The Unknown Region
3. To All, To Each

Premiere

W54a 20 March 1959: Canton, NY; Laurentian Singers.

Other Selected Performances

W54b 20 April 1966: Colorado Springs, CO; Jerald Lepinski's Classic Chorale. See: **B777**

W54c May 1986: Washington, DC; University of Maryland Chorus Chamber Singers; Paul Traver, conductor. See: **B846**

W54d 13 March 1988: St. Louis; St. Louis Symphony Chorus; Thomas Peck, conductor. See: **B791**

W54e 12 May 1990: New York; New York Virtuoso Singers; Harold Rosenbaum, conductor. See: **B177**

W54f 5 September 1991: Wooster, OH; The Choir of King's College, Cambridge; Stephen Cleobury, conductor. See: **B758**

W54g 15 September 1991: Washington, DC; The Choir of King's College, Cambridge; Stephen Cleobury, conductor. See: **B750**

W55 *THREE PIANO MOODS* (1958; Merion Music; 11 min.)
See: **D101, B849**
Movements: 1. Lyrical
           2. Pensive
           3. Dynamic

Premiere

W55a 2 December 1958: Athens, Greece; Joel Rosen.

W56 *WHEN JESUS WEPT* (1958; Merion Music; 5 min.)
For concert band.
The composer's arrangement of the second movement of *New England Triptych*.
Transcribed for organ by Samuel Adler.
See: **D122, B537, B709**
Premiere

W56a 18 June 1958: New York: Goldman Band; Richard Franko Goldman, conductor.

W57 *THE EARTH IS BORN* (1959; Ms; 30 min.)
Film score commissioned by the Time-Life Inc.

W58 *SYMPHONY NO. 7* (1960; Merion Music; 28 min.)
Commissioned for the seventy-fifth anniversary of the Boston Symphony Orchestra by the Koussevitzky Music Foundation in the Library of Congress.
See: **D91, D92, B452, B560, B633, B673**
Movements: 1. Largo assai
           2. Vigoroso
           3. Cantabile intensamente
           4. Scherzando brioso
              (played without pause)

Premiere

W58a 21, 22 October 1960: Boston; Boston Symphony Orchestra; Charles Munch, conductor. See: **B432, B485, B507**

Other Selected Performances

W58b December 1960: New York; Boston Symphony Orchestra; Charles Munch, conductor. See: **B317, B639, B642**

W58c 10 August 1985: Pittsburgh; Pittsburgh Symphony Orchestra; Lorin Maazel, conductor.

W59 *A SONG OF ORPHEUS* (1961; Merion Music; 21 min.)
Fantasy for Violoncello and Orchestra.
Commissioned for Leonard Rose by the Ford Foundation.
Dedicated to Frances Schuman on the occasion of the Schumans' twenty-fifth wedding anniversary.
Also arranged in 1978 for violoncello and chamber orchestra by Schuman and Jon Goldberg.
See: **D72**

Premiere

W59a 17 February 1962: Indianapolis; Indianapolis Symphony Orchestra; Leonard Rose, cello; Izler Solomon, conductor. See: **B209, B495, B516**

Other Selected Performances

W59b 25 April 1962: White Plains, NY; Symphony of the Air; Leonard Rose, cello; Simon Asen, conductor.

W59c 28 September 1962: New York; Juilliard Orchestra; Leonard Rose, cello; Jean Morel, conductor. See: **B512, B624**

W59d 9 January 1964: Cleveland; Cleveland Orchestra; Leonard Rose, cello; George Szell, conductor. See: **B701**

W59e December 1964: Los Angeles; University of California at Los Angeles. See: **B550**

W59f 30 July 1965: New York; New York Philharmonic Orchestra; Leonard Rose, cello; Lukas Foss, conductor.

W59g 17, 18, 19 December 1970: New York; New York Philharmonic Orchestra; Lorne Munroe, cello; Stanislaw Skrowaczewski, conductor. See: **B530**

W59h 8 November 1978: New York; Endymion Ensemble; Valentin Hirsu, cello; Jon Goldberg, conductor. Premiere of the 1978 version for cello and chamber orchestra.

W59i 21, 22 December 1985: New York; 92nd St. Y Chamber Orchestra; André Emelianoff, cello; Gerard Schwarz, conductor.

W59j 22, 24, 25 January 1986: San Francisco; San Francisco Symphony Orchestra; Michael Grebanier, cello; Stanislaw Skrowaczewski, conductor. See: **B532**

W59k 20 April 1991: Seattle; Seattle Symphony Orchestra; Cordelia Wikarski-Miedel, cello; Christopher Kendall, conductor. See: **B423**

W60   *SYMPHONY NO. 8* (1962; Merion Music; 31 min.)
Commissioned by the New York Philharmonic Orchestra for the inauguration of
Lincoln Center's Philharmonic Hall.
See: **D93, D94, B673**
Movements: 1. Lento sostenuto-Pressante vigoroso-Lento
2. Largo-Tempo più mosso-Largo
3. Presto-Prestissimo

Premiere

W60a 4, 5, 6, 7 October 1962: New York; New York Philharmonic Orchestra;
Leonard Bernstein, conductor. See: **B210, B512, B601, B661**

Other Selected Performances

W60b 30 November 1967: Chicago; Chicago Symphony Orchestra; Jean Martinon,
conductor.

W60c 21 December 1984: Philadelphia; Philadelphia Orchestra; William Smith,
conductor. See: **B694**

W60d 3, 4, 5 October 1985: New York; New York Philharmonic Orchestra; Zubin
Mehta, conductor.

W61   *DEO AC VERITATI* (1963; Merion Music; 3 min.)
For a cappella men's chorus.
Commissioned by Colgate University for the inauguration of its new president, Dr.
Vincent Barnett.

Premiere

W61a 19 April 1963: Hamilton, NY; Colgate University Glee Club; William Skelton,
conductor.

W62   *THE ORCHESTRA SONG* (1963; Merion Music; 4 min.)
An arrangement for orchestra of a traditional Austrian folksong.
Also arranged for concert band, *The Band Song*.

Premiere

W62a 11 April 1964: New York; Minneapolis Symphony Orchestra; André
Kostelanetz, conductor. See: **B211**

Other Selected Performance

W62b 29, 30, 31 May 1964: New York; New York Philharmonic Orchestra; André
Kostelanetz, conductor. See: **B549**

W63 *VARIATIONS ON "AMERICA"* (1963; Merion Music; 8 min.)
Orchestral arrangement of the organ composition by Charles Ives.
Commissioned by Broadcast Music, Inc. for the celebration of its twentieth
anniversary.
Also arranged for concert band (1968).
See: **D111, D112, D113, D114, D115, D116, D117, D118, D119, B556**

Premiere

W63a 20 May 1964: New York; New York Philharmonic Orchestra; André
Kostelanetz, conductor. See: **B211, B526**

Other Selected Performances

W63b 22 July 1986: Philadelphia; Philadelphia Orchestra; David Zinman, conductor.
See: **B548**

W63c 31 December 1989: St. Louis; St. Louis Symphony Orchestra; Leonard
Slatkin, conductor. See: **B704**

W63d 22 May 1990: Boston; Boston Pops Orchestra; Leonard Slatkin, conductor.
See: **B491**

W63e 14 June 1991: Meadow Brook Music Festival; Detroit Symphony Orchestra;
Neeme Järvi, conductor. See: **B514**

W63f 5 July 1991: Blossom Music Center; Cleveland Orchestra; Louis Lane,
conductor. See: **B515**

W63g 21 June 1993: Philadelphia; Philadelphia Orchestra; Lawrence Foster,
conductor. See: **B700**

W63h 18 September 1993; Houston; Houston Symphony Orchestra; Christoph
Eschenbach, conductor. See: **B466**

W64 *AMARYLLIS: VARIATIONS FOR STRING TRIO* (1964; Merion Music; 25 min.)
For string trio with three women's voices ad lib.
Commissioned by the Elizabeth Sprague Coolidge Foundation in the Library of
Congress in honor of the one hundredth anniversary of Coolidge's birth.
Dedicated to Elizabeth Sprague Coolidge and Harold Spivacke, Chief of the Music
Division of the Library of Congress.

Premiere

W64a 31 October 1964: Washington, DC; New York String Trio. See: **B725, B746**

Other Selected Performance

W64b 1965: New York; New Art String Trio. See: **B731**

W65 *PHILHARMONIC FANFARE* (1965; withdrawn by the composer; Ms.)
Written for the New York Philharmonic Orchestra Park Concerts.

Premiere

W65a 10, 11, 13, 14 August 1965: New York; New York Philharmonic Orchestra; William Steinberg, conductor. See: **B596**

W66 *THE WITCH OF ENDOR* (1965; Merion Music; 30 min.)
Ballet (also for orchestra alone).
Commissioned by Martha Graham.
See: **B822**

Premiere

W66a 2 November 1965: New York; Martha Graham, choreographer; Robert Irving, conductor. See: **B810**

W67 *DEDICATION FANFARE* (1968; Merion Music; 5 min.)
For concert band.
Commissioned for the opening celebration of the Gateway to the West Arch by the New Music Circle of St. Louis.

Premiere

W67a 4 July 1968: St. Louis; LaClede Band; Laurant Torno, conductor. See: **B212**

W68 *SYMPHONY NO. 9: LE FOSSE ARDEATINE* (1968; Merion Music; 30 min.)
Commissioned in memory of Alexander Hilsberg.
See: **D95, D96, B452, B575, B673**
Movements: 1. Anteludium
           2. Offertorium
           3. Postludium

Premiere

W68a 10 January 1969: Philadelphia; Philadelphia Orchestra; Eugene Ormandy, conductor. See: **B134, B212, B459**

Other Selected Performances

W68b 14 January 1969: New York; Philadelphia Orchestra; Eugene Ormandy, conductor. See: **B459, B518, B647**

W68c 13 November 1981: New York; New York Philharmonic Orchestra; Zubin Mehta, conductor. See: **B562**

W69 *TO THEE OLD CAUSE* (1968; Merion Music; 17 min.)
Evocation for oboe, brass, timpani, piano, and strings.
Commissioned by the New York Philharmonic Orchestra in celebration of its 125th anniversary.
See: **D106**

Premiere

W69a 3 October 1968: New York; New York Philharmonic Orchestra; Harold Gomberg, oboe; Leonard Bernstein, conductor. See: **B134, B212, B415, B433, B446, B458, B552, B646**

W70 *ANNIVERSARY FANFARE* (1969; Merion Music; 6 min.)
For brass and percussion ensemble.
Commissioned by the Metropolitan Museum of Art in honor of its centennial celebration.
See: **D8**

Premiere

W70a 13 April 1970: New York; brass and percussion ensemble; Frederik Prausnitz, conductor. See: **B213**

W71 *IN PRAISE OF SHAHN* (1969; Merion Music; 18 min.)
Canticle for orchestra.
Commissioned in memory of Ben Shahn by his friends.
See: **D38, D39, B676**

Premiere

W71a 29 January 1970: New York; New York Philharmonic Orchestra; Leonard Bernstein, conductor. See: **B167, B213, B373, B472, B497, B539, B542, B553, B612, B649**

Other Selected Performance

W71b 25 September 1973: London; London Symphony Orchestra; André Previn, conductor. See: **B513**

W72 *DECLARATION CHORALE* (1971; Merion Music; 8 min.)
For a cappella mixed chorus.
Text by Walt Whitman.
Commissioned by the Lincoln Center for the Performing Arts.

Premiere

W72a 30 April 1972: New York; International Choral Festival Choruses; Robert Shaw, conductor.

W73 *MAIL ORDER MADRIGALS* (1971; Merion Music; 12 min.)
For a cappella men's chorus, women's chorus, and mixed chorus.
Texts selected by Schuman from the 1897 Sears Roebuck Catalogue.
Commissioned, through a J.W. Fisher Foundation grant, by the Iowa State University
Department of Music for the Iowa State Singers.
See: **D45**
Movements: 1. Attention, Ladies! (TBB)
             2. Superfluous Hair (SSAA)
             3. Sweet Refreshing Sleep (SATB)
             4. Doctor Worden's Pills (SATB)

Premiere

W73a 12 March 1972: Ames, IA; Iowa State Singers; W. Douglas Pritchard,
conductor.

Other Selected Performance

W73b 12 May 1990: New York; New York Virtuoso Singers; Harold Rosenbaum,
conductor. See: **B177**

W74 *VOYAGE FOR ORCHESTRA* (1972; Merion Music; 25 min.)
Commissioned by the Eastman School of Music.

Premiere

W74a 27 October 1972: Rochester, NY; Eastman Philharmonic; Gustav Meier,
conductor.

W75 *CONCERTO ON OLD ENGLISH ROUNDS* (1973; Merion Music; 40 min.)
For viola, women's chorus, and orchestra.
Commissioned by the Ford Foundation for Donald McInnes.
See: **D28**
Movements: 1. Amaryllis-Introduction and Variations
             2. Great Tom Is Cast
             3. a. Who'll Buy Mi Roses
                b. Come, Follow Me
             4. Combinations
                a. Chorus
                b. Viola
                c. Orchestra
             5. Amaryllis-Recapitulation
               (played without pause)

Premiere

W75a 29 November 1974: Boston; Boston Symphony Orchestra; Radcliffe Choral
Society; Donald McInnes, viola; Michael Tilson Thomas, conductor. See: **B372,
B413**

Other Selected Performances

W75b 15 April 1976: New York: New York Philharmonic Orchestra; Abraham Kaplan Camerata Singers; Donald McInnes, viola; Leonard Bernstein, conductor. See: **B609, B668**

W75c 3 May 1976: New York; New York Philharmonic Orchestra; Abraham Kaplan Camerata Singers; Donald McInnes, viola; Leonard Bernstein, conductor. See: **B555, B610**

W75d 8 February 1979: Atlanta; Atlanta Symphony Orchestra; Donald McInnes, viola; Robert Shaw, conductor. See: **B643**

W75e 13 December 1985: New York; Juilliard Orchestra. See: **B598**

W76 *TO THY LOVE* (1973; Merion Music; 15 min.)
For a cappella women's chorus.
Text based on Old English Rounds.

W77 *PRELUDE FOR A GREAT OCCASION* (1974; Merion Music; 5 min.)
For brass and percussion ensemble.
Commissioned by the Hirshhorn Museum and Sculpture Garden of the Smithsonian Institution for its opening festivities.

Premiere

W77a 1 October 1974: Washington, DC; personnel of the National Symphony Orchestra; Antal Dorati, conductor.

W78 *BE GLAD THEN, AMERICA* (1975; Merion Music; 7 min.)
Schuman's arrangement for concert band of the first movement of *New England Triptych.*
See: **D9**

W79 *SYMPHONY NO. 10: AMERICAN MUSE* (1975; Merion Music; 33 min.)
Commissioned for the American Bicentennial celebration by the National Symphony Orchestra.
See: **D97, B673**
Movements: 1. Con fuoco
2. Larghissimo
3. Presto; Andantino; Leggero; Pesante; Presto possibile

Premiere

W79a 6, 7 April 1976: Washington, DC; National Symphony Orchestra; Antal Dorati, conductor. See: **B257, B286, B376, B599, B656**

Other Selected Performances

W79b 13 December 1985: New York; Juilliard Orchestra. See: **B598**

W79c 12 March 1987: Chicago; Chicago Symphony Orchestra; Edo de Waart, conductor. See: **B686**

W79d 2 November 1991: St. Louis; St. Louis Symphony Orchestra; Leonard Slatkin, conductor. See: **B706**

W80 *AMARYLLIS* (1976; Merion Music; 8 min.)
Variants on an Old English Round.
For string orchestra.

Premiere

W80a 27 July 1976: Philadelphia; Philadelphia Orchestra; André Kostelanetz, conductor.

Other Selected Performance

W80b 21 May 1977: New York; New York Philharmonic Orchestra; André Kostelanetz, conductor. See: **B468**

W81 *CASEY AT THE BAT* (1976; Associated Music Publishers; 40 min.)
A cantata for soloists, mixed chorus, and orchestra arranged from the opera *The Mighty Casey*.
Commissioned by the Norlin Corporation.
See: **D15**

Premiere

W81a 6, 7 April 1976: Washington, DC; Rosalind Rees and Robert Merrill, soloists; the Westminster Choir; National Symphony Orchestra; Antal Dorati, conductor. See: **B257, B286, B287, B376, B599, B656**

Other Selected Performances

W81b 10, 11 October 1980: Detroit; Detroit Symphony Orchestra; Antal Dorati, conductor. See: **B237**

W81c 22, 24 November 1985: New York; The Juilliard School.

W81d 10 August 1991: Blossom Music Center; Cleveland Orchestra; Leonard Slatkin, conductor. See: **B757**

W81e 11 February 1994: Chicago; William Ferris Chorale; William Ferris, conductor. See: **B789**

W82 *THE YOUNG DEAD SOLDIERS* (1976; Merion Music; 15 min.)
Lamentation for soprano, French horn, eight woodwinds, and nine strings.
Text by Archibald MacLeish.
Commissioned by the National Symphony Orchestra.
See: **D124**

Premiere

W82a 6, 7 April 1976: Washington, DC; Rosalind Rees, soprano; Edward C. Thayer, French horn; National Symphony Orchestra; Antal Dorati, conductor. See: **B257, B286, B376, B599, B656**

Other Selected Performances

W82b 24 October 1977: New York; Manhattan School of Music; Group for Contemporary Music; Rosalind Rees, soprano; Priscilla McAfee Rybka, horn. See: **B545**

W82c 5 October 1980: New York; Horblit Award Concert. See: **B723**

W83 *IN SWEET MUSIC* (1978; Merion Music; 23 min.)
Serenade on a setting of Shakespeare.
For voice, flute, viola, and harp.
Commissioned by the Chamber Music Society of Lincoln Center.
See: **D40, B740**

Premiere

W83a 29 October 1978: New York; Chamber Music Society of Lincoln Center; Jan DeGaetani, mezzo-soprano; Paula Robison, flute; Walter Trampler, viola; Osian Ellis, harp. See: **B288, B713, B715, B738, B739**

Other Selected Performances

W83b 5 October 1980: New York; Horblit Award Concert. See: **B723**

W83c 18 May 1983: Washington, DC; Rosalind Rees, soprano; Carol Wincenc, flute; Donald McInnes, viola; Susan Jolles, harp. See: **B815**

W83d 1, 3 November 1985: New York; Chamber Music Society of Lincoln Center.

W84 *XXV OPERA SNATCHES* (1978; Merion Music; 5 min.)
For unaccompanied trumpet; also arranged for unaccompanied flute.
Composed on request from the Metropolitan Opera Association for the 100th birthday of Eleanor Robson Belmont.

Premiere

W84a 10 January 1979: New York; Melvin Broiles, trumpet.

Other Selected Performances

W84b 1 October 1985: New York; Paula Robison, flute.

W84c 12 May 1990: New York; Marya Martin, flute. See: **B177**

W85   *THREE COLLOQUIES* (1979; Merion Music; 24 min.)
For French horn and orchestra.
In three movements to be played without interruption.
Commissioned by the New York Philharmonic Orchestra.
See: **D100**
Movements: 1. Rumination
            2. Renewal
            3. Remembrance

Premiere

W85a 24 January 1980: New York; New York Philharmonic Orchestra; Philip F.
Myers, French horn; Zubin Mehta, conductor. See: **B237, B289, B543, B546, B648**

Other Selected Performance

W85b June 1983: New York Philharmonic Orchestra; Philip F. Myers, French horn;
Zubin Mehta, conductor. See: **B500**

W86   *TIME TO THE OLD* (1979; Merion Music; 11 min.)
For voice and piano.
Texts by Archibald MacLeish.
See: **D31, D105**
Movements: 1. The Old Gray Couple
            2. Conway Burying Ground
            3. Dozing on the Lawn

Premiere

W86a 19 May 1980: Rosalind Rees, soprano; Thomas Muraco, piano. See: **B845**

Other Selected Performances

W86b 5 October 1980: New York; Horblit Award Concert. See: **B723**

W86c May 1986: Washington, DC; Rosalind Rees, soprano; Gary Steigerwalt, piano.
See: **B846**

W87   *AMERICAN HYMN* (1980; Merion Music; 9 min.)
For brass quintet.
Commissioned by the American Brass Quintet.
Also arranged for concert band.

W87a 30 March 1981: New York; American Brass Quintet.

W88 *AMERICAN HYMN: VARIATIONS ON AN ORIGINAL MELODY* (1981; Merion Music; 9 min.)
For concert band.
Commissioned for the fiftieth anniversary of the American Bandmasters Association by the American Bandmasters Association and the United States Air Force Band. Also for brass quintet.
See: **B438, B439**

W88a 5 March 1981: United States Marine Band; John Paynter, conductor.

W89 *AMERICAN HYMN: ORCHESTRAL VARIATIONS ON AN ORIGINAL MELODY* (1981; Merion Music; 26 min.)
For orchestra.
Commissioned by the St. Louis Symphony Orchestra for its centennial celebration.
See: **D7**

W89a 24 September 1982: St. Louis; St. Louis Symphony Orchestra; Leonard Slatkin, conductor. See: **B703**

W89b June 1985: San Francisco; San Francisco Symphony Youth Orchestra; David Milnes, conductor. See: **B360**

W89c 1 May 1986: Boston; Boston Composer's Orchestra; Gunther Schuller, conductor. See: **B488**

W90 *NIGHT JOURNEY* (1981; Merion Music; 20 min.)
Choreographic Poem for fifteen instruments.

W90a 27 February 1981: Albany, NY; Jon Goldberg, conductor.

W90b 18 May 1983: Washington, DC; Peabody Contemporary Music Ensemble; Frederik Prausnitz, conductor. See: **B815**

W90c 21 January 1988: San Francisco; San Francisco Chamber Orchestra; William McGlaughlin, conductor. See: **B808**

W91 *ESSES* (1982; Merion Music; 12 min.)
For a cappella mixed chorus.
Choral works on words beginning with S.
Commissioned by Ithaca College.
See: **D32**
Movements: 1. Suggestion
2. Serenata
3. Stillness
4. Singaling

Premiere

W91a 13 November 1982: Ithaca, NY; Ithaca College Choir; Lawrence Doebler, conductor.

W92 *PERCEPTIONS* (1983; Merion Music; 13 min.)
For a cappella mixed chorus.
Text by Walt Whitman.
Commissioned by the National Endowment for the Arts for the Gregg Smith Singers, Dale Warland Singers, I Cantori, and Philadelphia Singers.
See: **D63, D64**
Movements: 1. Thought
2. Beautiful Women
3. To Old Age
4. Each of Us
5. To the States
6. A Farm Picture
7. Whoever You Are
8. To You

Premiere

W92a 9 January 1983: Greenwich, CT; Gregg Smith Singers; Gregg Smith, conductor.

Other Selected Performances

W92b May 1986: Washington, DC; University of Maryland Chorus Chamber Singers; Paul Traver, conductor. See: **B846**

W92c 12 May 1990: New York; New York Virtuoso Singers; Harold Rosenbaum, conductor. See: **B177**

W93 *WHEN JESUS WEPT: PRELUDE FOR ORGAN* (1983; Merion Music; 5 min.)
Samuel Adler's organ transcription of the second movement of *New England Triptych*.
See: **D123**

W94   *DANCES* (1985; Merion Music; 10 min.)
Divertimento for wind quintet and percussion.
Composed for the Chamber Music Society of Lincoln Center.
See: **D30, B718**

Premiere

W94a 1 October 1986: New York; Chamber Music Society of Lincoln Center.
See: **B302, B734**

Other Selected Performance

W94b April 1990: Washington, DC; Capitol Woodwind Quintet. See: **B745**

W95   *ON FREEDOM'S GROUND* (1985; Merion Music; 40 min.)
An American Cantata for baritone, chorus, and orchestra.
Text by Richard Wilbur.
Commissioned by the Crane School of Music at SUNY Potsdam, the New York
Philharmonic Orchestra, the Albany Symphony Orchestra, the Atlanta Symphony
Orchestra, the Chicago Symphony Orchestra, the National Symphony Orchestra, the
Oregon Symphony Orchestra, the Pittsburgh Symphony Orchestra, and the St. Louis
Symphony Orchestra.
Dedicated to the composer's family.
Also available in a version for wind instruments.
Movements: 1. Back Then
           2. Our Risen States
           3. Like a Great Statue
           4. Come Dance
           5. Immigrants Still
              (played without pause between 1-2 and 4-5)

Premiere

W95a 28 October 1986: New York; New York Philharmonic Orchestra; Crane
School Chorus; Sherrill Milnes, baritone; Zubin Mehta, conductor. See: **B189, B264,
B396, B752, B760, B768, B770, B771, B774, B786, B790**

Other Selected Performances

W95b September 1987: Washington, DC; National Symphony Orchestra; Mstislav
Rostropovich, conductor. See: **B764**

W95c November 1987: Chicago; Chicago Symphony Orchestra; Leonard Slatkin,
conductor. See: **B787**

W96   *AWAKE, THOU WINTRY EARTH* (1986; Merion Music; 17 min.)
Duo for clarinet and violin.
Also available in a version for flute and bassoon.
Commissioned by the Walter W. Naumburg Foundation.

Premiere

W96a 10 March 1987: New York; Charles Neidich, clarinet; Curtis Macomber, violin. See: **B736**

W97 *SHOWCASE: A SHORT DISPLAY FOR ORCHESTRA* (1986; Merion Music; 4 min.)
For orchestra.
Commissioned by the Houston Symphony Orchestra for the Texas Sesquicentennial celebration.

Premiere

W97a 26 September 1986: Houston; Houston Symphony Orchestra; Sergiu Comissiona, conductor. See: **B264**

Other Selected Performances

W97b 30 April 1990: San Francisco; San Francisco Symphony Orchestra; Jahja Ling, conductor. See: **B453**

W97c 9 January 1991: Minneapolis; Minnesota Orchestra; Edo de Waart, conductor. See: **B502**

W97d 5 August 1992: Chicago; Grant Park Symphony; Jahja Ling, conductor. See: **B657**

W98 *COOPERSTOWN FANFARE* (1987; Merion Music; 1 min.)
For two trumpets and two trombones.
Composed for the opening of the Glimmerglass Opera's Alice Busch Opera Theater.

Premiere

W98a 28 June 1987: Cooperstown, NY.

W99 *STRING QUARTET NO. 5* (1987; Merion Music; 30 min.)
Commissioned for the First New York International Festival of the Arts by the Chase Manhattan Bank.
See: **D79**
Movements: 1. Introduction
2. Variations; Epilogue

Premiere

W99a 21 June 1988: New York; Orford String Quartet.

W100 *CHESTER: VARIATIONS FOR PIANO* (1988; Merion Music; 6 min.)
Based on a hymn by William Billings.
Commissioned for the Eighth Van Cliburn International Piano Competition.

Premiere

W100a 2 June 1989: Fort Worth, TX.

Other Selected Performance

W100b 12 May 1990: New York. See: **B177**

W101 *LET'S HEAR IT FOR LENNY!* (1988; Merion Music; 2 min.)
A set of orchestral variations on "New York, New York."
One of a collection of variations by several composers commissioned by the Boston
Symphony Orchestra in honor of Leonard Bernstein's 70th birthday.

Premiere

W101a 28 August 1988: Boston; Boston Symphony Orchestra; Seiji Ozawa,
conductor.

W102 *A QUESTION OF TASTE* (1988; Merion Music; 50 min.)
Opera in one act.
Libretto by J.D. McClatchy, based on the story "Taste" by Roald Dahl.
For soprano, two mezzo-sopranos, tenor, baritone, bass-baritone, and orchestra.
Commissioned by the Glimmerglass Opera through the Eugene V. and Clare Thaw
Charitable Trust.
See: **D71, B832**

Premiere

W102a 24 June 1989: Cooperstown, NY; Glimmerglass Opera; B. Rodney Marriott,
stage director; Stewart Robinson, conductor. See: **B827, B830, B844**

Other Selected Performance

W102b August 1991: New York; Juilliard School. See: **B826**

W103 *THE LORD HAS A CHILD* (1990; Merion Music; 6 min.)
For mixed chorus and brass quintet.
Text by Langston Hughes.
Also in versions by Schuman for chorus and voice.
Commissioned for the 350th anniversary of Greenwich, Connecticut.

Premiere

W103a 16 June 1990: Greenwich, CT; Greenwich Choral Society; Richard Vogt,
conductor.

Discography

This discography, presented in alphabetical order by composition, includes a listing of commercially-produced recordings, whether or not currently available. I should like to thank Karl Miller for sharing his extensive knowledge of Schuman recordings with me as I compiled this discography. See: **B21, B35, B36, B39, B40, B41**

AMERICAN FESTIVAL OVERTURE **(W14)**

D1   RCA Victor 18511 (78 rpm); Gramophone ED 350 (78 rpm); AF 562 (78 rpm), pre-1942.
National Symphony Orchestra; Hans Kindler, conductor.

D2   American Recording Society ARS 28, 1952; ARS 115, 1953.
Vienna Symphony Orchestra; Walter Hendl, conductor.
With: Roy Harris, *Third Symphony* (ARS 28 and ARS 115); Roger Sessions, Suite from *The Black Maskers* (ARS 115). See: **B16**

D3   Desto 404; 6404; 46404, stereo cassette, 1964 (reissue of ARS 28 and ARS 115).
Vienna Symphony Orchestra; Walter Hendl, conductor.
With: Roy Harris, *Third Symphony*; Roger Sessions, Suite from *The Black Maskers*.
See: **B16**

D4   Deutsche Grammophon 253 2085; 330 2085, cassette tape; 4133324-2 GH, compact disc, 1983.
Los Angeles Philharmonic Orchestra; Leonard Bernstein, conductor.
With: Samuel Barber, *Adagio for Strings*; Leonard Bernstein, Overture to *Candide*; Aaron Copland, *Appalachian Spring*.

D5   Deutsche Grammophon 423169-1 GH; 423169-4 GH, cassette tape, c. 1984.
Los Angeles Philharmonic Orchestra; Leonard Bernstein, conductor.
With: Samuel Barber, *Adagio for Strings*; Leonard Bernstein, Overture to *Candide*; Aaron Copland, *Appalachian Spring*.

D6   RCA (Red Seal) 09026 61282 2, compact disc, 1992.
St. Louis Symphony Orchestra; Leonard Slatkin, conductor.
With: William Schuman, *New England Triptych*, *Variations on "America,"* and
Symphony No. 10. See: **B585, B645, B655, B666**

AMERICAN HYMN (orchestral variations) **(W89)**

D7   Elektra/Nonesuch 79072-1; 79072-4, cassette tape, c. 1984 or 1985.
St. Louis Symphony Orchestra; Leonard Slatkin, conductor.
With: Joseph Schwantner, *Magabunda: Four Poems of Agueda Pizarro.* See: **B21**

ANNIVERSARY FANFARE **(W70)**

D8   Metropolitan Museum of Art "Centennial Fanfares" release AKS 10001, 1970.
Brass and Percussion Ensemble; Frederik Prausnitz, conductor.
With: Fanfares composed for the 100th anniversary of New York's Metropolitan
Museum of Art by Leonard Bernstein, Aaron Copland, Walter Piston, and Virgil
Thomson. See: **B213**

BE GLAD THEN, AMERICA (New England Triptych) **(W78)**

D9   Cornell University CUWE-19, 1976.
Album title: The Cornell University Wind Ensemble in Concert.
Cornell University Wind Ensemble; Marice Stith, conductor.
With: Howard Hanson, *Dies Natalis* and *Chorale and Alleluia*; Brian Israel, *Concerto
sacra*; Roger Nixon, *Fanfare and March*; John Philip Sousa, *George Washington
Bicentennial March.*

CAROLS OF DEATH **(W54)**

D10   Everest LPBR 6129; SDBR 3129, 1965; Everest LPBR 6129; SDBR 3129, 1972.
Album title: An American Triptych.
Gregg Smith Singers; Gregg Smith, conductor.
With: Samuel Barber, *Reincarnation*; Aaron Copland, *In the Beginning.* See: **B763**

D11   Bay Cities BCD 1022, compact disc, 1990.
Album title: American Voices II.
The Chorale of Roberts Wesleyan College; Robert Shewan and Stephen Shewan,
conductors.
With: William Schuman, *Perceptions* and *Te Deum*; Stephen Shewan, *Feast of
Carols*, *Awake My Soul*, *Morning Has Broken*, and *Sing Unto the Lord*; Leo
Sowerby, *O God, Our Help in Ages Past; Liturgy of Hope;* and *I Will Lift Up Mine
Eyes.* See: **B748, B759**

D12   CRI 615, compact disc, 1992.
Album title: To Orpheus.
New York Virtuoso Singers; Harold Rosenbaum, conductor.
With: Luigi Dallapiccola, *Prima serie dei cori di Michelangelo Buonarroti il Giovane*; Michael Dellaira, *Art and Isadora*; Hans Werner Henze, *Orpheus Behind the Wire*; David Lang, *By Fire*; George Perle, *Sonnets to Orpheus*. See: **B749**

D13   GSS 110.
Gregg Smith Singers; Gregg Smith, conductor.

D14   Angel (EMI) CDC 54188, compact disc.
The Choir of King's College, Cambridge; Stephen Cleobury, conductor.
With: Leonard Bernstein, *Chichester Psalms*; Aaron Copland, *In the Beginning*; Charles Ives, *Psalm 90*; Libby Larsen, *How It Thrills*. See: **B753**

CASEY AT THE BAT **(W81)**

D15   EAV LE 77410, cassette tape for filmstrip, 1980.
Long Island Symphonic Choral Association and Orchestra; Gregg Smith, conductor.
Cornell University Wind Ensemble; Marice Stith, conductor.
Soloists: Rosalind Rees, Richard Muenz, Brian Phipps, Walter Richardson, and Jay Willoughby.
Narration by William Schuman.

CHESTER OVERTURE (New England Triptych) **(W50)**

D16   Decca DL 8633; DL 78633, 1958.
The Goldman Band; Richard Franko Goldman, conductor.
With: works by William Bergsma, Anton Bruckner, Edwin Franko Goldman, François Joseph Gossec, Percy Grainger, Felix Mendelssohn, and Richard Wagner.
See: **B462**

D17   Century Records V 9091, 1959.
State University of New York College at Fredonia Concert Band; Herbert Harp, conductor.
With: Jerry Bilik, *Block M March*; Gustav Holst, *First Suite in E-flat*; William Latham, *Two Chorale Preludes*; Theodore Peterson, *Four Roses*; Peter Ilyich Tchaikovsky, *Marche Slav*; Jaromir Weinberger, "Polka and Fugue" from *Schwanda*.

D18   King 682, 1960.
University of Miami Symphonic Band.

D19   Vanguard VRS 9114; VSD 2124, 1963.
The University of Michigan Symphonic Band; William Revelli, conductor.

D20   Cornell University CUWE-10, 1973.
Cornell University Wind Ensemble; Marice Stith, conductor.
With: Paul Creston, *Prelude and Dance*; Percy Grainger, *Lads of Wampray March*; Howard Hanson, *March Carillon*; Healey Willan, *Royce Hall Suite*.

D21   Vogt Quality Recordings CSRV 2503, 1975.
Concord Band; William M. Toland, conductor.

D22   Klavier KCD 11048, compact disc.
Cincinnati College Conservatory of Music Wind Symphony; Eugene Corporon, conductor.
With: Leonard Bernstein, Overture to *Candide*; Aaron Copland, *An Outdoor Overture* and *El Salón México*; H. Owen Reed, *La Fiesta Mexicana*; William Schuman, *George Washington Bridge*.

CHORAL ETUDE (W9)

D23   Columbia C 17139D (78 rpm), pre 1942.
Madrigal Singers; Lehman Engel, conductor.
With: Charles Ives, *Psalm 67*.

CONCERTO FOR PIANO AND ORCHESTRA (W24)

D24   Turnabout TVS 34733; Murray Hill C 85783, cassette tape, 1979.
Massachusetts Institute of Technology Symphony; David Epstein, conductor; Gary Steigerwalt, piano.
With: Walter Piston, *Concertino for Piano and Chamber Orchestra* (Turnabout); works by Samuel Barber, Amy Beach, Aaron Copland, George Gershwin, Louis Moreau Gottschalk, Edward MacDowell, and Miklos Rózsa (Murray Hill).

CONCERTO FOR VIOLIN AND ORCHESTRA (W39)

D25   Deutsche Grammophon 2530103, 1971.
Boston Symphony Orchestra; Michael Tilson Thomas, conductor; Paul Zukofsky, violin.
With: Walter Piston, *Symphony No. 2*. See: **B471, B473, B594**

D26   Angel (EMI) CDC 49464, compact disc, 1989.
St. Louis Symphony Orchestra; Leonard Slatkin, conductor; Robert McDuffie, violin.
With: Leonard Bernstein, *Serenade for Violin, String Orchestra, Harp and Percussion*. See: **B430, B490, B523, B529, B557, B644, B652, B653, B664, B688**

D27   Deutsche Grammophon 429860 2 (reissue of DG 2530103), compact disc, 1990.
Boston Symphony Orchestra; Michael Tilson Thomas, conductor; Paul Zukofsky, violin.
With: Walter Piston, *Symphony No. 2*; Carl Ruggles, *Sun-treader*. See: **B471, B473, B594**

CONCERTO ON OLD ENGLISH ROUNDS (W75)

D28   Columbia M 35101, 1978.
New York Philharmonic Orchestra/The Camerata Singers; Leonard Bernstein, conductor; Donald McInnes, viola. See: **B437, B475, B559, B603**

CREDENDUM **(W49)**

D29 Columbia ML 5185, 1957; CML 5185, 1970; reissued as CRI S-308, 1973; CRI C-308, cassette tape.
Philadelphia Orchestra; Eugene Ormandy, conductor.
With: Leon Kirchner, *Piano Concerto* (Columbia); Andrew Imbrie, *Symphony No. 3* (CRI).

DANCES **(W94)**

D30 Crystal Records CD 752, compact disc, 1993.
Westwood Wind Quintet; Matthew Kocmieroski, percussion.
With: William Bergsma, *Concerto for Wind Quintet*; John Biggs, *Scherzo*; Elliott Carter, *Woodwind Quintet—1948*; Anthony Plog, *Animal Ditties*; George Rochberg, *To the Dark Wood*; Gunther Schuller, *Suite*. See: **B711**

DOZING ON THE LAWN (from *Time to the Old*) **(W86)**

D31 Elektra/Nonesuch 79178-1; 79178-2, compact disc; 79178-4, cassette tape, 1988.
Album title: Songs of America.
Jan DeGaetani, voice; Gilbert Kalish, piano.
With: songs by other American composers.

ESSES **(W91)**

D32 GSS 110.
Gregg Smith Singers; Gregg Smith, conductor.

FIVE ROUNDS ON FAMOUS WORDS **(W51)**

D33 GSS 110.
Gregg Smith Singers; Gregg Smith, conductor.

FOUR CANONIC CHORUSES (Nos. 1, 2, and 4) **(W3)**

D34 Concordia S-1, 1961.
Concordia Choir; Paul J. Christiansen, conductor. See: **B21**

GEORGE WASHINGTON BRIDGE **(W43)**

D35 Mercury MG 40006, 1953; EPI 5062; MG 50079, 1957; MMA 11009, 1959; SRI 75086, 1977.
The Eastman Wind Ensemble; Frederick Fennell, conductor.
With: Samuel Barber, *Commando March*; Robert Russell Bennett, *Suite of Old American Dances*; Morton Gould, *Ballad for Band*; Vincent Persichetti, *Divertimento for Band*; Walter Piston, *Tunbridge Fair*.

D36   KOCD 3562, compact disc, 1987.
Tokyo Kosei Wind Orchestra; Frederick Fennell, conductor.
With: Robert Russell Bennett, *Symphonic Songs for Band*; Aaron Copland, *An Outdoor Overture*; Morton Gould, *Ballad for Band*; Charles Ives, *Country Band March*; Ronald Lo Presti, *Elegy for a Young American*; Vincent Persichetti, *Masquerade*; Clifton Williams, *Pastorale*.

D37   Klavier KCD 11048, compact disc.
Cincinnati College Conservatory of Music Wind Symphony; Eugene Corporon, conductor.
With: Leonard Bernstein, Overture to *Candide*; Aaron Copland, *An Outdoor Overture* and *El Salón México*; H. Owen Reed, *La Fiesta Mexicana*; William Schuman, *Chester Overture*.

IN PRAISE OF SHAHN (W71)

D38   Columbia M 30112, 1970.
New York Philharmonic Orchestra; Leonard Bernstein, conductor.
With: Elliott Carter, *Concerto for Orchestra*. See: **B213, B524**

D39   New World NW 368-1; NW 368-2, compact disc, 1988.
Juilliard Orchestra; Otto Werner-Mueller, conductor.
With: Aaron Copland, *Connotations*; Roger Sessions, Suite from *The Black Maskers*.
See: **B506, B607, B615, B672, B677**

IN SWEET MUSIC (W83)

D40   CRI SD 439, 1980.
Rosalind Rees, soprano; Paula Robison, flute; Heidi Lehwalder, harp; Scott Nickrenz, viola.
With: William Schuman, *The Young Dead Soldiers* and *Time to the Old*. See: **B714, B719, B724, B726, B729, B733**

JUDITH (W42)

D41   Mercury MG 10088, 1951.
Louisville Orchestra; Robert Whitney, conductor.
With: William Schuman, *Undertow*. See: **B16, B794, B797, B814, B817, S18**

D42   Louisville 604, 1960.
Louisville Orchestra; Robert Whitney, conductor.
With: Gian Francesco Malipiero, *Piano Concerto No. 3*.

D43   CRI SD 500, 1984.
Eastman Philharmonic Orchestra; David Effron, conductor.
With: William Schuman, *Night Journey*. See: **B802, B803, B809**

D44 Delos DE 3115, compact disc, 1992.
Album title: A Tribute to William Schuman.
Seattle Symphony Orchestra; Gerard Schwarz, conductor.
With: William Schuman, *New England Triptych*, *Symphony No. 5*, and *Variations on "America."* See: **B585, B645, B666, B699**

MAIL ORDER MADRIGALS (W73)

D45 Vox SVBX 5354, 1979; GSS 110.
Album title: American Choral Music after 1950.
Gregg Smith Singers; Gregg Smith, conductor.
With: works by William Bergsma, Elliott Carter, Paul Chihara, Jacob Druckman, Lou Harrison, Michael Hennagin, Andrew Imbrie, Carolyn Madison, William Mayer, Edmund Najera, Ronald Roxbury, Gregg Smith, Donald Waxman.

THE MIGHTY CASEY (W45)

D46 Delos DE 1030, compact disc, 1990.
Juilliard Opera Center and Juilliard Orchestra; Gerard Schwarz, conductor.
With: William Schuman, *A Question of Taste*.

D47 Premiere Records PRCD 1009, 1991.
Excerpts from the opera.
Album title: Three American One-Act Operas.
Gregg Smith Singers; Gregg Smith, conductor.
With: Samuel Barber, *A Hand of Bridge*; Marc Blitzstein, *The Harpies*. See: **B840**

NEW ENGLAND TRIPTYCH (W53)

D48 Columbia ML 5347; MS 6040, 1959; Columbia Special Products 91A02007, 1972.
New York Philharmonic Orchestra; André Kostelanetz, conductor.
With: Samuel Barber, Intermezzo from Act 4 of *Vanessa*; Aaron Copland, *A Lincoln Portrait*.

D49 RCA Victor LM 2677; LSC 2677, 1963; LSC 3277, 1972.
"Chester" from *New England Triptych*.
Boston Pops Orchestra; Arthur Fiedler, conductor.

D50 Mercury MG 50379; SR 90379, 1964; SRI 75020, 1974.
Album title: Music by Three Americans.
Eastman-Rochester Symphony Orchestra; Howard Hanson, conductor.
With: Charles Tomlinson Griffes, *Poem for Flute and Orchestra*; Peter Mennin, *Symphony No. 5*.

D51 RCA Victor LSC 3060, 1969; SB 6798, 1969; 644529; LSC 3060.
Philadelphia Orchestra; Eugene Ormandy, conductor.
With: Charles Ives, *Symphony No. 3*.

D52   Decca DL 710168, 1970.
Cincinnati Symphony Orchestra; Max Rudolf, conductor.
With: Luigi Dallapiccola, *Variazioni per orchestra*; Peter Mennin, *Canto for Orchestra*; Anton Webern, *Passacaglia for Orchestra*.

D53   London OS 26442, 1977.
National Symphony Orchestra; Antal Dorati, conductor.
With: Robert Russell Bennett, *The Fun and Faith of William Billings, American*;
William Billings, *Be Glad Then, America*; *When Jesus Wept*; *Chester*.

D54   Mercury 432755 2 PM (reissue of Mercury MG 50379), compact disc, 1991.
Album title: Hanson Conducts Ives, Schuman, and Mennin.
Eastman-Rochester Symphony Orchestra; Howard Hanson, conductor.
With: Charles Ives, *Symphony No. 3* and *Three Places in New England*; Peter
Mennin, *Symphony No. 5*. See: **B565, B665**

D55   Delos DE 3115, compact disc, 1992.
Album title: A Tribute to William Schuman.
Seattle Symphony Orchestra; Gerard Schwarz, conductor.
With: William Schuman, *Judith*, *Symphony No. 5*, and *Variations on "America."*
See: **B474, B585, B645, B666, B699**

D56   Koch International Classics 3 7135 2 H1, compact disc, 1992.
Phoenix Symphony Orchestra; James Sedares, conductor.
With: Bernard Herrmann, *Symphony No. 1*. See: **B443, B564, B585, B654**

D57   RCA (Red Seal) 09026 61282 2, compact disc, 1992.
St. Louis Symphony Orchestra; Leonard Slatkin, conductor.
With: William Schuman, *American Festival Overture, Variations on "America,"* and
Symphony No. 10. See: **B585, B645, B655, B666**

NEWSREEL (orchestral version) **(W21)**

D58   Pro Arte PAD 102, 1984; CDS 102; CDS 3502, compact disc, 1984; PCD 102,
cassette tape.
Album title: American Festival
Milwaukee Symphony Orchestra; Lukas Foss, conductor.
With: Samuel Barber, *Adagio for Strings*; Leonard Bernstein, Overture to *Candide*;
Aaron Copland, *Fanfare for the Common Man* and *Variations on a Shaker Melody
from "Appalachian Spring"*; Henry Cowell, *Saturday Night at the Firehouse*; Charles
Ives, *The Circus Band March* and *The Unanswered Question*; Roger Ruggeri, *If . . .
then*. See: **B561, B670**

NIGHT JOURNEY **(W40)**

D59   CRI SD 500, 1984.
Album title: Music for Martha Graham.
Endymion Ensemble; Jon Goldberg, conductor.
With: William Schuman, *Judith*. See: **B802, B803, B809**

D60 Koch International Classics 37051-2, compact disc; 27051-4, cassette tape, 1991.
Album title: More Music for Martha Graham.
Atlantic Sinfonietta; Andrew Schenck, conductor.
With: Paul Hindemith, *Hérodiade*; Gian Carlo Menotti, *Errand into the Maze*. See:
B799, B807, B816, B818

ORPHEUS WITH HIS LUTE **(W33)**

D61 Turnabout TVS 34727, 1978.
Album title: Twentieth-Century Music for Voice and Guitar.
Rosalind Rees, soprano; David Starobin, guitar.

D62 GSS 110 (arrangement for chorus)
Gregg Smith Singers; Gregg Smith, conductor.

PERCEPTIONS **(W92)**

D63 GSS 110.
Gregg Smith Singers; Gregg Smith, conductor.

D64 Bay Cities BCD 1022, compact disc, 1990.
Album title: American Voices II.
The Chorale of Roberts Wesleyan College; Robert Shewan and Stephen Shewan,
conductors.
With: William Schuman, *Te Deum* and *Carols of Death*; Stephen Shewan, *Feast of
Carols*, *Awake My Soul*, *Morning Has Broken*, and *Sing Unto the Lord*; Leo
Sowerby, *O God, Our Help in Ages Past*; *Liturgy of Hope*; and *I Will Lift Up Mine
Eyes*. See: **B748, B759**

PRAYER IN TIME OF WAR **(W28)**

D65 Louisville S 721, 1973.
Louisville Orchestra; Jorge Mester, conductor.
With: John J. Becker, *Symphony No. 3*; Felix Labunski, *Canto di aspirazione*.

D66 Albany TROY O 27-2 (reissue of Louisville S 721), compact disc, 1990.
Louisville Orchestra; Jorge Mester, conductor.
With: John J. Becker, *Symphony No. 3*; Roy Harris, *Epilogue to Profiles in Courage:
JFK* and *When Johnny Comes Marching Home-An American Overture*; William
Schuman, *Symphony No. 4*. See: **B573, B632, B671, B698**

PRELUDE FOR VOICES **(W16)**

D67 Concordia S 6; CDLP 6, 1958.
Concordia Choir; Paul J. Christiansen, conductor.

D68 Vox SVBX 5353, 1979.
Gregg Smith Singers; Gregg Smith, conductor.

D69   GSS 110.
Gregg Smith Singers; Gregg Smith, conductor.

QUARTETTINO FOR FOUR BASSOONS (W18)

D70   New Music Quarterly Recording 1415 (78 rpm), 1939.
Sam Cohen, Jack Knitzer, Erika Kutzing, Leonard Sharrow.

A QUESTION OF TASTE (W102)

D71   Delos DE 1030, compact disc, 1990.
Juilliard Opera Center and Juilliard Orchestra; Gerard Schwarz, conductor.
With: William Schuman, *The Mighty Casey.*

A SONG OF ORPHEUS (W59)

D72   Columbia ML 6038; MS 6638, 1964; CX 1937; SAX 2575, 1965; Epic 82002; S
82002.
Cleveland Orchestra; George Szell, conductor; Leonard Rose, cello.
With: Samuel Barber, *Piano Concerto.*

STRING QUARTET NO. 2 (W12)

D73   Harmonia Mundi HMU 907114, compact disc, 1994.
Lydian String Quartet.
With: William Schuman, *String Quartet No. 3* and *String Quartet No. 5.* See: **B721,
B730, B742**

STRING QUARTET NO. 3 (W19)

D74   Concert Hall Society AB (78 rpm), 1946.
Gordon Quartet.

D75   RCA Victor LM 2481; LSC 2481, 1961.
Juilliard Quartet.
With: Elliott Carter, *String Quartet No. 2.* See: **B209, B432**

D76   Vox SVBX 5305, 1974.
Album title: American String Quartets, Volume II.
Kohon Quartet.
With: Aaron Copland, *Two Pieces for String Quartet*; George Gershwin, *Lullaby for
String Quartet*; Howard Hanson, *Quartet in One Movement*; Charles Ives, *Scherzo for
2 violins, viola, and cello*; Peter Mennin, *String Quartet No. 2*; Walter Piston, *String
Quartet No. 5*; Roger Sessions, *String Quartet No. 2*; Virgil Thomson, *String Quartet
No. 2.*

D77   Harmonia Mundi HMU 907114, compact disc, 1994.
Lydian String Quartet.
With: William Schuman, *String Quartet No. 2* and *String Quartet No. 5.* See: **B721,
B730, B742**

STRING QUARTET NO. 4 **(W44)**

D78   Columbia ML 4493, 1952.
Juilliard Quartet.
With: Ingolf Dahl, *Concertino a tre.* See: **B735**

STRING QUARTET NO. 5 **(W99)**

D79   Harmonia Mundi HMU 907114, compact disc, 1994.
Lydian String Quartet.
With: William Schuman, *String Quartet No. 2* and *String Quartet No. 3.* See: **B721,**
B730, B742

SYMPHONY NO. 3 **(W22)**

D80   Columbia ML 4413, 1951.
Philadelphia Orchestra; Eugene Ormandy, conductor. See: **B517, B618, B794, B817**

D81   Columbia ML 5645; MS 6245, 1961; CML 5645; CMS 6245, 1968; MS 7442, 1970.
New York Philharmonic Orchestra; Leonard Bernstein, conductor.
With: William Schuman, *Symphony for Strings* (MS 7442 only). See: **B209, B418,**
B432, B441, B498, B499, B520, B541, B551, B554, B572, B660

D82   Deutsche Grammophon 419780-1; 419780-2, compact disc, 1987.
New York Philharmonic Orchestra; Leonard Bernstein, conductor.
With: Roy Harris, *Symphony No. 3.* See: **B447, B522, B570, B586, B597, B663,**
B677, B678, B687, B689

SYMPHONY NO. 4 **(W23)**

D83   Louisville LS 692, 1969.
Louisville Orchestra; Jorge Mester, conductor.
With: Robert Bernat, *In memorium: John F. Kennedy.*

D84   Albany TROY O 27-2 (reissue of Louisville S721), compact disc, 1990.
Louisville Orchestra; Jorge Mester, conductor.
With: John J. Becker, *Symphony No. 3*; Roy Harris, *Epilogue to Profiles in Courage: JFK, When Johnny Comes Marching Home-An American Overture*; William Schuman, *Prayer in Time of War.* See: **B573, B632, B671, B698**

SYMPHONY NO. 5 (Symphony for Strings) **(W29)**

D85   Concert Hall Society A 11 (78 rpm), 1947; CHS 1078, 1951.
Concert Hall Symphony Orchestra; Edgar Schenkman, conductor.
With: Samuel Barber, *Capricorn Concerto.* See: **B448**

D86   Capitol P 8212, 1953; CTL 7039, 1953; Telefunken LCE 8212, pre 1956.
Pittsburgh International Festival of Contemporary Music CB 152, 1952.
Pittsburgh Symphony Orchestra; William Steinberg, conductor.
With: Ernest Bloch, *Concerto Grosso for String Orchestra and Piano.* See: **B16**

D87   Columbia MS 7442, 1970.
New York Philharmonic Orchestra; Leonard Bernstein, conductor.
With: William Schuman, *Symphony No. 3*. See: **B418, B441, B520, B554, B660**

D88   Delos DE 3115, compact disc, 1992.
Album title: A Tribute to William Schuman.
Seattle Symphony Orchestra; Gerard Schwarz, conductor.
With: William Schuman, *Judith*, *New England Triptych*, and *Variations on
"America."* See: **B474, B585, B645, B666, B699**

SYMPHONY NO. 6 **(W41)**

D89   Columbia ML 4992, 1955; CML 4992, 1968; AML 4992, 1974.
Philadelphia Orchestra; Eugene Ormandy, conductor.
With: Walter Piston, *Symphony No. 4*. See: **B16, B436**

D90   CRI SD 477 (reissue of Columbia ML 4992).
Philadelphia Orchestra; Eugene Ormandy, conductor.
With: William Schuman, *Symphony No. 9*. See: **B431, B558**

SYMPHONY NO. 7 **(W58)**

D91   Turnabout TVS 34447, 1971.
Utah Symphony Orchestra; Maurice Abravanel, conductor.
With: Ned Rorem, *Symphony No. 3*. See: **B442, B528, B679, B681**

D92   New World NW 348-1; NW 348-2, compact disc; NW 348-4, cassette tape, 1987.
Pittsburgh Symphony Orchestra; Lorin Maazel, conductor.
With: Leonardo Balada, *Steel Symphony*. See: **B536, B600, B641**

SYMPHONY NO. 8 **(W60)**

D93   Columbia ML 5912; MS 6512, 1963; CMS 6512, 1970.
New York Philharmonic Orchestra; Leonard Bernstein, conductor.
With: Samuel Barber, *Andromache's Farewell*. See: **B525**

D94   Odyssey Y 34140 (reissue of Columbia MS 6512), 1976.
New York Philharmonic Orchestra; Leonard Bernstein, conductor.
With: Robert Suderberg, *Concerto "within the mirror of time" for piano and
orchestra*.
SYMPHONY NO. 9 **(W68)**

D95   RCA Victor LSC 3212, 1971.
Philadelphia Orchestra; Eugene Ormandy, conductor.
With: Vincent Persichetti, *Symphony No. 9*. See: **B680**

D96   CRI SD 477 (reissue of RCA Victor LSC 3212).
Philadelphia Orchestra; Eugene Ormandy, conductor.
With: William Schuman, *Symphony No. 6*. See: **B431, B558**

SYMPHONY NO. 10 **(W79)**

D97   RCA (Red Seal) 09026 61282 2, compact disc, 1992.
St. Louis Symphony Orchestra; Leonard Slatkin, conductor.
With: William Schuman, *American Festival Overture, Variations on "America,"* and
New England Triptych. See: **B585, B645, B655, B666**

TE DEUM **(W35)**

D98   Aspen 1511, 1958.
Washington University Choir; Don Weiss, conductor.

D99   Bay Cities BCD 1022, compact disc, 1990.
Album title: American Voices II.
The Chorale of Roberts Wesleyan College; Robert Shewan and Stephen Shewan,
conductors.
With: William Schuman, *Perceptions* and *Carols of Death*; Stephen Shewan, *Feast of
Carols*, *Awake My Soul*, *Morning Has Broken*, *Sing Unto the Lord*; Leo Sowerby, *O
God, Our Help in Ages Past*; *Liturgy of Hope*; and *I Will Lift Up Mine Eyes.* See:
B748, B759

THREE COLLOQUIES FOR FRENCH HORN AND ORCHESTRA **(W85)**

D100 New World NW 326 1, 1985; NW 326 2, compact disc, 1988.
New York Philharmonic Orchestra; Zubin Mehta, conductor; Philip Myers, horn.
With: George Crumb, *A Haunted Landscape.* See: **B449, B494, B505, B519, B521,
B692, B695**

THREE PIANO MOODS **(W55)**

D101 Musical Heritage Society MHS 7534, 1986.
Includes only the third movement, "Dynamic."
With: piano music by other American composers. See: **B852**

THREE-SCORE SET **(W30)**

D102 Vox 174 (78 rpm), 1947.
Andor Földes, piano.

D103 Educo 3105, 1960's.
Richard Carpenter, piano.

D104 Vox SVBX 5303, 1976.
Roger Shields, piano.

TIME TO THE OLD **(W86)**

D105   CRI SD 439, 1980.
Rosalind Rees, soprano; Thomas Muraco, piano.
With: William Schuman, *In Sweet Music* and *The Young Dead Soldiers*. See: **B714, B719, B724, B726, B729, B733**

TO THEE OLD CAUSE **(W69)**

D106   Columbia MS 7392, 1970.
New York Philharmonic Orchestra; Leonard Bernstein, conductor; Harold Gomberg, oboe.
With: Randall Thompson, *Symphony No. 2.*

UNDERTOW **(W37)**

D107   Mercury MG 10088, 1951.
Louisville Orchestra; William Schuman, conductor.
With: William Schuman, *Judith*. See: **B16, B794, B797, B814, B817**

D108   Capitol P 8238, 1954.
Ballet Theatre Orchestra; Joseph Levine, conductor.
With: Aaron Copland, *Billy the Kid Ballet Suite*. See: **B800**

D109   Capitol HDR 21004 (reissue of Capitol P 8238), 1966.
Album title: Modern American Ballet.
Ballet Theatre Orchestra; Joseph Levine, conductor.
With: George Antheil, *Capital of the World*; Leonard Bernstein, *Facsimile*, *Fancy Free*; Aaron Copland, *Billy the Kid*, *Rodeo*; Morton Gould, *Fall River Legend*.

D110   New World 253 (reissue of Capitol P 8238), 1978.
Ballet Theatre Orchestra; Joseph Levine, conductor.
With: Morton Gould, *Fall River Legend.*

VARIATIONS ON "AMERICA" (after Charles Ives) **(W63)**

D111   Louisville First Editions 651, 1965.
Louisville Orchestra; Robert Whitney, conductor.
With: Alvin Etler, *Concerto for Wind Quintet and Orchestra*; Ulysses Kay, *Umbrian Scene.*

D112   RCA Victor LM/LSC 2893, 1966.
Chicago Symphony Orchestra; Morton Gould, conductor.
With: Charles Ives, *Symphony No. 1* and *The Unanswered Question.*

D113   Columbia MS 7289, 1969.
Philadelphia Orchestra; Eugene Ormandy, conductor.

D114   London 2246, 1976.
Los Angeles Philharmonic Orchestra; Zubin Mehta, conductor. See: **B574**

D115 Columbia MA 33728, 1976.
André Kostelanetz and His Orchestra; André Kostelanetz, conductor.

D116 London SPC 21178, 1978.
Boston Pops Orchestra; Arthur Fiedler, conductor.

D117 Delos DE 3115, compact disc, 1992.
Album title: A Tribute to William Schuman.
Seattle Symphony Orchestra; Gerard Schwarz, conductor.
With: William Schuman, *Judith*, *New England Triptych*, and *Symphony No. 5*. See: **B474, B585, B645, B666**

D118 RCA (Red Seal) 09026 61282 2, compact disc, 1992.
St. Louis Symphony Orchestra; Leonard Slatkin, conductor.
With: William Schuman, *American Festival Overture*, *New England Triptych*, and *Symphony No. 10*. See: **B585, B645, B655, B666**

D119 Teldec 174007-2 ZK, compact disc, 1992.
New York Philharmonic Orchestra; Kurt Masur, conductor.
With: Johannes Brahms, *Variations on a Theme by Haydn*; Max Reger, *Variations and Fugue on a Theme by Mozart*.

VOYAGE **(W47)**

D120 Columbia ML 4987, 1955; CML 4987, 1968; AML 4987, 1976.
Beveridge Webster, piano.
With: Virgil Thomson, *String Quartet No. 2*.

D121 Etcetera ETC 1036; KTC 1036, compact disc; XTC 1036, cassette tape, 1987.
Bennett Lerner, piano.
With: Samuel Barber, *Love Song*; Marc Blitzstein, *Three excerpts from "The Guests"*; Paul Bowles, *Dance, Cross-Country, Sonatina*; Aaron Copland, *Petit Portrait, Sentimental Melody, Sonnet II, Three Moods*; Roy Harris, *American Ballads*; Phillip Ramey, *Canzona*.

WHEN JESUS WEPT **(W56)**
(New England Triptych)

D122 Cornell University CUWE 9, 1971.
Cornell University Wind Ensemble; Marice Stith, conductor.
With: Gustav Holst, *Hammersmith* (prelude and scherzo); Richard Toensing, *Doxologies I*; Clifton Williams, *The Sinfonians*.

WHEN JESUS WEPT **(W93)**

(New England Triptych, organ transcription by Samuel Adler)

D123   Gasparo GS 258, compact disc, c. 1988.
Barbara Harbach, organ.
With: Samuel Adler, *Hymnset: Four Chorale Preludes on Old American Hymns*;
Gardner Read, *Preludes on Old Southern Hymns* and *Six Preludes on Old Southern Hymns*. See: **B850, B851, B855**

THE YOUNG DEAD SOLDIERS **(W82)**

D124   CRI SD 439, 1980.
White Mountains Festival Orchestra; Gerard Schwarz, conductor; Rosalind Rees, soprano; Robin Graham, horn.
With: William Schuman, *To Thee Old Cause* and *In Sweet Music*. See: **B714, B719, B724, B726, B729, B733**

Bibliography

Bibliographies, Catalogs, and Discographies

B1   *American Composers' Concerts and Festivals of American Music, 1925-1971:*
         Cumulative Repertoire. Rochester: University of Rochester, 1972. 75 pp. ML120
         U5 R6

         An alphabetical catalog by composer of compositions presented on the Eastman
         School of Music's American Composers' Concerts and Festivals from 1925 to 1971.
         Also includes student compositions performed from 1927 to 1964. Five Schuman
         works are listed on page thirty-six. In addition, a list of recordings of American
         music by the Eastman-Rochester Symphony Orchestra includes Schuman's *New
         England Triptych.* See: **D50**

B2   "Archives and Collections: Musicians' Papers in Archives." *Central Opera Service*
         27, no. 4 (1987): 38.

         Reports on the recent acquisition of a substantial collection of Schuman's papers by
         the New York Public Library at Lincoln Center.

B3   *ASCAP Symphonic Catalog: 1977.* 3rd. ed. New York: R.R. Bowker, 1977. 511 pp.
         ISBN 0 835 20910 5 ML128.05 A55 1977

         This listing of works by ASCAP members includes a Schuman entry (pp. 417-18) of
         sixteen items.

B4   Baron, John H. *Chamber Music: A Research and Information Guide.* Garland
         Reference Library of the Humanities, vol. 704. New York: Garland, 1987. 500 pp.
         ISBN 0 824 08346 6 ML128 C4 B37

         An annotated bibliography of writings on chamber music. Contains two entries
         which include information on Schuman.

B5   Borroff, Edith. *American Operas: A Checklist*. Detroit Studies in Music
Bibliography, vol. 69. Warren, MI: Harmonie Park, 1992. 334 pp. ISBN 0 899
90063 1 ML128.04 B58 1992

A comprehensive checklist of over four thousand operas written in the United States
from the end of the eighteenth century to the early 1990s. Organized alphabetically
by composer, Borroff includes basic information, if known, about each opera, without
annotation. Schuman's operas, *The Mighty Casey* and *A Question of Taste*, are listed
on pp. 267 and 268.

B6   Burnsworth, Charles C. *Choral Music for Women's Voices: An Annotated
Bibliography of Recommended Works*. Metuchen, NJ: Scarecrow, 1968. 180 pp.
ML128 V7 B87

Includes two compositions by Schuman: *Prelude for Voices* and *Requiescat* (pp. 106-
07). Also lists two choral arrangements by the composer on p. 132.

B7   Butler, Stanley. *Guide to the Best in Contemporary Piano Music*. 2 vols. Metuchen,
NJ: Scarecrow, 1973. 196, 172 pp. ISBN 0 810 80628 2 ML132 P3 B88

This helpful guide to twentieth-century piano music published since 1950 presents an
annotated listing of works organized alphabetically by composer within prescribed
levels of difficulty. Schuman works are found in volume one on pages 92 and 140
and in volume two on page 59. Also provides a glossary of terms, an index of
musical and pianistic features, an index to composers and compositions, and a list of
publishers.

B8   "Classified Chronological Catalog of Works by the United States Composer William
Schuman." *Inter-American Music Bulletin* 12 (July 1959): 34-41.

A chronological catalog arranged by genre of works composed by Schuman to 1959.
Cites year of composition, title, duration, publisher, and observations (dates of first
performances, orchestras and conductors, ensembles and conductors, information
about commissions, recordings). Concludes with a list of publishers' addresses and a
reproduction of the opening page of *Undertow*. See: **B11**

B9   Cohn, Arthur. *The Collector's Twentieth-Century Music in the Western Hemisphere*.
New York: J.B. Lippincott, 1961; reprint ed., New York: Da Capo, 1972, pp. 187-93.
ISBN 0 306 70404 8 ML156.4 N3 A5 1972

A concise introduction to the composer's music intended more for the general reader
than for the music specialist. Begins with the statement "Schuman is one of the big
names in American music." The bulk of the entry is given to a discussion of nine
Schuman works, all of which have been recorded. Provides analyses of the
compositions and includes information about the recordings.

B10   _____. *Recorded Classical Music*. New York: Schirmer, 1981. 2164 pp. ISBN
0 028 70640 4 ML156.9 C63

A voluminous annotated discography. Twenty-one Schuman recordings are listed and described on pp. 1660-66. In addition, a recording of Schuman's arrangement of Charles Ives's *Variations on "America"* is discussed on p. 928.

B11 *Composers of the Americas.* Vol. 5. Washington: Pan American Union, 1959. 107 pp. ML390 P16 v.5

Issued as a publication by the Pan American Union in their series devoted to providing biographical data and catalogs of works for composers of the Americas, this volume contains material on fourteen composers, including William Schuman. The Schuman entry (pp. 69-77) consists of a succinct biography in both Spanish and English, a facsimile of the first page from the composer's ballet *Undertow*, and a chronological listing of his works to 1959. The works catalog, which contains forty-nine items organized by genre, provides the year of composition, title, duration in minutes, publishers, and very brief observations, giving such information as date of first performance, performers, and details on commissions. See: **B8**

B12 Demakis, Louise W. *Inventory to the Papers and Records of William Schuman 1910-*. New York: The New York Public Library, 1989. 134 pp.

A comprehensive catalog of the William Schuman Collection located in the Music Division of the New York Public Library at Lincoln Center. According to the introduction, the listing includes "correspondence, photographs, scrapbooks, clippings, musical and non-musical programs, speeches, statements, magazine and newspaper articles, musical reviews and memorabilia," covering the years 1933 to 1986. Arranged in seven sections (each called Series), the first four present the items chronologically while the last two (Series V-William Schuman Music and Series VI-Schuman Family Papers) do not. Content notes about selected entries appear at the end of each series. Contains an index.

B13 Diamond, Harold J. *Music Analyses: An Annotated Guide to the Literature.* New York: Schirmer Books, 1991. 716 pp. ISBN 0 028 70110 0 ML128 A7 D5 1991

Documents, with brief commentaries, only three entries pertaining to Schuman literature (items 3641, 3642, and 3643).

B14 Dox, Thurston J. *American Oratorios and Cantatas: A Catalog of Works Written in the United States from Colonial Times to 1985.* 2 vols. Metuchen, NJ: Scarecrow, 1986. 709, 1306 pp. ISBN 0 810 81861 2 ML128 O45

A comprehensive catalog of American oratorios and cantatas divided into the following sections: oratorios, cantatas, ensemble cantatas, and choral theater. Some of the bibliographical entries contain excerpts from reviews or other writings. Schuman's cantatas are listed in volume two, pp. 954-56: *Casey at the Bat, A Free Song,* and *This Is Our Time.*

B15 Edmunds, John, and Boelzner, Gordon. *Some Twentieth Century American Composers: A Selective Bibliography*, with introductory essay by Nicolas Slonimsky, vol. 2. New York: New York Public Library, 1960. 55 pp. ML120 U5 Es v.2

A very selective, unannotated bibliography of seventeen composers. The Schuman portion (pp. 42-44) contains 92 items. Also includes two appendixes listing other American composers and an index.

B16   Ellsworth, Ray. "Americans on Microgroove, Part II." *High Fidelity Magazine* (August 1956): 60-65.

This narrative discography of recorded works by American composers contains a paragraph on Schuman in which the following works are enumerated: *American Festival Overture* (ARS 115), *Symphony for Strings* (Capital P 8212), *Undertow* (Mercury MG 10088), *Judith* (Mercury MG 10088), and the Sixth Symphony (Columbia ML 4992). Summarizes in scant fashion Schuman's musical style, noting such elements as dissonance, rhythm, and, in some scores, the presence of folklore materials or jazz. See: **D2, D3, D41, D86, D89, D107**

B17   Gleason, Harold, and Becker, Warren. *20th-Century American Composers*. 2nd ed. Music Literature Outlines, series iv. Bloomington: Frangipani, 1980. 232 pp. ISBN 0 899 17266 0 ML161 G53 ser. 4

A comprehensive bibliography of articles and books about seventeen composers. Though the bibliographic entries are presented without annotations, the authors also provide a chronology of biographical information, a quotation by the composer, an extensive list of works, and a helpful outline of musical style for each composer. The Schuman section (pp. 170-84) divides the bibliographic materials into five parts: books about William Schuman, articles by William Schuman, references to William Schuman in books and articles, references to works by William Schuman, and dissertations about William Schuman and his works.

B18   Gray, Michael, compiler. *Classical Music Discographies, 1976-1988: A Bibliography*. Greenwood Press Discographies, number 34. New York: Greenwood, 1989. 334 pp. ISBN 0 313 25942 9 ML128 D56 G7 1989

This bibliography of classical music discographies contains seven entries for William Schuman.

B19   *Guide to the Juilliard School Archives*, edited by Jane Gottlieb, Stephen E. Novak, and Taras Pavlovsky. New York: The Juilliard School, 1992. 113 pp. MT4 N5 J75 1992

An important new catalog which contains many references to Schuman. Presents a three-page chronology of prominent events in Juilliard's history, a listing of Juilliard administrators from 1905 to 1992, and an inventory of the school's substantial archival holdings (pp. 29-56). Also contains an appendix, a select bibliography, and a name index.

B20   Hall, David. *The Record Book: A Guide to the World of the Phonograph*. New York: Oliver Durrell, 1948; reprint ed., Westport, CT: Greenwood, 1978. 1394 pp. ISBN 0 313 20425 x ML156.2 H34 1978

After a discussion of the paucity of available recordings of Schuman's works and his musical style in general, four early Schuman recordings are listed.

B21 _____. "A Bio-Discography of William Schuman." *Ovation* 6 (August-September 1985): 8-14, 18-22.

Following an introduction on the current state of Schuman recordings, the author supplies an outstanding chronological overview of the composer's compositions and recorded works, together with pertinent biographical information, beginning with the *Chorale Canons* of 1932-33 and concluding with the *American Hymn: Orchestral Variations on an Original Melody* of 1981. Divided into two parts, this essay was written in honor of Schuman's seventy-fifth birthday. Also includes a select list of 1985/86 performances of the composer's music.

B22 Hinson, Maurice. *Guide to the Pianist's Repertoire.* Second, revised and enlarged edition. Bloomington: Indiana University Press, 1987. 856 pp. ISBN 0 253 32656 7 ML128 P3 H5 1987

An extensive annotated bibliography which contains three Schuman entries (p. 649): *Three-Score Set, Voyage,* and *Three Piano Moods.*

B23 _____. *The Pianist's Reference Guide: A Bibliographical Survey.* Los Angeles: Alfred, 1987. 336 pp. ISBN 0 882 84358 3 ML128 P3 H54 1987

An annotated bibliography of writings on the piano. Arranged alphabetically by author, the publication contains books, theses, and dissertations; each entry includes the standard bibliographical information. Concludes with a subject index, a composer index, and an appendix of a list of publishers. One entry (p. 14), a dissertation by Karen Elizabeth Bals entitled *The American Piano Concerto in the Mid-Twentieth Century*, deals with William Schuman. See: **B421**

B24 _____. *Music for Piano and Orchestra.* Enlarged edition. Bloomington: Indiana University Press, 1993. 359 pp. ISBN 0 253 33953 7 ML128 P3 H53 1993

An excellent reference work. This annotated bibliography includes an entry for Schuman's piano concerto (p. 263).

B25 Hovland, Michael. *Musical Settings of American Poetry: A Bibliography.* New York: Greenwood, 1986. 531 pp. ISBN 0 313 22938 4 ML128 V7 H67 1986

Contains seventeen entries for works by Schuman.

B26 Johnson, H. Earle. *Operas on American Subjects.* New York: Coleman-Ross, 1964. 125 pp. ML128 O4 J6

Organized alphabetically by composer, this is a helpful annotated catalog of operas based on American topics. Cites Schuman's *The Mighty Casey* (p. 89).

B27   Keats, Sheila. "Reference Articles on American Composers: William Schuman."
The Juilliard Review 1 (Fall 1954): 32.

Presents a listing of seven articles about Schuman published between 1942 and 1952.
A succinct annotation accompanies each entry.

B28   Kornick, Rebecca Hodell. *Recent American Opera: A Production Guide.* New York:
Columbia, 1991. 352 pp. ISBN 0 231 06920 0 MT955 K82 1990

Lists American operas premiered after 1972. Arranged alphabetically by composer,
each entry contains basic information about the libretto and the musical style of the
work; a synopsis of the plot; production requirements, such as ranges of the vocal
roles; and cites published reviews, complete with excerpts. Schuman's *A Question of
Taste* is examined on pages 277-79.

B29   Koshgarian, Richard. *American Orchestral Music: A Performance Catalog.*
Metuchen, NJ: Scarecrow, 1992. 762 pp. ISBN 0 810 82632 1 ML128.05 K67 1992

An important reference work for American music. The thirty-eight Schuman entries
(pp. 456-58) are arranged chronologically, without annotations. Cites the title, date
of composition, duration, instrumentation, and publisher.

B30   Krummel, D.W.; Geil, Jean; Dyen, Doris J.; and Root, Deane L. *Resources of
American Music History: A Directory of Source Materials from Colonial Times to
World War II.* Urbana: University of Illinois Press, 1981. 463 pp. ISBN 0 252
00828 6 ML120 U5 R47

An invaluable source for research in American music. Eight locations are listed
which contain Schuman materials in their collections.

B31   Lust, Patricia. *American Vocal Chamber Music, 1945-1980.* New York: Greenwood,
1985. 273 pp. ISBN 0 313 24599 1 ML128 V7 L8 1985

Schuman's *In Sweet Music* is listed as item 392 in this useful annotated bibliography.
The entry identifies the publisher, date of composition, text, instrumentation,
duration, and reprints the composer's dedication.

B32   Magi, Aldo P. "Thomas Wolfe: Say it with Music, Part One." *The Thomas Wolfe
Review* (Fall 1985): 11-26.

Catalogs, in chronological order, musical compositions set to texts by Thomas Wolfe.
Schuman's *Prelude for Voices* is the first work discussed.

B33   Mueller, Kate Hevner. *Twenty-Seven Major American Symphony Orchestras.*
Bloomington: Indiana University Press, 1973. 398 pp. ISBN 0 253 36110 9 ML128
O5 M75

Provides data on orchestral performances of works by numerous composers. The
Schuman citation, listing twenty-three compositions, is found on page 307.
Supersedes her husband's earlier work: John H. Mueller, *The American Symphony
Orchestra*.

B34   Nishimura, Mari. *The Twentieth-Century Composer Speaks: An Index of Interviews*.
Berkeley: Fallen Leaf Press, 1993. 189 pp. ISBN 0 914 91329 8 ML118 N57 1993

Catalogs interviews of twentieth-century composers printed in music journals, books,
and recordings from 1949 to 1987. Four Schuman entries (items 876-79) are listed on
pages 135-36.

B35   Oja, Carol J., ed. "William Schuman." *American Music Recordings: A Discography
of 20th-Century U.S. Composers*, pp. 267-70. Institute for Studies in American
Music. Brooklyn College of the City University of New York, 1982. ISBN 0 914
67819 1 ML 156.4 N3 U3

A first-rate discography which includes all Schuman recordings up to 1980. This
unannotated, alphabetical listing by title also contains the date of composition, the
ensembles and/or performers, record label, disc number, speed, and, if known, the
recording date, release date, and deletion date.

B36   Petersen, Barbara A. *William Schuman*. New York: *BMI*, 1990. 45 pp.

The most recent comprehensive catalog of Schuman's music is presented in this
brochure. Following an excellent account of the composer's life, a discussion of his
works, and a three-page listing of his honors and awards, the heart of the publication
is an extensive list of works which, arranged alphabetically by genre, identifies the
year of composition, publisher, time of performance, instrumentation, first
performance, and, if appropriate, information about the commission. Concludes with
a complete, though unannotated, discography.

B37   Phemister, William. *American Piano Concertos: A Bibliography*. Detroit:
Information Coordinators, Inc., 1985. 323 pp. ISBN 0 899 90026 7 ML128 P3 P5
1985

A useful catalog. Presents a citation (pp. 250-51) for Schuman's piano concerto of
1942. Identifies the publisher, date of publication, duration, information about the
first performance, and lists a recording. Reprints a substantial excerpt from an Olin
Downes review published in the 14 January 1943 *New York Times*. See: **W24a, B478**

B38   Rehrig, William H. *The Heritage Encyclopedia of Band Music: Composers and
Their Music*, edited by Paul E. Bierley. vol. 2. Westerville, OH: Integrity, 1991.
ISBN 0 918 04808 7

A valuable catalog. The Schuman entry (p. 677) includes an extremely brief and
incomplete biography, as well as a list of eleven band compositions.

B39   Rouse, Christopher. *William Schuman Documentary.* New York: G. Schirmer, 1980. 54 pp. ML410 S386 R7 1980

An indispensable monograph. Intended by the author as "a brief summation of the life and works of a figure vitally important to American music and letters." Valuable especially for the biography (pp. 1-26), which chronicles Schuman's life and career to 1980. Provides a basic, selective unannotated bibliography of only three and a half pages divided into "Writings about William Schuman" and "Writings by William Schuman." Presents a comprehensive catalog of the composer's compositions, organized chronologically by genre, and includes a discography arranged alphabetically by work. Devotes over two pages to a listing of Schuman's numerous degrees, honors, awards, and affiliations. Introductory remarks are given by Leonard Bernstein and Jacob Druckman.

B40   Weber, J.F. "A William Schuman Discography." *Journal of the Association for Recorded Sound Collections* 8 (September 1976): 74-81.

Compiled in celebration of the American bicentennial, this is Weber's original Schuman discography. Presents a list of recordings arranged by title in chronological order of composition. See: **B41**

B41   _____. *Carter and Schuman.* Discography Series XIX. Utica, NY: J.F. Weber, 1978. 20 pp. ML156.5 C27 W4

A comprehensive discography of all Schuman recordings to the time of publication. Each entry (items 101 to 152), presented by title in chronological order, includes the date of composition, the date of the first performance, and a listing of all known recordings. Also provides the date of recording, if known, and the dates of release and deletion. Identifies selected reviews. An expansion of the discography originally published in the September 1976 *Journal of the Association for Recorded Sound Collections.* See: **B40**

B42   Wenk, Arthur. *Analyses of Nineteenth- and Twentieth-Century Music: 1940-1985.* MLA Index and Bibliography Series, no. 25. Boston: Music Library Association, 1987. ISBN 0 914 95436 9 ML113 W45 1987

An alphabetical index by composer. Lists only four Schuman entries on page 256.

B43   White, J. Perry. *Twentieth-Century Choral Music: An Annotated Bibliography of Music Suitable for Use by High School Choirs.* 2nd ed. Metuchen, NJ: Scarecrow, 1990. 214 pp. ISBN 0 810 82394 2 ML128 C48 W53 1990

A valuable reference work for public school choral directors. Seven works by Schuman are included: *The Lord Has a Child*, "To All, to Each" from *Carols of Death*, "The Last Invocation" from *Carols of Death*, "The Unknown Region" from *Carols of Death*, "Thrift #2" from *Four Rounds on Famous Words*, "Health #2" from *Four Rounds on Famous Words*, and "Caution #3" from *Four Rounds on Famous Words*. Each entry, in addition to brief comments, identifies the composer, title, voicing, accompaniment, text, range, difficulty, style, publisher, usage, date of composition, and appropriate level.

Biographical Studies, General Stylistic Studies, and General References to Schuman

B44   "Academy of Arts Elects Six." *The New York Times*, December 10, 1973, p. 58.

Terse announcement of Schuman's election to the American Academy of Arts and Letters.

B45   "Advisers Are Named for U.S.-ANTA Plan." *The New York Times*, October 25, 1954, p. 30.

In this brief notice, Schuman, together with Olin Downes, Jay S. Harrison, Edwin Hughes, Paul Henry Lang, and Virgil Thomson, is listed as having been named to an advisory panel under the auspices of the American National Theatre and Academy, selected for the purpose of making recommendations to the State Department of musicians and ensembles for performance abroad.

B46   "American Composers—William Schuman." *The Musical Courier* 159 (January 1959): 41.

Venerates Schuman both as a composer and music educator. Presents a superficial overview of the composer's career. Recommends recordings of his music to young listeners.

B47   Anderson, E. Ruth. *Contemporary American Composers: A Biographical Dictionary*. 2nd ed. Boston: G.K. Hall, 1982, pp. 458-59. ISBN 0 816 18223 x ML390 A54 1982

Presents only the most basic biographical information and provides a list of the composer's works organized by genre.

B48   Anderson, W.R. "William Howard Schuman." *The Music Masters: The Twentieth Century*, edited by A.L. Bacharach. London: Cassell, 1954. Vol. 4, pp. 311-16. ML390 M76

A guide to Schuman's life and works written for the general reader rather than the music scholar.

B49   Apple, R.W., Jr. "City Ballet Battles Lincoln Center Plan to Control Theater." *The New York Times*, October 2, 1964, pp. 1, 29.

Relates the dispute between the Lincoln Center and the New York City Ballet. Prints excerpts from a letter by Schuman to the chairman of the City Center board regarding the situation.

B50   Archer, Eugene. "Lincoln Center to Show Movies." *The New York Times*, March 28, 1962, p. 34.

Deals with Schuman's decision to program motion pictures at the Lincoln Center.

B51   _____. "Major Film Fete Planned for City." *The New York Times*, May 1, 1963, p. 35.

Publicizes Schuman's announcement of an international film festival to be held at the Lincoln Center the following September.

B52   "The Arts." *Facts on File* (January 14, 1969): 857.

Briefly recognizes the need for greater funding for the arts based on several 1969 developments. Notes administrative changes at the Lincoln Center for the Performing Arts, including the resignation of William Schuman.

B53   "Arts Center Picks Chief of Finances." *The New York Times*, December 14, 1961, p. 52.

Presents comments by Schuman regarding his recommendation that Edgar B. Young, who was then acting president of Lincoln Center, join his new administration on January 1 as executive vice president of finance for Lincoln Center.

B54   Ayres, Alfred. "Schuman Honored at Kennedy Center." *The Juilliard Journal* 5 (December 1989-January 1990): 3.

Recognizes Schuman's selection as one of the Kennedy Center Honors recipients for 1989. Briefly recaps some of the highlights of the composer's career.

B55   Benjamin, Philip. "Composer to Head Lincoln Art Center." *The New York Times*, September 13, 1961, pp. 1, 51.

Provides details on the selection of Schuman as the president of the Lincoln Center for the Performing Arts. Includes comments on the composer by John D. Rockefeller III, chairman of the Lincoln Center board, and reprints excerpts from a letter written by Schuman to the Juilliard faculty in which he stated his reasons for accepting the new position.

B56   Block, Maxine, ed. "William (Howard) Schuman." *Current Biography: 1942*. New York: H.W. Wilson, 1942. 940 pp.

Sketches (pp. 746-48) the history of Schuman's career as a composer from his youth to his Fourth Symphony and *Newsreel*. Concludes with a short list of references.

B57   Bloom, Julius, ed. *The Year in American Music, 1946-1947*. New York: Allen, Towne & Heath, 1947. 571 pp. ML13 Y4 v. 1

Chronicles the year in music in the United States from September 1946 to May 1947. Several references are made to Schuman's activities and compositions.

B58   "BMI and Pulitzer/Tony/Obie." *BMI: The Many Worlds of Music* (1985): 38.

Includes a succinct notice of a special citation awarded to Schuman in April by the Pulitzer Prize committee.

B59   "BMI News: Schuman Takes Schuman Award." *BMI: The Many Worlds of Music* 2 (1982): 33.

Brief comments concerning the presentation of the William Schuman Award, granted by Columbia University, to Schuman.

B60   Borroff, Edith. *Music Melting Round: A History of Music in the United States*. New York: Ardsley House, 1995. 387 pp. ISBN 1 880 15717 9

This most recent survey of music in the United States includes a disappointingly brief discussion (p. 189) of William Schuman.

B61   "Brandeis Salutes 4 Creative Artists." *The New York Times*, March 6, 1957, p. 25.

Lists Schuman as one of the recipients of the first Brandeis University Creative Arts awards.

B62   "Brandeis to Honor Three." *The New York Times*, May 31, 1962, p. 13.

Short announcement indicating that Schuman was chosen to receive an honorary doctorate from Brandeis University.

B63   Broder, Nathan. "The Music of William Schuman." *The Musical Quarterly* 31 (January 1945): 17-28.

Although outdated, Broder's essay ranks as an early, major contribution to Schuman literature. Gives a good description of the composer's music up to 1945. Discusses salient characteristics of Schuman's compositional style: melody, harmony, rhythm, form, and orchestration. Argues that "the general character of his music . . . is far more than the sum of its parts. Its most prominent traits are boldness, originality, freshness, resourcefulness, and intensity of feeling." After a succinct biographical sketch, which concludes with an assessment of the Schuman-Roy Harris association, the author provides a list of works with publisher, date of composition, and information on first performance.

B64   _____. "Schuman, William Howard." *Die Musik in Geschichte und Gegenwart*, edited by Friedrich Blume. Kassel: Bärenreiter, 1949-. Vol. 12 (1965), cols. 260-61. ML100 M92

Presents a concise introduction to Schuman's life and works and includes a list of works by genre, a summary of musical style, and a modest bibliography.

B65   Brown, Michael R. "Enduring Wisdom from William Schuman." *The Instrumentalist* 48 (November 1993): 26-29.

A 1986 interview, never before published, conducted by the author at the composer's apartment in New York City. Emphasizes Schuman's experience as a composer for band.

B66   Brussel, James A. "Schizoid." *The New York Times Magazine*, January 14, 1962, p. 4.

A letter to the editor responding to criticisms of Schuman set forth in Harold Schonberg's letter to *The New York Times* of 31 December 1961, "Man to Orchestrate Lincoln Centre." Also includes a reply by Mr. Schonberg. See: **B324**

B67   Burkat, Leonard. "Current Chronicle: Boston." *The Musical Quarterly* 35 (April 1949): 285-87.

Lists Schuman as one of the composers whose works were presented on "American" programs by Koussevitzky and the Boston Symphony Orchestra.

B68   Butterworth, Neil. *A Dictionary of American Composers*. New York: Garland, 1984. 523 pp. ISBN 0 824 09311 9 ML106 U3 B87 1984

A brief discussion (pp. 412-14) of Schuman's life and works is presented in this biographical dictionary.

B69   "A Cake Surprises the Composer William Schuman." *The New York Times*, August 6, 1980, section 2, p. 4.

Reports that a birthday cake was given to the composer after a concert of his compositions at the Aspen Music Festival.

B70   Canby, Vincent. "Lincoln Center Upgrading Films." *The New York Times*, January 10, 1967, p. 34.

Discusses the appointment of William F. May to the board of directors of the Lincoln Center. His special responsibility was to develop the film area at Lincoln Center. Schuman is interviewed about the plans for the film department.

B71   "Casey at the Baton." *Time* 78 (September 22, 1961): 67-68.

Documents the appointment of Schuman to the presidency of Lincoln Center. Summarizes the important events of the composer's life.

B72   "Certificate of Merit to Schuman." *Pan Pipes of Sigma Alpha Iota* 60, no. 2 (1968): 42.

Acknowledges Schuman as the recipient of Sigma Alpha Iota's Certificate of Merit. Provides a listing of his most important works.

B73   Chapin, Louis. "Concert Music." *BMI: The Many Worlds of Music* (May 1967): 14.

Identifies Schuman as one of the composers commissioned to compose a work for the 125th anniversary of the New York Philharmonic. Also notes that Schuman was awarded both the Handel Medallion and the Concert Artists Guild Award at a dinner concert on March 12.

B74   _____. "William Schuman." *Broadcast Music, Inc.* (July 1967): 14.

Emphasizes the dual nature of Schuman's career as composer and administrator. Provides excerpts from a 1961 interview with Aaron Copland and Schuman. Notes the influence of both Roy Harris and Paul Hindemith on the composer's music. Includes some information on Schuman's career and musical style.

B75   Chase, Gilbert. *America's Music: From the Pilgrims to the Present.* New York: McGraw-Hill, 1955. 733 pp. ML 200 C5

A landmark study of music in America. Chase provides a general introduction to the music of Schuman (pp. 533-35) in a chapter entitled "The Eclectics." After presenting background information on the composer, the bulk of this section focuses on Schuman's orchestral compositions. *The Mighty Casey* is discussed (pp. 651-52) in the chapter "Toward an American Opera." See: **B76**

B76   _____. *America's Music: From the Pilgrims to the Present.* Revised Third Edition. Urbana: University of Illinois Press, 1987. 712 pp. ISBN 0 252 00454 x ML200 C5 1987

A magisterial revision of the earlier editions. Although the coverage of Schuman is not as extensive as in the previous editions, the composer is examined (pp. 572-73) in Chapter 31 entitled "The Grand Tradition." Following a paragraph devoted to Schuman's formative years, Chase includes a discussion of the composer's music, based largely on opinions offered by Bruce Saylor, Vincent Persichetti, and William Brooks. Argues that "Among the composers of the next generation, William Schuman (b. 1910) most dramatically and consistently expanded the heritage of the Grand Tradition within an essentially American context." See: **B75**

B77   Clark, John W. "William Schuman on His Symphonies: An Interview." *American Music* 4 (Fall 1986): 328-36.

A perceptive and informative interview which corroborates the notion that Schuman's principal interest as a composer is for the orchestra. Though Clark explores many issues related to the symphony in general and Schuman's symphonies specifically, the most enlightening discussion deals with the composer's opinions about form and one-movement symphonies. See: **B452**

B78   "Colgate Class Told Courage Is Needed." *The New York Times*, June 14, 1960, p. 34.

Schuman is listed as one of several dignitaries to receive an honorary degree from Colgate University.

B79   Commanday, Robert. "An American Original, Composer William Schuman Celebrated the Country in His Works." *San Francisco Chronicle*, February 20, 1992, section e, p. 3.

This obituary opens with the opinion that "the country lost the last composer of stature from the great between-the-wars generation of distinctly American composers."

B80   "Commencements: The Juilliard School." *The New York Times*, May 21, 1988, p. 34.

Mentions that Schuman, in his commencement address at Juilliard, gave a history of the school from its inception to the present.

B81   "Commencements: Yale University." *The New York Times*, May 31, 1988, section 2, p. 5.

Identifies the composer as one of the recipients of an honorary degree at Yale University's commencement exercises.

B82   "Committee Chosen for Hopkins Center." *The New York Times*, May 27, 1962, p. 96.

Calls attention to Schuman's appointment to the advisory board of Dartmouth College's Hopkins Center for the Performing Arts.

B83   "Composer and Administrator: William Schuman on His Music and His Work at the Juilliard School." *The Times*, September 27, 1960, p. 27.

The composer, in conversation with a special correspondent, discusses aspects of his career as a composer and as head of the Juilliard School.

B84   "Composer at Lincoln Sq.: William Howard Schuman." *The New York Times*, September 13, 1961, p. 51.

Written upon the occasion of Schuman's appointment as president of Lincoln Center, this somewhat substantial newspaper article recounts the major events of the composer's life and career.

B85 "Composer Finds Music Teaching Is Off Key in Public Schools Here." *The New York Times*, January 14, 1956, p. 21.

Summarizes a speech given before faculty and students at New Jersey's Trenton State College in which Schuman panned the state of music education in public schools.

B86 "Composer William Howard Schuman: Tribute to a Contemporary American Composer." *Music Clubs Magazine* 71 (Summer 1992): 9.

Dedicated to the memory of Schuman, this article provides a short survey of his career and music. Maintains that Schuman is one of the most notable composers in the history of American music.

B87 "Composers in Focus." *Broadcast Music, Inc.* (Winter 1976): 16-33.

Biographies of nineteen eminent composers (Schuman is discussed on pp. 29-30) are presented in this survey of the most-performed composers during the 1974-1975 concert season.

*   *Composers of the Americas.*

Cited as **B11**.

B88 "Composers Win Guggenheim Awards." *Musical America* 59 (April 10, 1939): 4.

Schuman, then on the faculty of Sarah Lawrence College, is named as one of four composers to be awarded a Guggenheim Fellowship. Includes discussion about the Guggenheim Foundation and Fellowships and gives meager information about each of the recipients.

B89 "Concert and Opera Asides." *The New York Times*, August 9, 1942, section 8, p. 5.

Remarks on the possibility of a forthcoming opera by William Schuman to be prepared in collaboration with the librettist Christopher La Farge.

B90 "Concert Music." *BMI: The Many Worlds of Music* (March 1969): 12.

A terse statement pertaining to Schuman's reasons for resigning from the Lincoln Center.

B91 Copland, Aaron. "From the '20's to the '40's and Beyond." *Modern Music* 20, no. 2 (1942-43): 78-82.

Surveys two decades of twentieth-century music, with emphasis on American composers. Schuman is mentioned as one of the most prominent young composers.

B92   _____, and Perlis, Vivian. *Copland: 1900 through 1942*. New York: St. Martin's/Marek, 1984. 402 pp. ISBN 0 312 16962 0 ML410 C75 A3 1984

References to Schuman are scattered throughout Copland's autobiography. Presents a section (pp. 350-55) by Schuman based, in part, on interviews conducted by Perlis on 2 June 1983 and 29 December 1983. See: **B93**

B93   _____. *Copland Since 1943*. New York: St. Martin's, 1989. 463 pp. ISBN 0 312 03313 3 ML410 C75 A3 1989

This second volume of Copland's autobiography, written with Vivian Perlis, contains numerous references to Schuman. See: **B92**

B94   "COS Salutes . . . " *Central Opera Service Bulletin* 29 (1989): 44.

Contains a brief notice that Schuman was the winner of the National Music Council's American Eagle Award.

B95   Danuser, Hermann; Kamper, Dietrich; and Terse, Paul, ed. *Amerikanische Musik seit Charles Ives*. Laaber: Laaber-Verlag, 1987. 439 pp. ISBN 3 890 07117 1 ML200 5 A43 1987

This substantial tome is a well-documented history of twentieth-century American music presented as a collection of articles by both German and American scholars. Divided into four parts, the third section reprints essays by selected composers ranging from Charles Ives to Steve Reich and George Crumb, while the fourth section of approximately one hundred pages presents biographical sketches of fifty-one composers. Schuman's biography (pp. 385-86), written by Thomas Seedorf, contains an incomplete list of works and a brief bibliography.

B96   "Dartmouth Ends Arts Ceremonies." *The New York Times*, November 19, 1962, p. 39.

Identifies Schuman as the main speaker for an academic convocation at Dartmouth College and states that he was awarded an honorary Doctor of Humane Letters degree.

B97   Davis, Peter G. "America's Senior Composers—Why Was Their Impact Profound?" *The New York Times*, September 28, 1980, section 2, pp. 25, 31.

Inspired by the birthdays in 1980 of Aaron Copland and Otto Luening, both born in 1900, and William Schuman and Samuel Barber, both born in 1910, this article focuses on the music and activities of the generation of composers born between 1890 and 1910.

B98 _____. "Fanfare for an Uncommon Man." *New York* 18 (December 2, 1985): 150-51.

Though the bulk of this article is concerned with the festivities and concerts honoring the eighty-fifth birthday of Aaron Copland, Davis also writes about the events surrounding the seventy-fifth birthday of William Schuman and the seventieth birthday of David Diamond. The author is especially flattering in his remarks about a recent performance of Schuman's Fifth Symphony presented in celebration of the composer. Commenting on Schuman's symphony and Copland's *Statements*, the reviewer remarks that they "accomplish what they set out to do with precision, skill, and expressive clarity—both scores, like so many others by these two composers, are beginning to sound more and more like American classics. . . . If the music of these two elder statesmen of American music now exudes a period flavor, perhaps the time has come to sit back, relax, and savor it. Bernstein is right: It is the best we have." See: **W29j**

B99 Davis, Ronald L. *A History of Music in American Life*, vol. 3: *The Modern Era, 1920-Present*. Malabar, FL: Robert Krieger, 1981. 444 pp. ISBN 0 898 74002 9 ML200 D3

Written by a non-music specialist, this history provides a survey of Schuman's life and works intended more for the general reader than for the music scholar (pp. 199-201).

B100 Dawson, Victoria. "11 Tapped for Medal of Arts." *The Washington Post*, June 11, 1987, section c, p. 1.

Notes that Schuman is one of eleven artists selected to receive a National Medal of Arts.

* Deimler, Kathryn George. "Quartal Harmony: An Analysis of Twelve Piano Compositions by Twentieth Century Composers."

Cited below as **B848**.

B101 Demuth, Norman. *Musical Trends in the 20th Century*. London: Rockliff, 1952; reprint ed., Westport, CT: Greenwood, 1975. 359 pp. ISBN 0 837 16896 1 ML197 D37 1975

Regards Schuman (pp. 317-19) as primarily a romantic composer, even to the point of suggesting, at least in some respects, a connection to Mahler. Contends that Schuman's style is more European than American.

B102 Deri, Otto. *Exploring Twentieth-Century Music*. New York: Holt, Rinehart and Winston, 1968. 546 pp. ML197 D39

A brief account of Schuman's style is provided in a paragraph on page 478.

B103   Dickinson, Peter. "William Schuman: An American Symphonist at 75." *The Musical Times* 126 (August 1985): 457-58.

Cognizant of Schuman's predilection for the symphony, Dickinson, in this essay intended as a tribute for the composer on his seventy-fifth birthday, provides a thorough overview of the composer's contributions in that medium. Acknowledges the debt of Schuman's symphonic style to Roy Harris; speculates on the influence of Paul Hindemith, especially regarding the neoclassicism of the Third Symphony. Considers these compositions from the standpoint of form, orchestration, harmony, melody, and rhythm. Recognizes the Sixth Symphony as a watershed work in Schuman's career. Prefacing the discussion of the symphonies is a survey of the composer's life and career.

B104   "Directors Named." *The New York Times*, April 5, 1970, section 3, p. 12.

Declares that the Videorecord Corporation of America has elected Schuman as its chairman.

B105   Downes, Edward. "Twenty-One Years of Composers Forums." *The New York Times*, October 7, 1956, section 2, p. 9.

A worth-while essay which deals with the invaluable contribution to American music of the Works Progress Administration. Relates an encounter between the young Schuman and Ashley Pettis, the director of the Composers Forum, which resulted in a concert featuring Schuman's works.

B106   "Dr. Schuman Heads Electronic Concern." *The New York Times*, March 3, 1970, p. 83.

Brief announcement of Schuman's appointment as chairman of the Videorecord Corporation of America.

B107   Dufallo, Richard. "William Schuman." *Trackings*. New York: Oxford, 1989, pp. 381-91. ISBN 0 195 05816 x ML390 D815 1989

A collection of interviews held with twenty-six contemporary composers. The interview with Schuman, which took place on 22 May 1986, sheds light on his associations with such important musicians as Aaron Copland, Roy Harris, Serge Koussevitzky, and others.

B108   Duke, Vernon. *Listen Here! A Critical Essay on Music Depreciation*. New York: Ivan Obolensky, 1963. 406 pp. ML197 D88

Provides an introduction (pp. 62-63, 317) to the works of Schuman. Mentions that his music tends "to be long-winded on occasion."

B109 Dyer, Richard. "Composer Reminisces." *Boston Globe*, October 7, 1980.

Reports on a talk given by Schuman to Boston University students.

B110 _____. "Schuman's Service to Music." *Boston Globe*, February 21, 1992, p. 37.

Written shortly after the death of the composer, Dyer recounts Schuman's career and attempts to assess Schuman's position as a major American composer.

B111 Edwards, Arthur C., and Marrocco, W. Thomas. *Music in the United States.* Dubuque, IA: Wm. C. Brown, 1968. 179 pp.

In their comments (pp. 126-127) on Schuman and his music, the authors regard the composer as essentially a neoclassicist. Contains a short Schuman discography (p. 157) of four items.

B112 "8 Awards in Arts Made by Brandeis U." *The New York Times*, December 27, 1956, p. 6.

Reports that Schuman was awarded a Creative Arts Award by Brandeis University.

B113 Ericson, Raymond. "Philharmonic Hall Acoustics Start Rumors Flying." *The New York Times*, December 4, 1962, p. 46.

Refutes several rumors concerning the acoustics at Philharmonic Hall. Presents opinions and a quotation by Schuman in the controversy.

B114 _____. "Schuman: No Pessimist He." *The New York Times*, January 19, 1969, section 2, pp. 13, 23.

Interview in which Schuman affirms his belief "in the future of the symphony orchestra." Recalls that Schuman in his younger days was judged a radical composer, but is now regarded as conservative. Speaks of the composer's interest in utilizing electronic music in the future.

B115 Erskine, John. *My Life in Music.* New York: William Morrow, 1950; reprint ed., Westport, CT: Greenwood, 1973. 283 pp. ISBN 0 837 16950 x ML429 E7 A3 1973

Erskine, who served as Juilliard's president from 1928 to 1937, provides his own account (pp. 254-58) of Schuman's appointment to the presidency of Juilliard.

B116 "Erudite Music Fan Is Schuman's Hope." *The New York Times*, October 4, 1951, p. 37.

Reports on the composer's address at the opening convocation ceremonies of the Juilliard School.

B117 Esterow, Milton. "Bing Attack Airs Dispute on Theater of Lincoln Center." *The New York Times*, December 5, 1964, pp. 1, 24.

Makes public the polemic concerning Schuman's efforts to hire Herman Krawitz as head of the Lincoln Center Repertory Theater.

B118 _____. "Lincoln Center Will Continue Seeking Director from Met." *The New York Times*, December 6, 1964, p. 88.

In this article, which deals with the efforts of the Lincoln Center to hire an assistant manager from the Metropolitan Opera to become the managing director of the Lincoln Center Repertory Theater and the ensuing controversy, Schuman defends his role in the proceedings.

B119 _____. "Lincoln Center Loses Whitehead." *The New York Times*, December 8, 1964, pp. 1, 55.

Reports on the resignation of Robert Whitehead from the Lincoln Center Repertory Theater amid the controversy surrounding the appointment of Herman Krawitz as managing director. Quotes several critical and disparaging remarks made by Whitehead about Schuman.

B120 Evett, Robert. "How Right Is Right?" *Score* 12 (June 1955): 33-37.

Loosely groups together the following American composers: William Schuman, Peter Mennin, Vincent Persichetti, Robert Palmer, and Samuel Barber. Points out similarities and differences among these six composers and acknowledges the influence of both Walter Piston and Roy Harris on this group. Compares the music of Schuman with that of Harris.

B121 Ewen, David, ed. *The Year in American Music, 1948 Edition.* New York: Allen, Towne & Heath, 1948. 551 pp. ML13 Y4 v. 2

Chronicles the year in music in the United States from 1 June 1947 to 31 May 1948. Several references are made to Schuman's activities and compositions.

B122 _____. *The Complete Book of 20th Century Music.* New York: Prentice-Hall, 1952; revised ed., London: Anthony Blond, 1961. 527 pp.

An appraisal (pp. 355-59) of Schuman's life and works intended more for the general reader than for the scholar. Includes discussion of eight compositions: *American Festival Overture*, String Quartet No. 3, Symphony No. 3, *A Free Song*, Symphony No. 5, *Undertow*, Concerto for Violin and Orchestra, and Symphony No. 6. See: **B124**

B123 _____. *The Home Book of Musical Knowledge.* New York: Prentice-Hall, 1954; reprint ed., London: Arco, 1957. 482pp. MT6 E95

A very superficial account of Schuman's music and career appears on page 121.

B124 _____. *The World of Twentieth-Century Music*. Englewood Cliffs, NJ: Prentice-Hall, 1968; 2nd ed., London: Robert Hale, 1991. 990 pp. ISBN 0 709 04398 8 ML390 E87 1991

An expansion of material which originally appeared in Ewen's *The Complete Book of 20th Century Music*. The Schuman entry (pp. 701-09) provides new information about the composer's life and adds analyses of the following works to the eight compositions described in the earlier volume: *Judith*, String Quartet No. 4, *Credendum*, *New England Triptych*, *A Song of Orpheus*, Symphony No. 8, and *Amaryllis* for String Trio. One work found in the earlier volume, String Quartet No. 3, is omitted. See: **B122**

B125 _____. *Composers Since 1900*. New York: H.W. Wilson, 1969, pp. 508-12. ML390 E833

Provides an overview of Schuman's life and works followed by a brief list of compositions and a sparse bibliography. See: **B126**

B126 _____. *Composers Since 1900: First Supplement*. New York: H.W. Wilson, 1981, pp. 253-56. ISBN 0 824 20664 9 ML390 E833 Suppl.

This supplement to Ewen's 1969 publication contains a discussion of compositions written by Schuman between 1968 and 1980. Also adds to the original list of works and bibliography. See: **B125**

B127 _____. *American Composers: A Biographical Dictionary*. New York: G.P. Putnam's Sons, 1982, pp. 571-76. ISBN 0 399 12626 0 ML390 E815 1982

Chronicles the life and works of the composer with many quotations from reviews of Schuman's music. Discusses several aspects of his style. Contends that Schuman is one of America's most important composers of orchestral music. Concludes with a statement by Schuman called "The Composer Speaks" and contains a list of works and a brief bibliography.

B128 Eyer, Ronald F. "William Schuman Is First Subject of Music Forum." *Musical America* 63 (January 25, 1943): 19.

Critiques the music forum held at Town Hall on January 13, at which a distinguished panel, including Schuman, listened to performances of several of his choral works and the Concerto for Piano and Small Orchestra. After the concert, those works were the topic of discussion for the panel, the audience, and the performers. The participants in the forum, in addition to Schuman, were Daniel Saidenberg, Virgil Thomson, Rosalyn Tureck, Robert Shaw, and Kenneth Klein. See: **W24a**

B129 _____. "Meet the Composer: William Schuman." *Musical America* 64 (January 25, 1944): 8, 25.

An early article providing a survey of Schuman's life and career, with emphasis on the composer's Tin Pan Alley days. Recounts the events surrounding Schuman's conversion to serious music. The last section of the essay presents Schuman's musical philosophy.

B130 _____. "William Schuman." *Musical America* 82 (September 1962): 26, 76.

An illuminating article dealing with Schuman's reasons for accepting the position of president at the Lincoln Center for the Performing Arts. Recaps the composer's career in music up to his appointment at Lincoln Center. Announces several new plans and programs to be implemented by Schuman at the arts center.

B131 "Faculty Honors Schuman." *The Juilliard Review* 9, no. 1 (1961): 3.

Publicizes the gift made to Schuman by the Juilliard faculty and staff of an endowed seat in the composer's name at Lincoln Center's Juilliard Theater. Also reprints a letter of congratulations from John D. Rockefeller III and a testimonial citation from the Juilliard faculty and staff.

B132 Feron, James. "Henry Moore, British Sculptor, to do a Lincoln Center Work." *The New York Times*, July 25, 1962, p. 30.

Presents several quotations by Schuman pertaining to the selection of the British sculptor Henry Moore to provide a sculpture for the Lincoln Center.

B133 "$50,000 Schuman Prize Is Awarded to Schuman." *The New York Times*, December 2, 1981, section 3, p. 23.

A brief notice that Schuman was to be the first composer honored with the William Schuman Award presented by Columbia University.

B134 "First Performances: Schuman, W." *The World of Music* 11, no. 1 (1969): 72.

Lists premiere performances of two Schuman works: *To Thee Old Cause* (3 October 1968, New York) and the Ninth Symphony (10 January 1969, Philadelphia). See: **W68a, W69a**

B135 Fleming, Michael. "Schuman Lives in the Harmony of Lincoln Center." *St. Paul Pioneer Press Dispatch*, February 23, 1992, section d, p. 6.

This substantial obituary reveres Schuman more as an arts administrator than as a composer.

B136 Fleming, Shirley. "William Schuman: Musician of the Month." *High Fidelity/ Musical America* 30 (August 1980): MA 4-5, 40.

Essentially based on an interview held with Schuman at his New York apartment, this article surveys the diversity and success of the composer's career. Schuman deplores the paucity of American music performances by our orchestras and decries the lack of interest in serious music by most record companies. The author reflects upon the many accomplishments achieved by Schuman at Juilliard, after which the composer discussed the Literature and Materials of Music program and the Juilliard String Quartet. In relating his experiences at Lincoln Center, Schuman remarked that "Those years at Lincoln Center were exciting years but not particularly happy ones." Describes several of Schuman's current activities, including his association with the Norlin Foundation; CBS; the Rockefeller Foundation; Broadcast Music, Inc.; and the McDowell Colony. After noting composition projects planned and in progress, this article, written in honor of Schuman's seventieth birthday, ends with the composer's description of his romanticism.

B137   Folkart, Burt A. "William Schuman; Famed U.S. Composer, Educator." *The Los Angeles Times*, February 17, 1992.

This obituary presents a summary of the composer's career.

B138   "Foundation Elects." *The New York Times*, October 25, 1961, p. 30.

Mentions the election of Leopold Mannes to the presidency of the Walter W. Naumburg Foundation, a position vacated by Schuman when he accepted his new job at Lincoln Center.

B139   Frankenstein, Alfred. "American Composers, XXII: William Schuman." *Modern Music* 22 (1944-45): 23-29.

This article, written shortly after Schuman's appointment as Director of Publications at G. Schirmer, asserts that he is a success as a composer. Describes a wide variety of stylistic characteristics found in the composer's music. Underscores the importance of Schuman's study with Roy Harris. Concludes with a selected list of works to 1944.

B140   _____. "Reviews of Books. *William Schuman*, by Flora Rheta Schreiber and Vincent Persichetti; *Samuel Barber*, by Nathan Broder." *The Musical Quarterly* 41 (January 1955): 105-06.

Compares favorably these biographies of the two composers. "The best section in either book is Persichetti's on the music of Schuman. This is a prime example of an extremely rare thing: musical analysis inspired by the love of music."

B141   Freedman, Guy. "Schuman at the Bat." *The Music Journal* 34 (July 1976): 14-16, 51.

An interview with Schuman held in January during the Bicentennial year of 1976. After a brief synopsis of the composer's career, Schuman answers questions dealing with various aspects of his musical style, American music, and music education. Observes the abundance of professional American composers active at that time.

B142 Funke, Lewis. "Flexible Theatre for Repertory Is Designed for Lincoln Center." *The New York Times*, November 14, 1961, pp. 1, 41.

Includes information provided by Schuman concerning the establishment of the Lincoln Center Repertory Company.

B143 Gamarekian, Barbara. "Performing Artists Honored in Words and Music." *The New York Times*, December 4, 1989, section c, p. 17.

A description of the festivities associated with the awards for artistic achievement presented by the John F. Kennedy Center for the Performing Arts. Schuman was one of the honorees.

B144 Gardner, Paul. "Reed Quits Lincoln Repertory Board." *The New York Times*, December 14, 1964, p. 49.

Written following the resignation of Joseph Varner Reed from the Repertory Theater's board of directors at Lincoln Center, this article prints Reed's criticism of Schuman's relationship with the theater's board.

B145 Garoutte, Nancy. "Bill Schuman." *Sarah Lawrence Alumni Magazine* (Fall 1944): 14, 22.

B146 Gay, Harriet. *The Juilliard String Quartet*. New York: Vantage, 1974. 89 pp. ISBN 0 533 01322 4 ML398 J84

Touches upon (pp. 3-11) Schuman's role in the establishment of the Juilliard String Quartet.

B147 Gelb, Arthur. "Lincoln Center Will Start Drive for Last 28 Million." *The New York Times*, May 7, 1962, pp. 1, 35.

Schuman comments on proposed festivals planned for the Lincoln Center in this article. He also stresses the importance of raising money for the Lincoln Center Fund.

B148 _____. "10 Million Lincoln Center Fund to be Headed by Mark Schubart." *The New York Times*, June 14, 1962, p. 25.

Notice that Schuman has appointed Mark Schubart to an administrative position at Lincoln Center responsible for the Lincoln Center Fund. Schuman accentuates the importance of the fund to the operation of Lincoln Center.

B149 Glock, William. "Music." *The Observer*, September 2, 1945, p. 2.

Attempts to present an evaluation of Schuman's music based on an examination of several of his most important early scores. Concludes that "Schuman, who writes without any dullness or half-measures, should, if not spoiled by success, become a major figure." The author was inspired to undertake this study after hearing a London performance of *A Free Song*. See: **W25c**

B150 Glueck, Grace. "A 'Knockout' Ends Sculpture Fight." *The New York Times*, November 16, 1965, p. 59.

Schuman voices his support for two controversial sculptures commissioned for the Lincoln Center.

B151 Goldin, Milton. *The Music Merchants*. London: Macmillan, 1969. 242 pp. ML200 G58

Offers useful information about Schuman's years at Lincoln Center.

B152 Goldman, Richard Franko. "American Music: 1918-1960. (i) Music in the United States." *The New Oxford History of Music*, edited by Martin Cooper, vol. 10: *The Modern Age, 1890-1960*. London: Oxford University Press, 1974, pp. 569-634. ISBN 0 193 16310 1 ML160 N44 vol. 10

Discusses the music of Schuman (p. 622) in a chapter devoted to American music. Compares the composer to Harris and supplies a compendious survey of Schuman's musical style.

B153 Goss, Madeleine. "William Schuman." *Modern Music-Makers: Contemporary American Composers*. New York: E.P. Dutton, 1952; reprint ed., Westport, CT: Greenwood, 1970, pp. 408-22. ISBN 0 837 12957 5 ML390 G69 1970

Among the earliest essays to include substantial biographical information about Schuman, this writing is based on material supplied by the composer. Concludes with a chronological catalog of works organized by genre.

B154 Gould, Jack. "Channel 13 Shifts Its Name to WNET." *The New York Times*, October 1, 1970, p. 83.

Reports Schuman's appointment to the board of the Educational Broadcasting Corporation.

B155 *Great Composers for Band*. 2nd ed. Bryn Mawr, PA: Theodore Presser, 1986. 16 pp.

Published to encourage the programming of band compositions by American composers, William Schuman (p. 11) is one of forty-one composers included. Contains brief information about Schuman and the following works: *American Hymn*; *The Band Song*; *Be Glad Then, America*; *When Jesus Wept*; *Chester*; *Dedication Fanfare*; and *Prelude for a Great Occasion*.

B156 Greene, David Mason, ed. "William Howard Schuman." *Greene's Biographical Encyclopedia of Composers*. London: Collins, 1985, pp. 1222-23. ISBN 0 004 34363 8 ML390 G84 1986

An appraisal of Schuman's life and works intended more for the general reader than for the music scholar. Although the article does not include a bibliography or a complete list of works, it does supply a list by genre of the composer's compositions which have been recorded.

B157 Grimes, Ev. "Conversations with American Composers." *Music Educators Journal* 72 (April 1986): 46-47, 50-54.

In this interview Schuman presents his views on music education. He also identifies the skills required to be a gifted music teacher.

B158 "G. Schirmer Announces Schuman Resignation." *Music Dealer* 5 (November 1951): 27.

B159 "Guggenheim Fund Names 69 Fellows." *The New York Times*, March 27, 1939, p. 21.

Lists individuals chosen to receive fellowships from the John Simon Guggenheim Memorial Foundation. In the area of musical composition, four applicants were selected: Ernst Bacon, Paul Creston, Anis Fuleihan, and William Schuman.

B160 Hall, David. Review of *William Schuman*, by Flora Rheta Schreiber and Vincent Persichetti. *Music Library Association Notes* 11 (September 1954): 560-61.

Compliments the authors for their volume on Schuman and evaluates the book (G. Schirmer, 1954) as a complete success. Centers on the section written by Persichetti on Schuman's musical style, praising Persichetti for his first-rate analyses, yet expressing regret that a more complete examination of the Sixth Symphony was not provided. Hall regards Schuman as one of the most significant composers and music educators of his time.

*   _____. "A Bio-Discography of William Schuman."

Cited as **B21**.

B161 Harrison, Max. "William (Howard) Schuman." *Contemporary Composers*, edited by Brian Morton and Pamela Collins. Chicago and London: St. James, 1992, pp. 831-35. ISBN 1 558 62085 0 ML105 C75 1992

Views Schuman as essentially a symphonist. Summarizes the important events of the composer's life and includes a good discussion of Schuman's compositions. Contains an extensive listing of awards and honors presented to the composer and includes an excellent catalog of works organized by genre.

B162 Haskell, Harry. "William (Howard) Schuman." *The New Grove Dictionary of Opera*, edited by Stanley Sadie. London: Macmillan, 1992. Vol. 4, pp. 252-53. ISBN 0 935 85992 6 ML102 D6 N5 1992

Following a concise account of Schuman's career, this dictionary article concentrates on the composer's two operas: *The Mighty Casey* and *A Question of Taste*. Includes a bibliography of four entries.

B163 Hayes, Sister Marie Therese. "The History of the Juilliard School from Its Inception to 1973." M.M. thesis, Catholic University of America, 1974. 216 pp.

Documents the development of the Juilliard School by focusing upon the men who have headed the institution. Following an introduction, the thesis consists of seven chapters (some with several subchapters): I. The Damrosch Years (1905-1937), II. The Hutcheson Years (1937-1945), III. The Schuman Years (1945-1962), IV. The Mennin Years (1962-), V. Overview of Departments of the Juilliard School, VI. Juilliard and the Lincoln Center Student Program, and VII. Conclusion. Divides the chapter dealing with Schuman into two parts: Schuman the Musician and Schuman the Administrator. Includes numerous footnotes, a good bibliography, and an appendix.

B164 Heinsheimer, H.W. "Bugles and Bells." *Musical Courier* 149 (March 1, 1954): 5-6.

Reflects upon the dearth of opera composition by modern American composers and contends that there is too much stress placed on the production of concert music in this country. Points out that Copland's first opera for the professional stage was written at the age of fifty-four and argues that Schuman's prolific output, with its complete avoidance of opera up to *The Mighty Casey*, is all too typical. Also discusses the careers of other composers.

B165 "Hemidemisemiquavers." *The New York Times*, September 21, 1980, section 2, p. 25.

Identifies Schuman as the winner of the Mark M. Horblit award for composition.

B166 Henahan, Donal. "Rome Opera to Inaugurate Lincoln Center Festival." *The New York Times*, February 27, 1968, p. 35.

Outlines the concerts planned as part of the 1968 Lincoln Center Festival. Schuman, in announcing the festival, raises concerns about the financial backing of the event.

B167 _____. "Schuman Now Basking in 'Total Sunshine.'" *The New York Times*, January 28, 1970, p. 48.

Written a little more than a year after Schuman's retirement from the Lincoln Center for the Performing Arts, this article includes the composer's reflections on past accomplishments and, at the same time, looks ahead to several future projects, including the world premiere of *In Praise of Shahn*, a proposed autobiography based on Schuman's memoirs, and other future commissions. See: **W71a**

B168   _____. "Chamber: Center Society." *The New York Times*, April 13, 1981, section 3, p. 14.

Discloses that Schuman, on April 12, was awarded a citation from the Chamber Music Society of Lincoln Center in honor of his role in establishing that organization. Reports that further recognition was given to the composer on that occasion with a performance of his Third String Quartet. Relates the style of Schuman's quartet to the 1930s neoclassicism of Paul Hindemith.

B169   Hershenson, Roberta. "At 80, a Modern Composer Persists in His 'Marvelous Indulgence.'" *The New York Times*, April 21, 1991, section 12, Westchester Weekly, pp. 1, 19.

Summarizes the composer's career and reports on forthcoming performances of Schuman's works. Based on an interview with the composer, this article was inspired by a recent performance of two Schuman compositions at Avery Fisher Hall by the New York Philharmonic. Mentions that approximately ninety-six orchestras across the United States have presented or will present Schuman pieces in this concert season.

B170   _____. "50th Reunion Pays Tribute to a Sarah Lawrence Music Teacher." *The New York Times*, June 21, 1992, section 13, Westchester Weekly, p. 16.

An account of the fiftieth reunion of the Sarah Lawrence College class of 1942. Schuman, who before his death in February was scheduled to participate in the celebration of a newly established William Schuman Scholarship, was fondly remembered by his former students. The composer was honored through concerts of his music and through the dedication of the recently refurbished William Schuman Music Library.

B171   Heyman, Barbara B. *Samuel Barber: The Composer and His Music*. New York: Oxford University Press, 1992. 586 pp. ISBN 0 195 06650 2 ML410 B23 H5

Heyman's definitive biography of Barber presents excerpts from several of Schuman's letters to Barber, all of which are preserved in the William Schuman Collection at the Music Division of the New York Public Library.

B172   Hitchcock, H. Wiley. "More than a Composer: William Schuman, Approaching Seventy." *Newsletter: Institute for Studies in American Music* 9 (May 1980): 1, 12.

Hitchcock's tribute to Schuman, though relatively short, is filled with admiration and respect for the man and for his accomplishments.

B173   _____. "William Schuman: Musical All-American." *Keynote* 4 (August 1980): 12-16.

A perceptive essay written in honor of the composer's seventieth birthday. Recognizes Schuman as an eminent composer, educator, and administrator. Summarizes Schuman's accomplishments and points out that his retirement since 1969 "has been one largely in name." Describes several interesting details about the composer's early career and mentions the importance of his association with Roy Harris. Emphasizes the significance of orchestral works in Schuman's output, focusing especially on the ten symphonies. Contends that "Schuman is no musical chauvinist, but many of his works lie very close to the bone of the American experience and could never have been conceived by anyone but an American."

B174   _____. *Music in the United States: A Historical Introduction*. 3rd ed., Englewood Cliffs, NJ: Prentice Hall, 1988. 365 pp. ISBN 0 136 08407 9 ML200 H58 1988

This highly-regarded survey of American music devotes just less than two pages (pp. 230-31) to a discussion of Schuman's music and style. Additional information about the composer is given on pages 220, 221, and 228.

B175 Hofmann, Paul. "Teachers Urged to Promote Arts." *The New York Times*, February 19, 1960, p. 20.

In this article on arts education at Lincoln Center, Schuman urges the exposure of schoolchildren to the arts.

B176   _____. "Kennedy Says U.S. Must Back Israel." *The New York Times*, June 11, 1967, p. 21.

Recognizes Schuman as the recipient of an honorary degree from Fordham University. Senator Robert F. Kennedy delivered the commencement address.

B177 Holland, Bernard. "The Bottom Line in Tune." *The New York Times*, May 17, 1990, section c, p. 18.

A review of a concert at Merkin Concert Hall on May 12 dedicated to Schuman in honor of his eightieth birthday. The New York Virtuoso Singers, conducted by Harold Rosenbaum, presented several of the composer's best-known choral works, including *Carols of Death*, *Perceptions*, *Five Rounds on Famous Words*, and *Mail Order Madrigals*. Also presented on the program was Schuman's latest piano composition, *Variations on Chester*, written for the Van Cliburn International Piano Competition, and *XXV Opera Snatches* for solo flute. See: **W51b, W54e, W73b, W84c, W92c, W100b**

B178 Hoover, Joanne Sheehy. "A Composer's View of Arts and Business." *The Wall Street Journal* 60 (August 15, 1980): 13.

Based upon an interview held with Schuman at the Aspen Music Festival, this article, which includes several quotations by the composer, concentrates on his dual career as creative artist and arts administrator. Contends that with the exception of Charles Ives, "no one else has combined business and music on an equal scale."

B179 Howard, John Tasker. *Our Contemporary Composers: American Music in the Twentieth Century.* New York: Thomas Y. Crowell, 1941; reprint ed., Freeport, NY: Books for Libraries Press, 1975. 447 pp. ISBN 0 518 10201 7 ML200 H8 C8 1975

Contains one of the earliest evaluations (pp. 225-26) of Schuman's music.

B180 _____. *Modern Music: A Popular Guide to Greater Musical Enjoyment.* New York: Thomas Y. Crowell, 1942; revised ed., New York: Thomas Y. Crowell, 1957; reprint ed., Westport, CT: Greenwood, 1978. 202 pp. ISBN 0 313 20556 6 ML197 H69 1979

Refers, in this short discussion (pp. 118-19) of Schuman's music, to the Third Symphony and the Sixth Symphony as "two of the most impressive utterances of the twentieth century." Includes a selective list of Schuman's recordings.

B181 _____, and Bellows, George Kent. *A Short History of Music in America.* New York: Thomas Y. Crowell, 1967. 496 pp. ML200 H82 1967

Gives a concise account (pp. 353-54) of Schuman's life and works. Contains a separate discussion (p. 394) of *The Mighty Casey.* Also includes a listing (p. 452) of Schuman recordings.

B182 Illson, Murray. "Dr. Hester Warns on College Costs." *The New York Times,* June 7, 1962, p. 27.

Includes Schuman as one of eight persons who received an honorary doctorate from New York University.

B183 "In Memoriam." *Das Orchester* 40 (1992): 655.

Contains a short obituary of Schuman.

B184 "In the News: William Schuman." *Broadcast Music, Inc.* (October 1971): 7.

Brief notification of Schuman's commencement address to the Peabody Conservatory's class of 1971. Also refers to the fact that Schuman was awarded the twelfth Edward MacDowell Medal on August 8.

B185 "An Influential American." *Baltimore Morning Sun,* February 22, 1992, section a, p. 6.

This obituary refers to Schuman as "among this century's most important composers of the modern American school."

B186 "Inside Job." *Newsweek* 64 (December 21, 1964): 74-75.

Extensively discusses the controversy at Lincoln Center surrounding the Repertory Theater. Prints inflammatory remarks by Rudolf Bing and Robert Whitehead dealing with Schuman's attempt to hire Herman Krawitz as the managing director of the Repertory Theater.

B187 "Inside Stuff—Music." *Variety* 224 (September 20, 1961): 50.

Briefly discusses Schuman's early career in popular music and his collaborations with Edward B. Marks, Jr. and Frank Loesser. Mentions two songs, *Who'll Close the Window in the Morning* and *Waitin' for the Moon*, composed by Schuman, the former to a libretto by Marks and the latter to a libretto by the composer.

B188 "Institute of Arts Names 15 Members." *The New York Times*, December 28, 1945, p. 13.

Recognizes Schuman as one of the persons chosen for membership in the National Institute of Arts and Letters.

B189 "An Interview with William Schuman." *The Podium: Magazine of the Fritz Reiner Society* (Fall-Winter 1987): 9-16.

Following an introduction, this substantial interview offers insightful information on a variety of topics, especially Schuman's relationships with Fritz Reiner and with Roy Harris, as well as commenting on composers and conductors such as Leonard Bernstein, Antal Dorati, Leopold Stokowski, Aaron Copland, John Adams, Leonard Slatkin, and Jean Martinon. This interview was conducted shortly after the premiere performance on 28 October 1986 of Schuman's *On Freedom's Ground.* See: **W95a**

B190 Jacobi, Peter. "Schuman of the Center." *The Music Magazine and Musical Courier* 164 (September 1962): 8-11.

Offers an interview between Schuman and the magazine's editor, Peter Jacobi. Provides insight into Schuman's decision to leave the Juilliard School for the presidency of Lincoln Center. Schuman discusses several projects planned for Lincoln Center and states his views on composition.

B191 "Juilliard Graduates 120." *The New York Times*, May 31, 1958, p. 6.

Briefly reports on a speech given by Schuman at Juilliard's commencement exercises.

B192 "Juilliard Names Head." *The New York Times*, December 20, 1961, p. 37.

Reports that Mark Schubart will replace Schuman as interim director of the Juilliard School. Communicates Schuman's appointment as president emeritus and indicates that he will continue to serve on the Juilliard board of directors. Announces that the Juilliard School is providing money to establish an endowed seat in honor of Schuman in the Lincoln Center's Juilliard Theatre.

B193 "Juilliard President Asks Government Aid to Music." *Down Beat* 21 (July 14, 1954): 1.

Schuman's commencement address at Juilliard featured a plea for government support of the arts.

B194 "Juilliard School Adds 28 to Staff." *The New York Times*, May 6, 1946, p. 17.

This article reports on announcements made the day before by Schuman regarding the appointment of several new distinguished faculty to the Juilliard School, among them Beveridge Webster, piano; Joseph Fuchs, violin; Leonard Rose, cello; Milton Katims, viola; and Robert Shaw, choral music. In addition, the formation of the new Juilliard String Quartet is declared.

B195 "Juilliard School of Music—New York." *Daughters of the American Revolution Magazine* (January 1963): 74-75.

Gives a thumbnail sketch of the Juilliard School, with emphasis on the planned move to Lincoln Center. Highlights Schuman's role as Juilliard's president.

B196 "Juilliard School of Music to Alter Program in Fall, with Literature Added to Studies." *The New York Times*, May 13, 1947, p. 30.

Announcement by Schuman of several changes scheduled to take place at the Juilliard School in the next academic year, particularly the implementation of the new Literature and Materials of Music program. Recognizes the appointment of eleven new faculty members to the school, among them the composers Vincent Persichetti, Robert Goeb, Robert Ward, Peter Mennin, and Richard Franko Goldman.

B197 "Juilliard Schools Now a Single Unit." *The New York Times*, January 16, 1946, p. 19.

Announces, under the leadership of Schuman, the merger of the Juilliard Graduate School and the Institute of Musical Art into the Juilliard School of Music.

B198 Kearns, William. Review of *William Schuman Documentary*, by Christopher Rouse. *The Sonneck Society Newsletter* 12 (Summer 1986): 62.

A complimentary review of Rouse's book.

B199 Keats, Sheila. "William Schuman." *Stereo Review* (June 1974): 68-77.

Published as the twenty-first entry in *Stereo Review's* American Composer Series, this article chronicles the career of Schuman from his youth to the age of sixty-three. Combines an account of the composer's life with a discussion of several major works. Also contains a subsection entitled "On Listening to William Schuman's Music," focusing on an appraisal of the *American Festival Overture*.

B200   "The Kennedy Center Announces '89 Awards." *The New York Times*, August 8, 1989, section c, p. 14.

Identifies Schuman as one of five individuals slated to receive a 1989 Kennedy Center Honors award.

B201   King, William G. "Music and Musicians." *The New York Sun*, February 16, 1940, p. 26.

Takes note of the forthcoming premiere performance of Schuman's Third String Quartet at New York's Town Hall on February 27. See: **W19a**

B202   Kingman, Daniel. *American Music: A Panorama*. New York: Schirmer, 1979; 2nd ed., New York: Schirmer, 1990. 684 pp. ISBN 0 028 73370 3 ML200 K55 1990

Examines Schuman's Third String Quartet (pp. 485-86) from the standpoint of form, rhythm, melody, and harmony. Advocates that the work is representative of both "classicism and Americanism." Mentions other compositions by Schuman in discussions of American contributions to band, symphony, opera, and concerto literature.

B203   Klein, Howard. "Schuman vs. Pulitzer." *The New York Times*, June 20, 1965, section 2, p. 13.

Underscores Schuman's disgust with the Pulitzer Prize Advisory Board for failing to select a winner in music. According to Klein, Schuman argued for "the establishment of a mechanism whereby a comprehensive survey of music published and performed during the year under consideration can be presented to the jury; and he urged that the jury not contain men openly hostile to the newest music."

B204   Kozinn, Allan. "William Schuman Is Remembered with Selections of His Own Music." *The New York Times*, April 3, 1992, section a, p. 17.

A performance review of a memorial concert of Schuman's music at the Juilliard Theater conducted by Leonard Slatkin and Harold Rosenbaum. In addition to the selections presented on the program, a number of persons, among them Joseph Polisi, Christopher Rouse, and Leonard Slatkin, remembered the composer to those in attendance.

B205   Kyle, Marguerite K. "AmerAllegro: William Schuman." *Pan Pipes of Sigma Alpha Iota* 46 (January 1954): 59.

Supplies information about the May 4, 5, and 6 premiere performances in Hartford, Connecticut, of *The Mighty Casey*. Notes performances of five other Schuman compositions and lists new recordings of three of his works. See: **W45a**

B206   _____. "AmerAllegro: William Schuman." *Pan Pipes of Sigma Alpha Iota* 48 (January 1956): 71.

Presents information about Schuman premieres (*Credendum*) and performances (*Judith, The Mighty Casey*). See: **W49a**

B207   _____. "AmerAllegro: William Schuman." *Pan Pipes of Sigma Alpha Iota* 49 (January 1957): 68.

Takes note of several activities concerning Schuman's works, including premieres, performances, publications, and recordings.

B208   _____. "AmerAllegro." *Pan Pipes of Sigma Alpha Iota* 51 (January 1959): 82.

A brief note about performances, recordings, and other news of several Schuman compositions.

B209   _____. "AmerAllegro." *Pan Pipes of Sigma Alpha Iota* 54 (January 1962): 70.

Briefly notes several activities related to the composer and his works: the premiere of *A Song of Orpheus* by the Indianapolis Symphony; the performances of eight Schuman compositions, including the Seventh Symphony; the recordings of the Third Symphony, issued by Columbia Records, and the Third String Quartet, presented by RCA Victor; and the appointment of Schuman as president of Lincoln Center. See: **W59a, D75, D81**

B210   _____. "AmerAllegro." *Pan Pipes of Sigma Alpha Iota* 55, no. 2 (1963): 68-69.

Includes information about the premiere performance of Schuman's Symphony No. 8 given by the New York Philharmonic with Leonard Bernstein conducting, as well as information on performances of other works by the composer. See: **W60a**

B211   _____. "AmerAllegro." *Pan Pipes of Sigma Alpha Iota* 57, no. 2 (1965): 78.

A concise report of the premieres of two Schuman works: *The Orchestra Song* and the *Variations on "America."* Also notes other performances, publications, and recordings of Schuman works, as well as news concerning the composer's activities. See: **W62a, W63a**

B212   _____. "AmerAllegro: William Schuman." *Pan Pipes of Sigma Alpha Iota* 61, no. 2 (1969): 74.

Lists Schuman premieres in St. Louis, New York, and Philadelphia of *Dedication Fanfare, To Thee Old Cause,* and the Ninth Symphony. See: **W67a, W68a, W69a**

B213   _____. "AmerAllegro: William Schuman." *Pan Pipes of Sigma Alpha Iota* 63, no. 2 (1971): 76.

Concise mention of Schuman premieres (*In Praise of Shahn, Anniversary Fanfare*) and recordings (*In Praise of Shahn, Anniversary Fanfare*). See: **W70a, W71a, D8, D38**

B214 LaFave, Ken. "Schuman Death Ends Renaissance." *The Phoenix Gazette*, section c, p. 3.

Contends that Schuman was part of "the great renaissance of American music" between the wars.

B215 Lambert, Bruce. "William Schuman Is Dead at 81; Noted Composer Headed Juilliard." *The New York Times*, February 16, 1992, section 1, p. 48.

Schuman's obituary, published the day following Schuman's death from complications associated with hip surgery, paid tribute to the composer both for his compositions and for his role as a champion of American music. Includes an overview of Schuman's career. See: **B216**

B216 _____. "The New York Times Recounts Mr. Schuman's Life." *The Juilliard Journal* 7 (March 1992): 3.

A reprint of the obituary published in *The New York Times* on 16 February 1992 entitled "William Schuman is Dead at 81; Noted Composer Headed Juilliard." See: **B215**

B217 Leichtentritt, Hugo. *Serge Koussevitzky, the Boston Symphony Orchestra, and the New American Music*. Cambridge: Harvard University Press, 1946; reprint ed., New York: AMS Press, 1978. 199 pp. ISBN 0 404 14680 5 ML422 K7 L4 1978

This book, devoted to an account of the Koussevitzky years in Boston and the promotion of American music during that time, contains helpful information about Schuman and his relationship to Koussevitzky. Especially valuable is the section dealing with the introduction of Schuman's music in Boston from 1939 to 1944 (pp. 137-141).

B218 Levin, Hillel. "The Selling of Lincoln Center." *New York* 13 (November 3, 1980): 66-72.

Considers the financial and artistic problems associated with managing Lincoln Center. Looks upon the Schuman years of leadership as mostly positive, especially in terms of artistic programs.

B219 "Lewis Lusardi Is Appointed by Lincoln Center Fund." *The New York Times*, November 2, 1966, p. 35.

Succinct report of an earlier announcement made by Schuman naming Lewis Lusardi to a position at Lincoln Center.

B220 "Library Acquires Papers of Lincoln Center Chief." *The New York Times,* February 23, 1987, section 3, p. 13.

A concise article revealing that the collected papers of Schuman would now be housed in the New York Public Library.

B221 "Library-Museum of the Arts Opens at Lincoln Center." *The New York Times*, December 1, 1965, p. 55.

Comments on the dedication ceremonies held in conjunction with the opening of the Lincoln Center Library and Museums. Schuman was the master of ceremonies for this event.

B222 "Lime Light: The Mighty Schuman." *Symphony* 41 (January-February 1990): 19.

Observes that Schuman was honored on 6 December 1989 with a Kennedy Center Honors award. Includes a very brief summary of the composer's career.

B223 "Lincoln Center Denies Beaumont Theater Delay." *The New York Times*, April 1, 1965, p. 31.

Schuman confirms that the Lincoln Center's Vivian Beaumont Theater will be open by June 1.

B224 "Lincoln Center Head Sees Humphrey About Europe Trip." *The New York Times*, March 17, 1967, p. 35.

Notice of a meeting between Schuman and Vice President Humphrey, held for the purpose of discussing the composer's forthcoming European trip.

B225 Lipman, Samuel. "American Music: The Years of Hope." *Commentary* 71 (March 1981): 56-61.

Although primarily devoted to a defense of twentieth-century American music, Lipman's essay provides a thumbnail sketch of the attainments of eleven significant American composers, among them William Schuman. Characterizes Schuman's original style as a "combination of motor energy and a melodic line . . . drawn from popular American music." Argues, however, that his later works portray a "tragic, tightly dark-hued mood." Concludes that Schuman's music has not yet received the acclaim which it deserves.

B226 "List of Recipients of Honorary Degrees at Columbia." *The New York Times*, January 12, 1954, p. 16.

Cites Schuman and Richard Rodgers as recipients of the Doctor of Music degree.

B227 Lowell, John H. Review of *The Juilliard Report on Teaching the Literature and Materials of Music*. *The Musical Quarterly* 40 (April 1954): 248-50.

An objective discussion of Juilliard's then novel approach to undergraduate music training. Credits Schuman as the originator of the idea for the Literature and Materials of Music curriculum.

B228 Lowens, Irving. "From the Mail Pouch: Another Viewpoint on Contests." *The New York Times*, April 12, 1942, section 8, p. 6.

This letter attacks Schuman for opinions expressed by the composer in a letter published a week earlier in *The New York Times* dealing with a composition contest supported by the New Opera Company. See: **S8**, **S9**

*   McClatchy, J.D. "William Schuman: A Reminiscence."

Cited as **B832**.

B229 "MacDowell Medal to Schuman." *Pan Pipes of Sigma Alpha Iota* 64, no. 2 (1972): 20-21.

Reports on the selection of William Schuman as the 1971 winner of the Edward MacDowell Medal, presented to the composer on 8 August 1971. Prints comments made about Schuman by Aaron Copland, who gave the address at the ceremony, and Russell Lynes, the president of the MacDowell Association. Provides brief information on the MacDowell Colony.

B230 Machlis, Joseph. "William Schuman." *Introduction to Contemporary Music.* New York: Norton, 1961, pp. 516-20; 2nd ed., New York: Norton, 1979, pp. 584-85. ISBN 0 393 09026 4 ML197 M11 I5 1979

A valuable introduction to the composer and his music. Asserts that "The music of William Schuman stems from a temperament that is optimistic, assertive, and thoroughly at home in the world. It has vigor and energy, and is planned on a large scale." Regards *Credendum*, with "Its vaulting melodies, athletic rhythms, orchestral brightness, and general exuberance," as typical of Schuman's musical style. Incorporates separate discussions of his life, his music, and *Credendum*. The second edition (1979) of this well-known text omits the chapter on the composer, opting instead to include a succinct entry (pp. 584-85) in the composer dictionary at the end of the volume.

B231 _____. "William Schuman." *American Composers of Our Time.* New York: Thomas Y. Crowell, 1963; reprint ed., Westport, CT: Greenwood, 1990, pp. 137-48. ISBN 0 313 22141 3 ML 390 M175 A4 1990

Sixteen American composers are represented in this collection of biographies. The essay devoted to Schuman, Chapter 12, contains an appraisal of the composer's life and works intended more for the general reader than for the music scholar. According to Machlis, "Schuman's music reflects the man. It is the music of an active personality—optimistic, vigorous, assertive. It is planned on a large scale."

B232 McKinnon, George. "Symphony to Fete William Schuman." *Boston Globe,* September 10, 1980.

Provides information about the forthcoming October 2, 3, 4, and 7 performances of Schuman's Third Symphony by the Boston Symphony Orchestra. Recalls that the symphony was premiered by the orchestra on 17 October 1941. See: **W22v**

B233   McLellan, Joseph. "William Schuman, Freshman of Composition." *The Washington Post Show*, December 3, 1989, section g, pp. 1, 4.

Written upon the occasion of Schuman receiving a Kennedy Center Honor, this ample article is based on an interview conducted by the author in the composer's New York City apartment. Portrays Schuman as an indefatigable administrator and composer.

B234   _____. "Schuman's American Song: Remembering the Composer and His Musical Lives." *The Washington Post*, February 18, 1992, section d, p. 1.

This substantial eulogy begins with the observation that Schuman, though not as well known as Leonard Bernstein and Aaron Copland, possibly had a greater impact "on American musical life."

B235   "Maestro in Play Clothes." *Newsweek* 26 (August 13, 1945): 100-01.

Enthusiastically reports on the appointment of Schuman as president of the Juilliard School of Music. Contains a succinct list of the most important awards won by the composer up to that time. Provides a brief overview of Schuman's career.

B236   "Mannes Music School Receives a Charter as College, Will Offer 5-Year B.S. Courses." *The New York Times*, April 28, 1953, p. 31.

Reproduces remarks made by Schuman at a party held at the Mannes College of Music celebrating that institution's new charter and academic status granted by the state of New York.

B237   "Many Happy Returns for Barber, Copland et al." *Symphony Magazine* 31 (December 1980): 45-46, 61.

Acknowledges that "A unifying theme of this season's orchestral programming is the celebration of milestone birthdays," particularly noting concerts honoring Aaron Copland, William Schuman, Samuel Barber, and Isaac Stern. Also discusses concerts given in tribute of the centennial birthday celebrations of Ernest Bloch and Béla Bartók. Devotes entire sections in the article to Copland, Schuman, and Barber respectively. Refers to several performances and honors given Schuman: the October 10 and 11 performances of the cantata *Casey at the Bat* by Antal Dorati and the Detroit Symphony Orchestra, the premiere of *Three Colloquies for French Horn and Orchestra* by the New York Philharmonic, the publication of Christopher Rouse's *William Schuman Documentary*, and the presentation of the Horblit Award to the composer by the Boston Symphony Orchestra. See: **W81b, W85a**

B238   Martin, William R., and Drossin, Julius. *Music of the Twentieth Century*. Englewood Cliffs, NJ: Prentice-Hall, 1980. ISBN 0 136 08927 5 ML197 MN1745

A useful introduction to the music of Schuman (pp. 264-69) which views the composer essentially as a neoclassicist. After a brief biographical and stylistic discussion, including mention of his best-known works, the authors offer a descriptive analysis of the Third Symphony, complete with musical examples.

B239 Marx, Henry. "We Note That . . . " *Music News* 42 (December 1950): 4.

Reports on a convocation speech given by Schuman at the Juilliard School of Music.

B240 Mayer, Martin. "Music Mailbag: William Schuman Protests a 'Completely False History.'" *The New York Times*, October 26, 1969, section 2, p. 29.

A reply, in which Mayer defends his article "Are the Trying Times Just Beginning," to Schuman's letter to the editor. See: **S56**

B241 "Mayor Inducts Hult in Public Works Job." *The New York Times*, April 1, 1967, p. 18.

The Mayor of New York City announced that Schuman would be New York's "cultural ambassador" to Europe.

B242 Mellers, Wilfrid. *Music and Society: England and the European Tradition.* London: Dennis Dobson, 1946; 2nd ed., London: Dennis Dobson, 1950. 230 pp. ML3795 M4 1950

Compares the music of Schuman (pp. 222-23) to that of Harris and Copland. Provides a discussion of the Third Symphony and briefly describes the choral style of the composer.

B243 _____. *Music in a New Found Land.* New York: Hillstone, 1975. 545 pp. ISBN 0 883 73023 5 ML200 M44 1975

Provides a fairly substantial, but generally negative, description of Schuman's style (pp. 78-79). "William Schuman has stamina in plenty, but—even in his best pieces—seldom attains vision."

B244 "Merger Proposed for Arts Schools." *The New York Times*, December 12, 1958, p. 2.

Announces Schuman's proposal to combine the High School of Performing Arts with the High School of Music and Art.

B245 Milburn, Frank, Jr. "The Juilliard School of Music—Its First 50 Years." *Musical America* 76 (February 15, 1956): 30, 140, 227.

A useful account of the history of the Juilliard School of Music written on the occasion of its fiftieth anniversary. Recognizes many of the important personages associated with the school and recounts several notable events in the life of the institution. Includes "A Message from the President" provided by William Schuman.

B246 Miller, Karl F. "William Schuman at 75: An Appreciation." *Symphony Magazine* (June-July 1985): 28-31, 161.

A well-written, informative essay that summarizes the accomplishments of Schuman's multifarious career and surveys the composer's most significant compositions, with emphasis on the orchestral works. Contends that optimism is a characteristic common to much of Schuman's output. Argues that his works are representative "of the times in which they were written." Believes that *To Thee Old Cause* ranks as possibly Schuman's preeminent achievement in terms of emotion.

B247 _____. "William Schuman: 1910-1992." *The American Record Guide* 55 (July-August 1992): 29-31.

A thoughtful consideration of the composer's music from one who has a thoroughgoing interest in and knowledge of Schuman's works. Voices the opinion that "the human voice and the orchestra" were at the heart of the composer's creative outlook. Attests that the Sixth Symphony is "one of the most profound expressions in 20th Century orchestral literature."

B248 Miller, Margo. "MacDowell Colony Taps New Leaders." *Boston Globe*, December 17, 1984, section 3, p. 27.

Announces that Varujan Boghosian and Edwin Cohen will succeed Schuman as the chairman of the MacDowell Colony. Notes Schuman's service to the colony.

B249 Mitgang, Herbert. "Arts and Letters Group Gives Award to Knopf." *The New York Times*, May 20, 1982, section 3, p. 15.

Reports that several awards were recently granted by the American Academy and Institute of Arts and Letters. Among the recipients was Schuman, who received a gold medal prize for music.

B250 "Mixing Business and Art." *Business Week* (August 3, 1963): 42-45.

A thorough discussion of Schuman the executive. After an introduction, the article is divided into three sections: I. "One of a kind," II. "Talent on board," and III. "Stopwatch operation." Describes the composer's schedule in his position as president of Lincoln Center.

B251 Molotsky, Irvin. "National Medal of Arts Awarded to 11 by Reagan." *The New York Times*, June 11, 1987, section 3, p. 25.

Declares that Schuman is one of the winners of the National Medal of Arts.

B252 "A Mu Phi Epsilon Citation of Merit Awarded to William Schuman." *The Triangle of Mu Phi Epsilon* 82, no. 2 (1988): inside front cover.

Proclaims Schuman the winner of a Citation of Merit awarded by Mu Phi Epsilon. Presents a superficial account of the composer's life and works.

B253 "Music Conference at the 92d Street Y." *The New York Times*, December 20, 1980, p. 18.

Announces that Schuman is scheduled to speak at a forthcoming luncheon at the 92d Street Y.

B254 "Music Journal's 1972 Gallery of Living Composers." *Music Journal* 30 (July 1972): 34-62.

William Schuman is one of fifty composers included in this extensive article. Each entry, though rather short, covers pertinent information on the composer's education, career, awards, and compositions, as well as printing a current address and recent photograph.

B255 Myers, Rollo H., ed. *Twentieth Century Music*. London: Calder, 1960; 2nd revised and enlarged ed., London: Calder and Boyars, 1968. 289 pp. ML197 M95 1968

This survey of twentieth-century music consists of twenty-one chapters, each written by a different scholar or pair of scholars. Chapter nineteen, entitled "Music in the United States," by Robert Layton and Wilfrid Mellers, devotes an extended paragraph (p. 237) to Schuman.

B256 "National Symphony Orders 12 Works for the Bicentenary." *The New York Times*, April 24, 1974, p. 49.

Gives notice that Schuman was one of eleven composers chosen to receive a commission from the National Symphony Orchestra to compose works for the Bicentennial celebration.

B257 "National Symphony Premieres 'Casey at the Bat' Cantata Commissioned by Norlin Corp." *The Music Trades* 124 (May 1976): 126.

Recognizes the premieres of three Schuman works on a 6 April 1976 Bicentennial concert at the Kennedy Center: *Casey at the Bat*, *The Young Dead Soldiers*, and the Tenth Symphony. At the time of these performances, Schuman was serving as Chairman of the Board of the Norlin Foundation. See: **W79a**, **W81a**, **W82a**

B258 "Nation's Musicians Celebrate William Schuman's Birthday." *The Triangle of Mu Phi Epsilon* 79, no. 3 (1985): 3.

Written in honor of the composer's seventy-fifth birthday, this article provides a concise introduction to Schuman's life and works and includes a list of his most renowned compositions. Concludes with a brief mention of the organizations involved in the birthday celebration.

B259 "New Juilliard President." *The Musician* 50 (August 1945): 161.

Notes Schuman's appointment to the presidency of the Juilliard School of Music. Also provides brief biographical information and a concise, incomplete list of the composer's works.

B260 "New Title for Schuman." *The New York Times*, September 23, 1961, p. 17.

Reports that Schuman would be awarded the title of President Emeritus at Juilliard upon leaving the institution at the end of the year.

B261 "New York: Schuman to Leave Lincoln Center." *Opera* (February 1969): 113.

Succinctly announces the resignation of Schuman from the presidency of the Lincoln Center.

B262 "Newsbriefs: William Schuman 75th Birthday." *The Choral Journal* 26 (October 1985): 24.

Takes note of the composer's seventy-fifth birthday and mentions several honors received by Schuman.

B263 "988 Are Graduated at Adelphi College." *The New York Times*, June 13, 1963, p. 22.

Lists Schuman as one of the recipients of an honorary Doctor of Fine Arts degree from Adelphi College.

B264 "1986-87 Premieres and Season Highlights." *Symphony Magazine* 37, no. 5 (1986): 16-26.

This extensive listing of scheduled programs by 124 orchestras includes two planned Schuman performances: *Showcase: A Short Display for Orchestra* by the Houston Symphony Orchestra on 26 September 1986 and *On Freedom's Ground* by the New York Philharmonic on 28 October 1986. Also contains a parallel article by Leona Francombe entitled "Highlights of the Season." See: **W95a, W97a**

B265 "1977 ACDA National Convention." *The Choral Journal* 17 (December 1976): 18-21.

In this article dealing with the forthcoming National American Choral Directors Association Convention in Dallas, Schuman is identified as the keynote speaker for the event. Provides a summary of the composer's career and includes quotations lauding Schuman by Harold Schonberg and Aaron Copland. Also gives information on recent performances of some of Schuman's latest works, such as the Tenth Symphony, *The Young Dead Soldiers*, and *Casey at the Bat*.

B266 Norman, Gertrude, and Schrifte, Miriam Lubell, editors. *Letters of Composers*. Reprint ed., Westport, CT: Greenwood, 1979. 422 pp. ISBN 0 313 20664 3 ML90 N67 1979

One letter (pp. 411-12) of Schuman's is reprinted in this volume. Dated 21 March 1942, the composer's correspondence to Robert Beckhard is in response to an inquiry regarding the *American Festival Overture.*

B267 "Notes of Musicians." *The New York Times,* April 17, 1938, section 10, p. 6.

A concise article which mentions that Schuman, then a faculty member at Sarah Lawrence College, was the first prize winner in a composition contest supported by the Musicians Committee to Aid Spanish Democracy. The winning work was the composer's Second Symphony.

B268 "Notes on People." *The New York Times,* January 1, 1977, p. 12.

Mentions that Schuman was named treasurer of the American Academy and Institute of Arts and Letters.

B269 "Obituaries: William Howard Schuman." *The Sonneck Society Bulletin* 18 (Spring 1992): 23.

A somewhat matter-of-fact obituary which lists the composer's most significant accomplishments.

B270 "Obituaries: William Schuman." *The American Organist* 26 (May 1992): 55.

A eulogy which summarizes the varied accomplishments of Schuman.

B271 "Obituaries: William Schuman." *The Gramophone* 69 (April 1992): 29.

A concise survey of Schuman's life and career is given in this obituary.

B272 "Obituaries: William Schuman." *The Instrumentalist* 46 (April 1992): 74-75.

Devotes a column and a half to Schuman's obituary.

B273 Page, Tim. "William Schuman at 75." *The New York Times,* August 4, 1985, section 2, pp. 17-18.

Dedicated to Schuman in honor of his seventy-fifth birthday, this article observes that the composer has been a major figure in American music for more than forty years. Points out that numerous performances of Schuman's compositions have taken place and are yet to take place in this anniversary year. Briefly mentions that, at present, Schuman is preparing two new works.

B274 Palatsky, Eugene. "The Lincoln Center Situation." *Dance Magazine* 37 (May 1963): 36-38.

Answers rumors concerning the future of dance at the new Lincoln Center for the Performing Arts. Refers to an announcement by Schuman indicating hope that the New York City Ballet would be a constituent member of the Lincoln Center. Enthusiastically provides ideas and several quotations by the composer regarding the future of the center.

B275 Parmenter, Ross. "First Winner of Critics Circle Prize." *The New York Times*, May 31, 1942, section 8, p. 6.

Parmenter recognizes Schuman as the initial recipient of the New York Music Critics Circle award for his Third Symphony. After a biographical overview and general remarks about the composer's completed symphonies, Parmenter briefly discusses the award-winning work, writing that Schuman "had the passacaglia melody long before he began the work and then he derived the chorale melody from it and also used it as the fugue subject."

B276 _____. "The World of Music." *The New York Times*, June 6, 1948, section 2, p. 7.

Identifies Schuman as the winner of a $1,000 commission from the Dallas Symphony Society to compose a work for orchestra.

B277 _____. "Philharmonic Acoustical Work Now Turns to Correcting Echo." *The New York Times*, July 26, 1963, p. 16.

Describes the corrective work being done on the acoustics of Philharmonic Hall. Schuman's satisfaction with the work is noted in the article.

B278 "Party of the Season; BMI Honors Pulitzer Prize Winners." *BMI: The Many Worlds of Music* (June 1983): 22-25.

Describes a reception given by BMI for its composers and lyricists who have won the Pulitzer Prize. In attendance were thirteen previous winners, including Schuman, who won the very first Pulitzer Prize in music in 1943, and the 1983 recipient, Ellen Taaffe Zwilich. Schuman recounts how, forty years ago, he learned that he had won the award. Includes several photographs of the event.

B279 Perlis, Vivian. "A Life Spent on One Musical Path." *The New York Times*, August 12, 1990, section 2, pp. 23-24.

Based on an interview conducted in honor of Schuman's eightieth birthday, this tribute acknowledges that Schuman's path as a composer "has been constant, within traditional forms and tonal systems." Briefly presents significant information about the composer's most recent works and about the latest performances of those compositions. Repeats a lengthy quotation by Leonard Slatkin on Schuman's musical style. Also presents a brief subsection entitled "A Word on Words," which offers Schuman's thoughts on collaborating with a librettist.

B280 Persichetti, Dorothea. "William Schuman." *The International Cyclopedia of Music and Musicians*, edited by Oscar Thompson and Bruce Bohle. Updated 11th ed. New York: Dodd, Mead, 1985, pp. 2003-08. ISBN 0 396 08412 5 ML100 I57 1985

Duplicates Persichetti's article published in the ninth edition of 1964. Combines an excellent account of Schuman's life with a discussion of his works. Contains an out-dated list of works.

B281 "Personalia." *Mens en melodie* 47 (March 1992): 186. In Dutch.

Includes an announcement of Schuman's death.

*   Petersen, Barbara A. *William Schuman.*

Cited as **B36**.

B282 Pettis, Ashley. "The WPA and the American Composer." *The Musical Quarterly* 26 (1940): 101-12.

Chronicles the activities of the Composers Forum Laboratory, established in 1935 under the auspices of the WPA Federal Music Project. Cites Schuman, one of the young composers to benefit from these sessions, as a significant case study in the Composers Forum Laboratory. Closes with a discussion of characteristic traits exhibited by most of the best composers associated with this project.

B283 Polisi, Joseph W. "William Schuman: Juilliard President Emeritus Dies, a Tribute." *The Juilliard Journal* 7 (March 1992): 1.

Celebrates the late composer as one who "helped America and the world to better appreciate the performing arts through his compositions, his vision and his abiding belief in the goodness of the human spirit." Reflects upon Schuman's numerous accomplishments, both as a composer and as an administrator.

B284 Poole, Jane L. "Obituary: William Schuman." *Opera News* 57 (July 1992): 45.

Gives only the most basic facts about Schuman's career.

B285 Porter, Andrew. *Music of Three More Seasons: 1977-1980.* New York: Alfred A. Knopf, 1981. 613 pp. ISBN 0 394 51813 6 ML60 P894

A collection of essays that were first presented in *The New Yorker*. Contains a couple of general references to Schuman and two reviews of Schuman works.

B286 "Premieres." *Music Educators Journal* 63 (December 1976): 14.

Briefly notes the world premiere performances of three of Schuman's compositions at the Kennedy Center in Washington, D.C.: *Casey at the Bat*, *The Young Dead Soldiers*, and *Symphony No. 10*. See: **W79a, W81a, W82a**

B287 "Premieres." *Symphony News* 28 (June 1977): 47, 49-50.

An extensive listing of premieres. Includes a citation for the 6 April 1976 performance of *Casey at the Bat* by the National Symphony Orchestra, the Westminster Choir, and with Antal Dorati conducting. See: **W81a**

B288 "Premieres." *Symphony News* 30 (June 1979): 80, 82.

The 29 October 1978 premiere of *In Sweet Music* is included in this list of premieres. The performance was by the Chamber Music Society of Lincoln Center and mezzo-soprano Jan DeGaetani. See: **W83a**

B289 "Premieres." *Symphony News* 31 (1980): 46, 57.

This substantial list of new performances covers the 24 January 1980 premiere of *Three Colloquies* for horn and orchestra. Zubin Mehta conducted the New York Philharmonic Orchestra and Philip Myers was the French horn soloist. See: **W85a**

B290 "The Pulitzer Prizes (Some Winners in Music): William Schuman." *Broadcast Music, Inc.* (1974): 21.

In addition to a photograph of Schuman, the entire entry consists of a single paragraph on the composer and his music.

B291 "Pulitzer Winner William Schuman Headed Juilliard, Lincoln Center." *Boston Globe*, February 16, 1992, p. 51.

The Associated Press obituary praises Schuman's contributions to American music.

B292 Ramey, Phillip. "Malign Neglect." *Keynote* 7 (April 1983): 12-17.

Advocates the performance of mainstream twentieth-century music and argues against the continuation of the "Masterpiece Syndrome" in our concert halls and recital halls. Surveys the neglected music of thirty-one contemporary composers, with a decided preference for American composers. William Schuman is described as a composer whose "inspiration shows no sign of lessening."

B293 Read, Gardner. *Style and Orchestration.* New York: Schirmer, 1979. 304 pp. ISBN 0 028 72110 1 ML455 R4

Presents a valuable examination of Schuman's orchestration style (pp. 227-32).

B294 Rees, C.B. "Impressions . . . Dr. William Schuman of the Lincoln Centre." *Musical Events* (July 1967): 8-9.

An entertaining, tongue-in-cheek interview with Schuman held at the Savoy Hotel in London. Although the author admits to a lack of knowledge concerning Schuman's career as a composer and arts administrator, he expresses admiration for the composer in his role as spokesman and president of the Lincoln Center.

B295 Reich, Howard. "Century's Top Composers? Try Copland, Bernstein and Bill Schuman." *Chicago Tribune*, April 27, 1986, Arts section, p. 16.

Argues that Schuman, in light of his accomplishments, should "be as famous as Aaron Copland or Leonard Bernstein or any of the other remaining icons of American musical culture." Replete with quotations by the composer.

B296 _____. "Composer William Schuman, 81; Legend in American Symphony." *Chicago Tribune*, February 17, 1992, Chicagoland section, p. 7.

This obituary proclaims the composer "a towering figure among American symphonists and a protean force on music in America."

B297 Reis, Claire R. "William Howard Schuman." *Composers in America*. New York: MacMillan, 1947, pp. 319-20.

Originally published in 1930 as *American Composers*, this volume contains biographical information about more than three hundred American composers. The essay devoted to Schuman contains a short discussion of his life and works. Concludes with a list of the composer's works, which also provides the duration, the publisher, and the date of composition.

B298 _____, and Helm, Everett. "Previously Unpublished Composer's Letters as Written to Claire R. Reis." *Musical America* 83 (January 1963): 14-17.

Publishes for the first time letters written to Claire Reis, one of the co-founders and leaders of the League of Composers, by fourteen composers. One letter, dated 9 February 1962, was written by Schuman to Reis in appreciation for her work with contemporary composers. Each letter in this article is preceded by a commentary.

B299 RePass, Richard. "American Composers of Today." *London Musical Events* 8 (December 1953): 25.

B300 Rich, Alan. "Schuman Speaks to Music Critics." *The New York Times*, November 3, 1962, p. 16.

A condensed account of Schuman's address to the tenth annual conference of the Music Critics Association. Rich stresses that Schuman "spoke as composer, rather than as president of Lincoln Center."

B301 Robertson, Nan. "Schuman Attacks Congress on Arts." *The New York Times*, May 20, 1967, p. 39.

A thorough report of Schuman's speech to the Friends of the Kennedy Center on May 19. Focuses, with the help of several quotations from the composer, on Schuman's criticism of Congress for its role in the support of the arts.

B302 _____. "William Schuman Offers a Birthday Gift to Friends." *The New York Times*, October 2, 1985, section 3, p. 16.

Lincoln Center was the scene of a spectacular birthday gala held in honor of Schuman (although his birthday was almost two months earlier). Several distinguished speakers praised the composer, and the evening was capped with a concert of selected Schuman works. As a surprise gift to the birthday guests, Schuman composed a wind quintet and percussion piece entitled *Dances*, which received its premiere as the final selection on the evening's concert. See: **W94a**

B303 _____. "Artists in Old Age: The Fires of Creativity Burn Undiminished." *The New York Times*, January 22, 1986, section 3, pp. 1, 10.

Looks at twelve creative artists, among them the composers Gian Carlo Menotti, William Schuman, and Morton Gould, and investigates why each continues to strive for more accomplishments in their elderly years.

B304 Robinson, Harlow. "William Schuman." *High Fidelity/Musical America* 35 (August 1985): MA 4-5, 9.

Written in honor of the composer's seventy-fifth birthday, this essay, based on a recent interview, describes how Schuman carefully planned his career in order to allow time for composition. Asserts that Schuman "happily embraces the label of 'American composer'" and, at the same time, recognizes that "American music still has a long way to go in overcoming the bias towards the European repertoire." Reports that he is unwilling to denounce avant-garde trends in music.

B305 Roca, Octavio. "Schuman, Orchestral Music's Man." *The Washington Times*, November 28, 1989.

Written in anticipation of the Kennedy Center Honors ceremony, this article attempts to evaluate Schuman's contribution to American music.

B306 Rockwell, John. "William Schuman—'The Continuum Has Been Composition.'" *The New York Times*, August 3, 1980, section 2, pp. 19, 22.

Sheds light on Schuman's philosophy of the art of composition. Laments the paucity of recordings of American serious music.

B307 "Rodgers Gives $15,000 for Juilliard Students." *The New York Times*, May 4, 1962, p. 25.

Publicizes the establishment of a fund for needy students at the Juilliard School given by Richard Rodgers in honor of Schuman.

B308 Roeder, Michael Thomas. *A History of the Concerto*. Portland, OR: Amadeus, 1994. 480 pp. ISBN 0 931 34061 6 ML1263 R64 1994

Discusses, in the chapter entitled "The Concerto in the United States," Schuman's Violin Concerto, Piano Concerto, and *Concerto on Old English Rounds*. Considers the latter work "among the most unusual concertos in the history of the form." Describes the composer's overall style as "rigorous, economical, and highly rhythmic."

B309 Rosenberg, Donald. "Schuman to Celebrate 80th Birthday." *The Pittsburgh Press*, July 30, 1990, section d, p. 2.

Notes performances this season by the Pittsburgh Symphony of Schuman works, including *American Festival Overture, Variations on "America,"* and *Casey at the Bat*.

B310 Rosenwald, Hans. "Speaking of Music." *Music News* 43 (April 1951): 10-11.

In this discussion of several composers, among them Randall Thompson, Morton Gould, John Cage, Gian Carlo Menotti, and Marc Blitzstein, Schuman is hailed as one of the very best of the younger generation. Believes that Schuman's Tin Pan Alley background is expressed in his compositions and highlights, too, the "academicism—in the best sense of the word—to be found in his music."

B311 Rothstein, Edward. "A Composer with many Public Faces." *The New York Times*, March 8, 1992, p. 29.

Reflects upon Schuman's multifaceted career, claiming that he was "the most important musical administrator of the 20th century" and speculating that "At one time, he was probably the most powerful figure in the world of art music." Details several of Schuman's accomplishments at the Juilliard School and at Lincoln Center. Praises the composer's "consistent practical vision" and declares this trait to be present in his Third Symphony and Seventh Symphony. Criticizes the composer's music for a shallowness of passion and emotion. Believes that Schuman's death has left a void which "will not soon be filled."

*   Rouse, Christopher. "Expansion of Material in the Seventh Symphony of William Schuman."

Cited as **B633**.

*   _____. *William Schuman Documentary*.

Cited as **B39**.

B312 _____. "Schuman and His Generation: Finding an American Voice." *Symphony Magazine* 36 (October-November 1985): 6, 8, 74.

A valuable essay providing great insight into Schuman's music and work. After affectionately recounting his own youthful introduction to the composer and his music, Rouse traces the development of an "American Music" during the first decades of the twentieth century, noting that "It was into this milieu that Schuman entered in 1938." Cites, among others, the following individuals as important in promoting the compositions of Schuman early in his career: Aaron Copland, Serge Koussevitzky, and Paul Rosenfeld. Compares the music of Schuman with that of his contemporaries: "Unlike that of his colleagues, Schuman's music was clearly urban in character. While most sought to evoke the spirit of rural America, Schuman, though only rarely writing specifically of cities or city life, nonetheless produced an enervated, syncopated music teeming with the energy and brisk metabolism of the metropolis." Regards the Sixth Symphony of 1948 as a pivotal work; observes that after 1958 "there began an overall process of simplification." Summarizes the salient features of the composer's music in the following felicitous statement: "Perhaps the principal virtue is the simple honesty of the music. There is nothing false here, no attempt nor desire to deceive. This music speaks plainly, but eloquently. . . . Schuman's music, like that of his contemporaries, also tenaciously refuses to cloy. It is neither glib nor recondite nor exotic. It is meaningful. It has *meaning* . . . clear, concise, and, for me, deeply moving." This article is based upon the author's participation in a presentation to the American Symphony Orchestra League Conference entitled "William Schuman and His Generation: Composers Reflect on Making Music in America."

B313 Sabin, Robert. "The Dangers of Being a Destructive Reactionary." *Musical America* 81 (February 1961): 8, 60.

Written in critical response to Winthrop Sargeant's polemical article in the 10 December 1960 issue of *The New Yorker,* which attacked Schuman and his Seventh Symphony. Sabin vehemently defends Schuman as one of America's foremost composers. See: **B642**

B314 _____. "Lincoln Center Challenge." *Musical America* 82 (February 1962): 6.

This editorial praises the selection of Schuman as the president of the Lincoln Center for the Performing Arts.

B315 _____. "Juilliard at the Crossroads." *Dance Magazine* (July 1968): 33-36, 38-39, 76-79.

Written at a time when the future of Juilliard's Dance Department was in doubt, this lengthy article presents a convincing case for the continuation of the department and, at the same time, includes an outstanding overview of the dance program's history. Contains information about Schuman's role in the development of dance at Juilliard.

B316 Salazar, Adolfo. *Music in Our Time: Trends in Music Since the Romantic Era.* New York: W.W. Norton, 1946; reprint ed., Westport, CT: Greenwood, 1970. 367 pp. ISBN 0 837 13014 x ML196 S252 1970

Translated from the Spanish by Isabel Pope, Salazar's study devotes a paragraph to Schuman, which mainly consists of a listing of his best-known works to 1945.

B317 Salzman, Eric. "He Marks Milestones." *The New York Times*, November 27, 1960, section 2, p. 9.

Inspired by the forthcoming performance in New York of the composer's new Seventh Symphony by the Boston Symphony Orchestra, the author focuses on Schuman's self discipline as a composer and on his administrative accomplishments at the Juilliard School. The article, which includes several quotations by the composer, is based on a recent interview with Schuman. See: **W58b**

B318 _____. "Lincoln Center to Aid Teachers." *The New York Times*, March 18, 1962, p. 85.

A somewhat detailed account of Schuman's speech at the 1962 Chicago convention of the Music Educators National Conference in which the composer presented his plans for the Lincoln Center Teachers Institute.

B319 Saminsky, Lazare. *Living Music of the Americas*. New York: Howell, Soskin and Crown, 1949. 284 pp. ML198 S3

Includes a generous, though dated, examination (pp. 69-74) of Schuman's musical style. Calls Schuman "the American Hindemith."

B320 Sargent, David. "Celebration! An American Tradition Is Reborn." *Vogue* 170 (October 1980): 53-54.

Recognizes the birthdays of three American music luminaries: William Schuman, Samuel Barber, and Aaron Copland. Views each of these composers as a product of the 1930s and argues that their conservative style has recently not been in vogue. Points to a revival of the most successful compositions by these men, such as Schuman's Third Symphony, and contends that "the work of these older composers is, at its best . . . music of demonstrable worth, and almost guaranteed to be played and admired for generations."

B321 Saylor, Bruce. "William Schuman." *The New Grove Dictionary of Music and Musicians*, edited by Stanley Sadie. London: Macmillan, 1980. Vol. 16, pp. 825-27. ISBN 0 333 23111 2 ML100 N48

Views Schuman as one of the most celebrated and significant composers in the United States. Summarizes the important events in the composer's multifarious career and attempts a brief description of Schuman's musical style, especially as demonstrated in his orchestral music. Points to the composer's success as an educator and arts administrator. Includes a list of his works, a selected list of Schuman's writings, and a selective bibliography.

B322 _____. "William (Howard) Schuman." *The New Grove Dictionary of American Music*, edited by H. Wiley Hitchcock and Stanley Sadie. London: Macmillan, 1986. Vol. 4, pp. 166-69. ISBN 0 943 1836 2 ML101 U6 N48 1986

Presents a slight expansion of Saylor's article in *The New Grove Dictionary of Music and Musicians*. Contains a revised list of Schuman's works and increases the size of the bibliography.

B323 Schonberg, Harold C. "Juilliard to Move to Lincoln Sq. and Add Training in the Drama." *The New York Times*, February 7, 1957, pp. 1, 20.

In this article Schonberg describes in some detail the plans to relocate the Juilliard School of Music in the Lincoln Center for the Performing Arts. Also included are several opinions and quotations by Schuman regarding the change.

B324 _____. "Man to Orchestrate Lincoln Center." *The New York Times*, December 31, 1961, section 6, pp. 8, 28-30.

Published on the eve of Schuman's official appointment as the new president of Lincoln Center, this article focuses on Schuman's organizational abilities, his skill as an impromptu speaker, his contributions to the Juilliard School, and concludes with a brief biography and short evaluation of his compositional style. See: **B66**

B325 _____. "Increasing Interest in Cultural Matters Demands Body of Informed Opinion." *The New York Times*, November 11, 1962, section 2, p. 9.

Inspired by and written in response to a recent address by Schuman given to the Music Critics Association, Schonberg demurs at the composer's description of the ideal music critic and, at the same time, agrees with Schuman's contention that music critics must be better informed.

B326 "School Merger Pends." *The New York Times*, January 9, 1959, p. 12.

Reports that Schuman's proposal to merge the High School of Performing Arts with the High School of Music and Art was approved.

B327 Schreiber, Flora Rheta. "A Model for Music Teachers." *Music Journal* 13 (October 1955): 28-29.

Recounts the unusual circumstances related to Schuman's decision to embark on a career in music. Argues that the composer's pragmatic philosophy has contributed to his success in so many diverse areas. Written shortly after the publication of a biography on William Schuman by the author and Vincent Persichetti. See: **B328**

B328 _____, and Persichetti, Vincent. *William Schuman*. New York: G. Schirmer, 1954. 139 pp. ML410 S386 S3

A seminal contribution to Schuman literature, recognized especially for Persichetti's thoughtful discussion of the composer's works. Divided into two parts, the first written by Schreiber and the second by Persichetti, part one provides an authoritative account of Schuman's life and career; part two, subdivided into smaller sections, considers different aspects of Schuman's musical style, such as melody, harmony, rhythm, and form, as well as presenting perceptive analyses, illustrated copiously with musical examples, of *American Festival Overture*, the Third Symphony, the *Symphony for Strings*, *Undertow*, and *Judith*. The appendix includes lists of works and records and a bibliography organized into articles written by Schuman and those written about him. Also contains an index.

B329 "Schuman Awarded MacDowell Medal." *The New York Times*, August 9, 1971, p. 21.

Announces that Schuman was the winner of the Edward MacDowell Medal.

B330 "Schuman Drops Schirmer Post." *The New York Times*, September 30, 1951, p. 61.

Succinctly proclaims Schuman's resignation from G. Schirmer as director of publications.

B331 "Schuman Gets Dallas Award." *The New York Times*, May 14, 1948, p. 28.

Notes that Schuman is the winner of a $1000 commission from the Dallas Symphony Society to compose a composition for orchestra.

B332 "Schuman Gets Schirmer Post." *The New York Times*, September 30, 1944, p. 16.

A terse notice of Schuman's selection to the post of director of publications at G. Schirmer.

B333 "Schuman Heads Music Fund." *The New York Times*, April 18, 1975, p. 22.

Short announcement of Schuman's appointment as chairman of the board of the Norlin Foundation.

B334 "Schuman Is Named to M'Dowell [*sic*] Post." *The New York Times*, January 24, 1974, p. 44.

Announcement of Schuman's appointment as the MacDowell Colony's board chairman.

B335 "Schuman Named Lincoln Center President." *The Music Magazine and Musical Courier* 163 (October 1961): 2.

Announces the appointment of Schuman to the presidency of the Lincoln Center. Includes a statement by the composer on the center's leadership role in the performing arts.

B336 "Schuman, No Kin." *Time* 39 (April 20, 1942): 60.

The title of this article refers to confusion between Robert Schumann and William Schuman. Reports that Schuman's Second Symphony, the winning composition in a contest to promote Spanish democracy, never received the expected performance and publication as promised. Recognizes Schuman's profitable relationship with Serge Koussevitsky. Provides a sketchy synopsis of Schuman's career (he was then at Sarah Lawrence College) and comments on the *American Festival Overture*.

B337 "Schuman on Cultural Panel." *The New York Times*, February 11, 1959, p. 32.

Identifies Schuman as being selected to serve on the Advisory Committee on Cultural Information in Washington.

B338 "Schuman Receives Kennedy Center Award." *The Juilliard Journal* 5 (February 1990): 1.

Recognizes Schuman as one of five individuals honored by the Kennedy Center on 3 December 1989. On that occasion, the Juilliard Orchestra played two movements from the composer's *New England Triptych*. The entire program was later broadcast by CBS television on December 29. See: **W53w**

B339 "Schuman Receives MacDowell Medal." *The Triangle of Mu Phi Epsilon* 66, no. 1 (1971): 27.

Informative article dealing with the presentation of the twelfth Edward MacDowell Medal to Schuman at the MacDowell Colony. The main speaker for the ceremonies was Aaron Copland, who commented that "Schuman's works celebrate America . . . A positive feeling comes from Schuman's music. It is a celebration of life."

B340 "Schuman Requests Freedom of Artists." *The New York Times*, October 12, 1950, p. 42.

Reports on the composer's address at the 1950 opening convocation ceremonies of the Juilliard School.

B341 "Schuman Scores Pulitzer Awards." *The New York Times*, June 14, 1965, p. 44.

In this report of Schuman's commencement address to the graduating class at Brandeis University, the composer takes the Pulitzer Prize Advisory Board to task for not selecting a winner in music.

B342 "Schuman 75th Birthday Celebrations." *BMI: The Many Worlds of Music*, Issue No. 3, 1985, p. 13.

Written in commemoration of Schuman's seventy-fifth birthday on August 4. Enumerates several ways in which the composer is to be honored during the 1985-1986 musical season.

B343 "Schuman Signs Exclusive Contract." *Etude* 74 (March 1956): 9.

Notice of Schuman's agreement to have his compositions published exclusively by the Theodore Presser Company.

B344 "Schuman Symphony in Premiere." *The New York Times*, November 13, 1943, p. 19.

A short notice of the premiere performance in Boston on 12 November 1943 of Schuman's Fifth Symphony by Serge Koussevitsky and the Boston Symphony Orchestra. See: **W29a**

B345 "Schuman to be Honored by Concert Artists Guild." *The New York Times*, January 20, 1967, p. 26.

An announcement that Schuman was selected to receive the Concert Artists Guild Award for 1967.

B346 "Schuman to Head Juilliard School." *The New York Times*, August 1, 1945, p. 15.

Makes public Schuman's appointment to the presidency of the Juilliard School of Music. Supplies information on the composer's educational background, his career, his awards, and his works.

B347 "Schuman to Head Lincoln Center." *Musical America* 81 (October 1961): 16.

An announcement that Schuman is to become the president of the Lincoln Center for the Performing Arts. Offers quotations from the composer's letter of resignation to the Juilliard School of Music.

B348 "Schuman to Head Naumburg Board." *The Musical Courier* 160 (December 1959): 5.

A condensed statement concerning Schuman's election to the presidency of the Naumburg Musical Foundation board.

B349 "Schuman to Lincoln Center." *The New York Times*, September 13, 1961, p. 44.

Comments on Schuman's appointment to head the Lincoln Center. Remarks that it is unusual in the United States for the creative artist to fill an administrative post. Believes that Schuman's selection will benefit the arts in this country.

B350 "Schuman Wins First Pulitzer Music Prize." *Musical America* 63 (May 1943): 25.

Observes that Schuman was the winner of the first Pulitzer Prize in music for his cantata *A Free Song*. Provides a brief biographical sketch and lists several of the composer's honors and awards.

B351 "Schuman Wins Prize." *The New York Times*, November 5, 1939, section 9, p. 7.

Announces Schuman's selection as the first winner of a composition award, for a commissioned work yet to be composed, given by the Town Hall and the League of Composers. Also includes a brief paragraph on the composer's career.

B352   Shepard, Richard F. "Morris Endorses the City Center." *The New York Times*, October 10, 1964, p. 19.

Focuses on the controversy surrounding the control of the New York State Theater. Refers to Schuman's role in the argument.

B353   _____. "Schuman Discusses His Plans for Lincoln Center Harmony." *The New York Times*, January 12, 1965, p. 32.

Reports on Schuman's first press conference as the president of the Lincoln Center.

B354   _____. "Schuman Finds Europe Knows Little of Arts in U.S." *The New York Times*, May 2, 1967, p. 54.

Schuman is interviewed after returning from a month-long trip to Europe. He discusses the misconceptions that Europeans, in general, have about music in America and recounts the purpose of his tour. The composer challenges the U.S. Congress to provide more funds for cultural exchanges between the United States and Western Europe.

B355   _____. "Deficit Can't Hide Festival Success." *The New York Times*, July 14, 1967, p. 18.

Prints several comments by Schuman explaining the deficit resulting from the Lincoln Center Festival of 1967.

B356   _____. "Schuman Quitting Lincoln Center Post." *The New York Times*, December 5, 1968, pp. 1, 61.

Schuman's resignation as president of the Lincoln Center is made known in this newspaper interview. Discusses the financial problems of Lincoln Center at that time and mentions the composer's plans for the future. Applauds Schuman's contributions to the success of the Lincoln Center.

B357   _____. "Lincoln Center—The First 20 Years." *The New York Times*, May 20, 1979, section 2, pp. 1, 28.

Written in anticipation of Lincoln Center's twentieth anniversary celebration, this article provides a history of the arts center. Highlights Schuman's role in the development of the institution.

B358   "Shiny New Image." *Newsweek* (January 25, 1965): 84-85.

Airs Schuman's frustration with the problems and controversies associated with the new Lincoln Center.

B359 "Sigma Alpha Iota Award." *Music of the West Magazine* 6 (January 1951): 6.

Briefly mentions that Schuman was awarded a commission to compose a new work by the American Music Awards program of the Sigma Alpha Iota Foundation.

B360 Sigman, Matthew. "Conference 1985: Building New Audiences." *Symphony Magazine* 36, no. 4 (1985): 30-33, 36-37.

A thorough summary of events associated with the fortieth National Conference of the American Symphony Orchestra League. Substantial discussion (complete with photographs) is given concerning the presentation of the Gold Baton Award to William Schuman. The presenter, Peter Kermani, stated: "William Schuman is a great composer. One does not call Beethoven a great German composer, Berlioz a great French composer, or Prokofiev a great Russian composer. They are simply great composers. So is William Schuman." In addition, the composer was honored with performances of his works by the San Francisco Symphony Youth Orchestra, which played *New England Triptych* and *American Hymn*; with a session chaired by Christopher Rouse entitled "Schuman and His Generation: Composers Reflect on Making Music in America"; and by tributes prepared by Morton Gould and Hugo Weisgall. See: **W53m**, **W89b**

B361 Slatkin, Leonard. "William Schuman: An Appreciation." *Symphony* 43 (May-June 1992): 22-24.

A tribute written soon after Schuman's death by one of the leading interpreters of the composer's music. Extols Schuman as one of several important American symphonists active during the mid-twentieth century. Reflects upon Schuman's numerous accomplishments at the Juilliard School and at the Lincoln Center. Proposes that "If Charles Ives was this country's musical father and Aaron Copland its dean, then William Schuman was certainly its CEO." Recollects that "composition was his first love." Includes a list of Schuman's compositions for orchestra.

B362 Slepian, Dorothy. "Polyphonic Forms and Devices in Modern American Music." *The Musical Quarterly* 33 (July 1947): 311-26.

Considers Schuman to be one of the leading contemporary American composers whose compositions demonstrate a propensity for polyphony. Among the composer's works cited are *American Festival Overture*, the Third Symphony, the Second String Quartet, the Third String Quartet, and the Concerto for Piano and Small Orchestra. Categorizes composers as follows: "those who use such devices frequently, those who employ them moderately, and those who do not use them at all. Piston, Harris, and Schuman are in the first group."

B363 Slonimsky, Nicolas. "William Howard Schuman." *Baker's Biographical Dictionary of Musicians*. 8th ed. New York: Schirmer, 1992, pp. 1654-55. ISBN 0 028 72415 1 ML105 B16 1991

A concise examination of Schuman's life and works. In his closing assessment of the composer's style Slonimsky writes: "In several of his works he employs American melo-rhythms, but his general style of composition is cosmopolitan, exploring all viable techniques of modern composition." Concludes with a list of works and a brief bibliography.

B364 _____. *Music Since 1900*. 5th ed. New York: Schirmer Books, 1994. 1260 pp. ISBN 0 028 72418 6 ML197 S634 1994

This copious chronicle of musical events from 1900 to 1969 contains twenty-eight entries about Schuman, most of which provide information about premiere performances of the composer's works.

B365 Stambler, Bernard. "Four American Composers." *The Juilliard Review* (Winter 1955): 7-16.

Compares, largely on the basis of four biographies published between 1953 and 1955, the careers and music of these composers: Aaron Copland, William Schuman, Samuel Barber, and Charles Ives. Asserts, "These four, covering as they do, in time, the span from the closing years of the past century to the present day and, in background before turning to composition, the span of Americana from the village band to Tin Pan Alley, tempt one into anatomizing the living American composer—examining, to borrow Robert Burton's terms, his Causes in general, his Symptoms or signs, his Prognosticks or indications, and his Cures." The source for information on Schuman is Flora Rheta Schreiber's and Vincent Persichetti's *William Schuman*, published in 1954 by G. Schirmer. See: **B328**

B366 "State Tests Urged in Music Teaching." *The New York Times*, June 2, 1951, p. 13.

A report of Schuman's commencement address at the Juilliard School.

* Stedman, Preston. *The Symphony*.

Cited as **B673**.

B367 Steele, Jonathan. "William Schuman's Literature and Materials Approach: A Historical Precedent for Comprehensive Musicianship." Ph.D. dissertation, University of Florida, 1988. 159 pp. UM Order No. 89-24027 ML410 S34 S814

According to the author's abstract, this investigation "documents William Schuman's early development of the Literature and Materials approach, his implementation of this program at Juilliard, some associations of the program with the origins of the Contemporary Music Project of the sixties, and a comparison of the Literature and Materials approach at Juilliard to the Comprehensive Musicianship movement in music education." Notes, bibliography, appendixes, and an index.

B368 "Stevenson Cast as Concert Star." *The New York Times*, February 20, 1962, p. 31.

Describes the concerts planned for the opening of Lincoln Center's Philharmonic Hall. Schuman is cited as providing the organizational details for the initial week of the new concert hall.

B369 Stoddard, Hope. "William Schuman—Discusses Problems in the Field of Music Education." *International Musician* (March 1961): 22-23.

Interviews Schuman about a variety of matters dealing with music education in the United States. For example, in answering a question about school music curricula, the composer offered the following as part of his response: "Music must be regarded as one of the great spiritual and intellectual achievements of man, comparable to achievements in literature and the visual arts." Also includes a concise biography of Schuman.

B370 Sullivan, Dan. "Priority for Arts in Schools Asked." *The New York Times*, June 27, 1967, p. 34.

Sullivan notes that Schuman, in a keynote address given at the New York State Theater to the Teacher's Convocation on the Performing Arts, implored music educators to raise the level of the arts in the public schools.

B371 "Swanson's Short Symphony Wins Music Critics Circle Award Here." *The New York Times*, January 8, 1952, p. 23.

Recognizes the recipients of the New York Music Critics Circle awards. Schuman's *Judith* is noted as the winner in the category of music for the dance. The composer's Sixth Symphony is mentioned as one of the compositions considered for the best orchestral work prize.

B372 "Symphonic Highlights: Premieres." *International Musician* 73 (December 1974): 15.

Mentions very briefly the world premiere on November 29 of *Concerto on Old English Rounds*, played by the Boston Symphony Orchestra. See: **W75a**

B373 "Symphony Premieres." *Facts on File*, January 29, 1970, p. 213.

Notes the premiere performance of Schuman's orchestral work *In Praise of Shahn*, commissioned in honor of the painter Ben Shahn. See: **W71a**

B374 "Ten Works Are Commissioned by the Philharmonic for 1962-63." *The New York Times*, January 25, 1962, p. 24.

Lists Schuman as one of ten prominent composers commissioned to compose a work for the New York Philharmonic Orchestra's first season in Lincoln Center's Philharmonic Hall.

B375 Terry, W. "William Schuman at 75." *BMI: The Many Worlds of Music* (June 1985): 19.

An article of general interest written in honor of the composer's birthday.

B376 "Things You Should Know: Premieres." *Music Journal* 34 (May 1976): 38.

Provides perfunctory information about the 6 and 7 April 1976 premieres of three Schuman works at the Kennedy Center by Antal Dorati and the National Symphony Orchestra: *The Young Dead Soldiers*, the Tenth Symphony, and *Casey at the Bat*. See: **W79a, W81a, W82a**

B377 "Third St. Music School Honors Schuman, Segal." *The New York Times*, November 12, 1981, section 3, p. 17.

Notes that Schuman was awarded the Third Street Music School Settlement's 1981 award "for distinguished achievement in music and the arts." Also presented with an award was Martin E. Segal, the chairman of Lincoln Center.

B378 Thomson, Virgil. *The Musical Scene.* New York: Alfred A. Knopf, 1945; reprint ed., New York: Greenwood, 1968. 301 pp. ML60 T5 1968

Contains essays and reviews which were originally published in the *New York Herald Tribune*. Reviews a 1943 performance of *A Free Song.* See: **W25b**

B379 _____. "'Theory' at Juilliard." *New York Herald Tribune*, May 18, 1947.

Discusses the new Literature and Materials of Music curriculum implemented by Schuman at Juilliard.

B380 _____. *The Art of Judging Music.* New York: Alfred A. Knopf, 1948; reprint ed., New York: Greenwood, 1969. 318 pp. ML60 T4.8 1969

A collection of music reviews and essays by the distinguished composer and music critic of the *New York Herald Tribune*. Contains reviews of performances of Schuman works.

B381 _____. *Music Right and Left.* New York: Henry Holt, 1951; reprint ed., New York: Greenwood, 1969. 214 pp. ML60 T49 1969

Another collection of essays which were first presented in the *New York Herald Tribune*. Contains references to Schuman in two essays.

B382 _____. *Music Reviewed, 1940-1954.* New York: Vintage, 1967. 422 pp. MT 125 T515 M9 1967

A book of reviews originally published in the *New York Herald Tribune*.

B383 _____. *Twentieth-Century Composers: American Music Since 1910.* New York: Holt, Rinehart and Winston, 1971. 204 pp. ISBN 03 076465 3 ML200.5 T5

While there are several references to Schuman scattered throughout this narrative, the best discussion of his style occurs on pages 86-87. Also included is a short biography and list of works (p. 172).

B384 "Three Premieres: Composers Schuman, Gaburo, Willis." *Pan Pipes of Sigma Alpha Iota* 45, no. 4 (1953): 3-4.

Contains information on the premiere performance of Schuman's new piano composition, *Voyage*. See: **W47a**

B385 Tober, Marie. "What About Art?" *The New York Times*, October 13, 1963, Magazine section, pp. 102, 104.

A letter to the editor written in response to Schuman's article "Have We Culture? Yes, and No." See: **S42**

B386 "The Two Schumans." *Time* 80 (October 12, 1962): 54.

Acknowledges Schuman's dual career as a composer and administrator. Discusses rehearsals and the approaching premiere of the composer's Eighth Symphony. Remarks that the new work "was a typically Schuman-crafted product" and provides insight into Schuman's administrative style and compositional style.

B387 "U.S. Arts Medals Presented." *The New York Times*, June 19, 1987, section 3, p. 26.

Calls attention to the June 18 White House ceremony at which Schuman was awarded a National Medal of Arts.

B388 Vancea, Zeno. "La journée internationale de la musique." *Muzica* 29 (November-December 1979): 71-72.

Concludes with a discussion of Schuman, evidently inspired by a performance of the finale to the composer's Third Symphony. Includes scant information about Schuman's background and comments on the structure of the movement.

B389 "Ventilation for Juilliard." *Time* 46 (October 22, 1945): 57.

Emphasizes some of the new reforms in curriculum initiated by Schuman at Juilliard.

B390 von Rhein, John. "Who Will Last? - Sound Survivors: 14 Master Composers Score a Place in History." *Chicago Tribune*, May 17, 1987, Arts section, p. 18.

Predicts that Schuman will be one of fourteen living composers whose music will endure.

B391 _____. "Ferris Chorale Commissions Fanfares for 20th Year." *Chicago Tribune*, May 9, 1991, Tempo section, p. 12.

Announces that Schuman is one of eight composers commissioned to compose a choral fanfare for the William Ferris Chorale.

B392 "Wants Music Expansion." *The New York Times*, October 10, 1945, p. 23.

In this short notice of a talk made by Schuman to students at Juilliard's Institute of Musical Art, remarks by the composer are quoted which, while recognizing the abundance of music and the arts in large cities like New York, observe the paucity of musical activity in the life of many smaller American communities.

B393 "We Salute—William Schuman." *Music Clubs Magazine* 37 (September 1957): 12.

Published as the fifth essay in a series on contemporary American composers, this article presents a cursory overview of the composer's career. Closes with a paragraph which stresses his accomplishments at the Juilliard School of Music to that time.

B394 Webster, Daniel. "Schuman: Activist, Composer." *The Philadelphia Inquirer*, February 18, 1992, section c, p. 1.

Written shortly after the death of the composer, this appreciative article focuses on Schuman's accomplishments as an arts administrator, teacher, and composer.

B395 Weisgall, Hugo. "William Schuman." *Dictionary of Contemporary Music*, edited by John Vinton. New York: E.P. Dutton, 1974, pp. 664-65. ISBN 0 525 09125 4 ML100 V55

After a brief, biographical introduction of only one paragraph, this article (pp. 664-65) discusses several aspects of the composer's style. Cites Schuman, along with Roger Sessions, as the American composers whose symphonic works best represent a continuation of the tradition of Bruckner, Mahler, and their predecessors. Concludes with a list of principal compositions and a very short bibliography.

B396 "What's the Score?: Double Debut." *The Instrumentalist* 41 (December 1986): 85.

Makes mention of three Schuman performances: the premiere of the cantata *On Freedom's Ground* in Avery Fisher Hall, the composer's arrangement of a suite from the cantata for wind quintet and percussion presented on October 1 by the Chamber Music Society, and the divertimento from the suite played on November 2 by the Chamber Music Society. See: **W95a**

B397 "Wilder Play, Sinclair Novel Are Pulitzer Prize Winners." *The New York Times*, May 4, 1943, pp. 1, 12.

This copious newspaper article announces the 1942 Pulitzer Prize winners and provides a biographical sketch for each recipient. Schuman is noted as the first composer to win the prize in the field of music.

B398 "William Schuman." *Pan Pipes of Sigma Alpha Iota* 43 (December 1950): 129.

B399 "William Schuman." *Pan Pipes of Sigma Alpha Iota* 44 (January 1952): 44.

Furnishes news about performances of Schuman's Sixth Symphony, Third Symphony, and Fourth String Quartet, as well as providing a list of new Schuman recordings.

B400 "William Schuman." *Pan Pipes of Sigma Alpha Iota* 47 (January 1955): 64-65.

Succinct report of new publications (*Voyage*, *The Mighty Casey*) and projected recordings (*Voyage*, Symphony No. 6) of compositions by Schuman.

B401 "William Schuman Elected President of Lincoln Center." *The Juilliard Review* 9, no. 3 (1961): 3-4.

Reprints as part of this announcement a statement by John D. Rockefeller III, chairman of the Lincoln Center board, concerning the Schuman appointment. Also prints a portion of Schuman's resignation letter to the Juilliard School faculty and provides a closing quotation praising the composer by James P. Warburg, Juilliard's chairman of the board.

B402 "William Schuman Elected to American Academy of Arts and Letters." *The Diapason* 65 (March 1974): 1.

Identifies Schuman as the fifth composer to be elected to the prestigious American Academy of Arts and Letters.

B403 "William Schuman Gets Music Prize." *The New York Times*, May 15, 1942, p. 24.

This article, acknowledging Schuman as the winner of the first New York Music Critics Circle award for his Third Symphony, was published the day following the vote by the members of the Circle.

B404 "William Schuman Honored by Concert Artists Guild." *The New York Times*, March 13, 1967, p. 47.

Report of the dinner concert at which Schuman was awarded the Concert Artists Guild Award for 1967.

B405 "William Schuman Is Recipient of CMA's National Service Award." *Chamber Music Magazine* 2, no. 4 (Winter 1985): 35.

Primarily an announcement about Schuman receiving the National Service Award from Chamber Music America. Presents a short paragraph which gives some of the composer's accomplishments.

B406 "William Schuman ist tot." *Neue Musikzeitung* 41 (April-May 1992): 2.

Prints a short Schuman obituary.

B407 "William Schuman Juilliard's President." *The Juilliard Review* 8, no. 3 (1961): 6-7.

Prints two pages of photographs showing Schuman in various activities. Each photograph is accompanied by an explanatory caption.

B408 "William Schuman Testimonial Dinner." *The Juilliard Review* 9, no. 2 (1962): 4-5.

Reports on a dinner held in Schuman's honor after his resignation from Juilliard to celebrate his years of leadership to the institution. Announces the creation of a William Schuman Fund at Juilliard, which was established with a $15,000 donation from Richard Rodgers.

B409 "William Schuman Wins $5,000 Mark Horblit Prize." *The New York Times*, September 18, 1980, section 3, p. 7.

Announces that Schuman is the 1980 recipient of the Boston Symphony's Mark M. Horblit award.

B410 "William Schuman Wins New Composer's Award." *Musical America* 59 (November 10, 1939): 11.

Identifies Schuman as the initial winner "of the new award in composition offered under the joint auspices of the Town Hall and the League of Composers." Indicates that he received a commission to compose a work appropriate for a Town Hall performance. Gives scant attention to the composer's career.

B411 "Winter Meeting: January 12, 1977." *National Music Council Bulletin* 36, no. 2 (1977): 6.

Includes a succinct interview with the composer, with questions posed by Robert Sherman.

B412 "Wisconsin to Honor Schuman." *The New York Times*, May 15, 1949, p. 79.

In this short announcement, Schuman is recognized as having been selected to receive an honorary doctorate from the University of Wisconsin in June.

B413 "World Premieres." *Symphony News* 25, no. 6 (1974): 27.

A terse announcement of the 29 November 1974 premiere performance of *Concerto on Old English Rounds*. See: **W75a**

B414 Young, Edgar B. *Lincoln Center: The Building of an Institution.* New York: New York University Press, 1980. 334 pp. ISBN 0 814 79656 7 PN1588 N5 Y68

Documents the history of the Lincoln Center for the Performing Arts from its origins to 1980.

Works: Orchestral and Band Music

B415 Anderson, Owen. "New Works: Orchestral Premieres." *Music Journal* 26 (December 1968): 105-06.

Relates with enthusiasm an account of the premiere performance of *To Thee Old Cause*, played by Leonard Bernstein and the New York Philharmonic. Compares this "somber, elegiac" score to Schuman's Eighth Symphony. See: **W69a**

B416 Archibald, Bruce. Review of William Schuman: *The Orchestra Song* and *Variations on "America."* *Music Library Association Notes* 23 (September 1966): 157.

Archibald's review is basically unsympathetic to both works. In his evaluation of *The Orchestra Song*, he doubts that either performers or listeners will find the composition very interesting.

B417 Artner, Alan G. "Pianist Takes New Direction with Prokofiev." *Chicago Tribune*, February 7, 1986, Chicagoland section, p. 9.

A favorable review of the February 6 concert by the Chicago Symphony Orchestra. One of the works on the program was Schuman's Third Symphony, successfully interpreted by guest conductor Leonard Slatkin. See: **W22z**

B418 _____. "Basically the Best; Dipping into the Currents Helps Define Mainstream." *Chicago Tribune*, October 29, 1989, Arts section, p. 10.

Artner's list of recommended recordings of twentieth-century music includes the CBS LP MS 7442 release of Schuman's Third Symphony and *Symphony for Strings*. See: **D81, D87**

B419 "Atlanta Symphony Orchestra Performance Calendar." *Atlanta Journal*, September 2, 1990, section n, p. 8.

Notes that Robert Shaw will conduct a performance of Schuman's *American Festival Overture* on September 27, 28, and 29. See: **W14p**

B420 B., J. "Music: Concert in Park." *The New York Times*, June 20, 1957, p. 24.

Pans, in this performance review, the first New York hearing of Schuman's *Chester Overture*, which was played in Central Park by the Goldman Band. Describes the composition as "a somewhat perfunctory rehash of the Billings tune." See: **W50b**

B421 Bals, Karen Elizabeth. "The American Piano Concerto in the Mid-Twentieth Century." D.M.A. dissertation, University of Kansas, 1982. 124 pp. UM Order No. 83-01668

Traces the history of the piano concerto in America to 1970. The third chapter, entitled "The Piano Concerto in America from 1940 to 1960," incorporates an analysis of Schuman's *Concerto for Piano and Small Orchestra* (pp. 35-45). Includes footnotes, musical examples, and a selected bibliography.

B422 Bargreen, Melinda. "Youth Symphony Shines." *The Seattle Times*, May 23, 1989, section c, p. 5.

Reviews the May 21 concert of the Seattle Youth Symphony Orchestra, which included a performance of William Schuman's *New England Triptych*. The concert was conducted by Rubin Gurevich. See: **W53t**

B423 _____. "Kendall's Versatility Shines." *The Seattle Times*, April 22, 1991, section f, p. 3.

Reviews the April 20 concert of the Seattle Symphony Orchestra, with Christopher Kendall conducting. One of the selections on the program was Schuman's *A Song of Orpheus*, performed by the symphony and cellist Cordelia Wikarski-Miedel. See: **W59k**

B424 _____. "Recordings." *The Seattle Times*, July 2, 1992, section f, p. 3.

Presents a review of the new Delos disc by Gerard Schwarz and the Seattle Symphony entitled "A Tribute to William Schuman." See: **D44, D55, D88, D117**

B425 Barry, Malcolm. "Concerts: Modern." *Music and Musicians* 23 (October 1974): 56-58.

A negative response to the first London hearing of Schuman's *Symphony for Strings*. The reviewer, in his concluding comments on the performance by Neville Marriner and the Los Angeles Chamber Orchestra, characterizes the work as having "just enough spice to make the piece sound modern, enough notes to demonstrate the players' techniques, but also enough disposability to make the piece completely forgettable." Reviews of three other compositions appear in this article. See: **W29h**

B426 Battisti, Frank L. "William Schuman: When Jesus Wept." *BDGuide* (January-February 1990): 13-15.

After a concise discussion of Schuman's version of this work for band, including statements about the composition by the composer, the author offers rehearsal suggestions for band directors, organized according to the major sections of the score. Points out two mistakes in the printed version of the score and suggests a few changes in instrumentation, generally based on the orchestral version of the work. Credits Schuman as being one of the significant composers for band during the 1940s and 1950s.

B427 Bendheim, Anne. "Financial News Good, Too: Cellist, PSO Offer Splendid Night." *The Phoenix Gazette*, April 3, 1987, section f, p. 5.

A positive review of the April 2 concert by the Phoenix Symphony Orchestra. Reports that Schuman's *New England Triptych* was the opening selection. See: **W53q**

*   Berger, Arthur. "Spotlight on the Moderns."

Cited as **B794**.

B428 Bernstein, Leonard. "The Latest from Boston." *Modern Music* 16, no. 3 (1938-39): 182-84.

Examines three works performed at a festival of American music by Koussevitzky and the Boston Symphony Orchestra: John Alden Carpenter's Concerto for Violin, William Schuman's Second Symphony, and Roy Harris's Third Symphony. Offers generally positive remarks about the Schuman composition. See: **W13c**

B429 _____. "Young American—William Schuman." *Modern Music* 19 (1942): 97-99.

Inspired by Boston Symphony Orchestra performances of the Third Symphony, Bernstein, then an assistant to Koussevitzky, comments on aspects of the work. Criticizes Schuman for certain general compositional traits, yet overall, praises his achievement.

B430 Berrett, Joshua. Review of William Schuman: *Concerto for Violin and Orchestra*, recorded by the St. Louis Symphony Orchestra, conducted by Leonard Slatkin, with Robert McDuffie, violin. *American Music* 9 (Fall 1991): 335-37.

This cogent review of the 1989 EMI Angel CDC 49464 2 recording of Schuman's Concerto for Violin traces the evolution of the work from the original commission by Samuel Dushkin through the subsequent revisions leading to the 1959 final version, which, as the reviewer observes, was "substantially different from the original." Bemoans the paucity of commercial recordings, reporting that the only previous recording of the composition is no longer available. Remarks that both Slatkin and Robert McDuffie, the violinist, "have impressive credentials as champions of American music." Observes that Richard Freed's program notes are, on the whole, adequate. Leonard Bernstein's *Serenade for Violin, String Orchestra, Harp and Percussion* appears with the Schuman concerto on this release. See: **D26**

B431 Blois, Louis. Review of William Schuman: *Symphony No. 6* and *Symphony No. 9 "Le Fosse Ardeatine,"* recorded by the Philadelphia Orchestra, conducted by Eugene Ormandy. *The American Record Guide* 47 (May 1984): 43-44.

An informative and complimentary review. Suggests that Schuman's symphonies "are among the major representatives of the form in America, with a strength and attractiveness capable of bringing them wide appeal." Believes that the Sixth Symphony "is closest to the Romantic vision of the Third" and calls the Ninth "a masterpiece of economy and craftmanship." Recorded on CRI SD-477. See: **D90, D96**

B432 "Boston Premiere for Schuman's 'Seventh.'" *Pan Pipes of Sigma Alpha Iota* 54, no. 2 (1962): 3, 5.

Furnishes recent information about three Schuman compositions: the 21 and 22 October 1960 premiere of the composer's Seventh Symphony by the Boston Symphony Orchestra, a work written on commission from that organization, conducted by Charles Munch; the review in this same journal of the Columbia Records recording of Schuman's Third Symphony; and the review, also in this same journal, of the RCA Victor recording of the composer's Third String Quartet. See: **W58a, D75, D81**

B433 Breuer, Robert. "Berichte aus dem Ausland." *Melos* 35 (December 1968): 487-88.

Comments on the New York City premiere performance of *To Thee Old Cause*. See: **W69a**

B434 Brillhart, Jerome Bellamy. "Comparative Analysis of Two Symphonies by William Schuman as Documentation of a Critical Judgment." M.M. thesis, University of Texas at Austin, 1960.

B435 Broder, Nathan. "Current Chronicle: New York." *The Musical Quarterly* 36 (April 1950): 279-82.

An informative, enthusiastic review of Schuman's Concerto for Violin, complete with musical examples. Calls attention to the importance of the solo instrument and summarizes techniques used to unify the composition.

B436 _____. "Reviews of Records." *The Musical Quarterly* 41 (October 1955): 551-55.

Review of several recordings by a diverse group of twentieth-century composers. Schuman's Sixth Symphony is paired with Walter Piston's Fourth Symphony (Columbia ML 4992) and Schuman's *Voyage* is coupled with Virgil Thomson's Second String Quartet (Columbia ML 4987). Describes Schuman's Sixth Symphony as "one of Schuman's finest works, powerful and passionate. More subtle and complex than his earlier symphonies, it does not yield all of its secrets on one or two hearings. Once one becomes acquainted with the themes, following what happens to them becomes an exciting adventure." See: **D89, D120**

B437 Bronston, Levering. Review of William Schuman: *Concerto on Old English Rounds*, recorded by the New York Philharmonic Orchestra and the Camerata Singers, conducted by Leonard Bernstein, with Donald McInnes, viola. *The New Records* (August 1978): 7.

A positive, albeit brief, review of the Columbia M35101 recording. See: **D28**

B438 Brown, Michael R. "The Band Music of William Schuman: A Study of Form, Content and Style." Ed.D. dissertation, University of Georgia, 1989. 224 pp. UM Order No. 90-03372

A thorough examination of three works for band by Schuman: *George Washington Bridge*, *Chester*, and *American Hymn: Variations on an Original Melody*. After three introductory chapters, chapter four presents detailed analyses of the compositions. Particularly noteworthy is the penultimate chapter (chapter 5), which "endeavors to place the band compositions analyzed within the context of William Schuman's general style of instrumental music." The final chapter (chapter 6) is a summary twenty pages in length. Includes chapter references, extensive musical examples, a bibliography, and six appendixes.

B439 _____. "Analysis: *American Hymn: Variations on an Original Melody* by William Schuman." *Journal of Band Research* 27 (1992): 67-79.

Examines Schuman's last work for band, with emphasis on a structural analysis. Stresses that the form of Schuman's hymn, "The Lord Has a Child," upon which the band composition is based, provides the overall structure of *American Hymn: Variations on an Original Melody*.

B440 _____. "Conducting Schuman's Chester Overture." *The Instrumentalist* 48 (November 1993): 29-36.

Provides an illuminating discussion of Schuman's well-known band transcription of the third movement from his own *New England Triptych*.

B441 Brown, Royal S. Review of William Schuman: *Symphony No. 3* and *Symphony No. 5*, recorded by the New York Philharmonic Orchestra, conducted by Leonard Bernstein. *High Fidelity* (November 1970): 96.

Discusses the Columbia MS 7442 issue of Schuman's third and fifth symphonies. Argues that the composer is among the best twentieth-century symphonists and contends that the Fifth Symphony is a masterpiece. See: **D81**, **D87**

B442 _____. Review of William Schuman: *Symphony No. 7*, recorded by the Utah Symphony Orchestra, conducted by Maurice Abravanel. *High Fidelity* 22 (December 1972): 104, 106.

Reviews the Turnabout (TVS 34447) recording of Schuman's Seventh Symphony. Does not regard this work as one of Schuman's finest symphonies. See: **D91**

B443 _____. Review of William Schuman: *New England Triptych*, recorded by the Phoenix Symphony Orchestra, conducted by James Sedares. *Fanfare* (September-October 1992): 259-60.

Contends that "much of Schuman's characteristic style, with its rich, often polytonal chordal harmonies, gets smoothed over in this work by the various references to the music of the early American composer William Billings." A review of the Koch International Classics disc. See: **D56**

B444 Brown, Steven. "FSO's Rachmaninoff Has Power." *The Orlando Sentinel*, March 13, 1993, section a, p. 2.

Reviews the March 11 and 12 concerts by the Florida Symphony Orchestra, under the direction of Andrews Sill. One of the works performed on the program was Schuman's *American Festival Overture*, described as a composition demonstrating "vigor and brilliance." See: **W14u**

B445   _____. "Galway's Style Range Matches each Moment Playing with the Jacksonville Symphony." *The Orlando Sentinel*, March 30, 1993, section a, p. 2.

Brown's concert review of a March 29 Orlando concert by the Jacksonville Symphony Orchestra features discussion of James Galway playing Ellen Taaffe Zwilich's flute concerto. Conductor Lawrence Leighton Smith also led the orchestra in a performance of Schuman's *New England Triptych*. See: **W53dd**

B446   Brozen, Michael. "New York Philharmonic (Bernstein)." *High Fidelity/Musical America* 18 (December 1968): MA-16.

To Thee Old Cause, composed for the 125th anniversary of the New York Philharmonic, is reviewed in this article after early October performances of the work by Leonard Bernstein and the New York Philharmonic. See: **W69a**

B447   C., D.C. Review of William Schuman: *Symphony No. 3*, recorded by the New York Philharmonic Orchestra, conducted by Leonard Bernstein. *HighPerformance Review* 5 (July-September 1988): 80-81.

Compares, in this recording review of Deutsche Grammophon 419780-1, the Schuman Third Symphony with the Roy Harris Third Symphony. See: **D82**

B448   Canby, Edward Tatnall. "Schuman's Synthesis." *Saturday Review of Literature* 30 (November 1, 1947): 46.

Maintains that Schuman's *Symphony for Strings* is a pivotal work in the development of an American style in modern music. Presents a keen description of the composer's musical language, arguing that in the Fifth Symphony he "is moving towards a farther sense of line. His music, concurrently, has grown deeper, his style more clear, and his speech concentrated." Concludes, however, that Schuman is still searching for a mature musical style, one which would assimilate the American and European traditions. A recording review of the Concert Hall release. See: **D85**

*   _____. Review of William Schuman: *Judith* and *Undertow*, recorded by the Louisville Orchestra, conducted by Robert Whitney.

Cited as **B797**.

B449   _____. Review of William Schuman: *Three Colloquies for Horn and Orchestra*, recorded by the New York Philharmonic Orchestra, conducted by Zubin Mehta, with Philip Myers, horn. *Audio* 69 (December 1985): 110-11.

Contends that Schuman's music is "competent in every technical sense but somehow chilly and academic." A review of the New World recording. See: **D100**

B450 Carter, Elliott. "Coolidge Crusade; WPA; New York Season." *Modern Music* 16 (November-December 1938): 33-38.

Considers, in this survey of new music recently heard in New York, Schuman's *Pioneers* and his Second Symphony. Carter's response to the Westminster Choir performance of the choral work was that it "left by far the best impression and fully confirmed Copland's enthusiastic review of it in the last issue." The reviewer's opinion of the symphony, as performed by the Greenwich Orchestra at a WPA concert under Schenkman, was, however, less favorable, complaining that it "suffers from the opposite fault of a too obvious plan, the plan being filled with ideas often of no very great interest." Mentions the debt of Schuman to Roy Harris. See: **W10a, W13a**

B451 _____. "Forecast and Review: American Music in the New York Scene." *Modern Music* 17, no. 2 (1939-40): 93-101.

After an opening section in which the author attempts to re-evaluate American music, the discussion focuses on recently performed compositions by several well-known composers. Emphasizes the Roy Harris Third Symphony and works by Roger Sessions. Describes Schuman's *American Festival Overture*, observing that "it has vitality and conviction behind it."

* Chase, William W. Review of William Schuman: *In Sweet Music*, *The Young Dead Soldiers*, and *Time to the Old*, recorded by Rosalind Rees and the Orpheus Trio, the White Mountains Festival Orchestra, and pianist Thomas Muraco.

Cited as **B714**.

B452 Clark, John W. "The One-Movement Symphony in America, 1937-1976: With Analyses of Works by Roy Harris, William Schuman, Vincent Persichetti, and Peter Fricker." Ph.D. dissertation, University of California at Santa Barbara, 1982. 308 pp. UM Order No. 83-10224

Examines single-movement American symphonies composed during the mid-twentieth century, providing penetrating analyses of thirteen works by four major composers. Four of Schuman's symphonies (2, 6, 7, 9) are included in this investigation. Appendix II contains a biographical sketch of Schuman and a transcription of a 15 December 1980 interview held with the composer in New York City. Clark's study, consistently well written and discerning, represents a significant contribution to Schuman research. See: **B77**

* _____. "William Schuman on His Symphonies: An Interview."

Cited as **B77**.

B453 Commanday, Robert. "Flashy Briton Prodigy Introduces Hummel Concerto." *San Francisco Chronicle*, March 2, 1990, section e, p. 6.

Reviews an April 30 concert by the San Francisco Symphony that included three of the fanfares commissioned by the Houston Symphony for the 1986 Texas Sesquicentennial, among them Schuman's *Showcase: A Short Display for Orchestra*. The reviewer remarked that "It's lively, brilliant and episodic, draws in syncopation from the jazz of Schuman's younger days and winds up with a whiz-bang, applause-machine ending." The concert was under the direction of guest conductor Jahja Ling. See: **W97b**

B454 _____. "First Test of Symphony at Walnut Creek." *San Francisco Chronicle*, November 12, 1990, section f, p. 3.

Praises a November 10 concert presented by conductor Gary Sheldon and the Marin Symphony, which included a "strong and secure" performance of Schuman's *New England Triptych*. See: **W53x**

B455 _____. "First Test of Symphony at Walnut Creek." *San Francisco Chronicle*, November 13, 1990, section e, p. 3.

Commanday's review of the November 11 concert by the California Symphony, conducted by Barry Jekowsky, at Walnut Creek in the Hofmann Theater at the Regional Center for the Arts, argues that the performance of Schuman's *New England Triptych* "was good without being stirring." See: **W53y**

B456 _____. "Edo de Waart's Return Features American Works." *San Francisco Chronicle*, April 5, 1991, section e, p. 6.

A concert review of the April 3 San Francisco Symphony program conducted by guest conductor Edo de Waart. Schuman's Sixth Symphony was heard for the first time in San Francisco. See: **W41k**

B457 _____. "Pisek, McDuffie Bring Out Symphony's Best." *San Francisco Chronicle*, November 13, 1992, section c, p. 4.

An enthusiastic review of a November 12 performance of Schuman's Concerto for Violin by the San Francisco Symphony and violinist Robert McDuffie. The orchestra was conducted by guest conductor Libor Pisek. Commanday writes that "This Schuman Concerto deserves to be planted firmly in the repertory. It's bold, romantic and contains some of the most personal and tender music Schuman ever wrote for orchestra. . . . There is character in this stuff, with phrases and lines of inspired breadth and shape." See: **W39g**

B458 "Concert Music in the News." *BMI: The Many Worlds of Music* (November-December 1968): 40.

Provides information about a 3 October 1968 performance of *To Thee Old Cause* by Leonard Bernstein and the New York Philharmonic Orchestra. Mentions that the work was commissioned for the 125th anniversary season of the orchestra and that it was composed in memory of Robert F. Kennedy and Martin Luther King. Closes with an excerpt from a review of the performance by Harriett Johnson published in the *New York Post*. See: **W69a**

B459 "Concert Music in the News." *BMI: The Many Worlds of Music* (March 1969): 14.

Primarily a review of the Ninth Symphony inspired by two recent performances: the 10 January 1969 premiere by Eugene Ormandy and the Philadelphia Orchestra and the 14 January 1969 New York presentation of the work by the same orchestra. Gives important background information about the composition, as well as printing several comments on the symphony by the composer. Also contains complimentary remarks describing the work reprinted from the newspaper reviews of four critics. See: **W68a, W68b**

B460 "Contrast in Cabrillo Concerts." *San Jose Mercury News*, August 19, 1985, section b, p. 10.

Notes a performance of Schuman's Concerto for Violin at the Cabrillo Music Festival on August 16. The violinist Maryvonne Le Dizes-Richard "gave an exciting performance" of the concerto. The conductor was John De Main. See: **W39e**

B461 Cowell, Henry. "Current Chronicle: New York." *The Musical Quarterly* 42 (July 1956): 386-89.

Cowell's discerning review of *Credendum* lauds the composition and comments in general on the musical style of the work. Concludes with the following assessment: "The total work is impressive, large-scaled, Schuman's *magnum opus.*" See: **W49b**

B462 _____. "Reviews of Records." *The Musical Quarterly* 44 (July 1958): 402-03.

A complimentary review of a recording (Decca DL 8633) of band compositions performed by the Goldman Band under the direction of Richard Franko Goldman. Ranging from works by Gossec and Mendelssohn to a march by Edwin Franko Goldman, the album also includes Schuman's *Chester Overture* for band. See: **D16**

B463 Cranfill, Mabel. "Schuman Premiere Presented in Dallas." *Musical America* 69 (April 15, 1949): 27.

The reviewer notes the world premiere performance in Dallas of Schuman's Sixth Symphony, performed by the Dallas Symphony Orchestra under the direction of Antal Dorati. See: **W41a**

B464 Crankshaw, Geoffrey. "Two Sides of Previn." *Music and Musicians* 17 (May 1969): 63.

Briefly reports on a February 24 performance of Schuman's Third Symphony by the London Symphony Orchestra, conducted by André Previn. Suggests that the composition is lacking in memorable melodies. Applauds, however, the composer's vigorous use of the orchestra, commenting on the enthusiastic playing by the members of the orchestra. See: **W22t**

*   Croan, Robert. "Rhythm Strength: Maazel's Mastery Ties Three Pieces into One Package."

Cited as **B798**.

B465 Cunningham, Carl. "Symphony Mixes Social Justice with Music." *The Houston Post*, June 29, 1992, section d, p. 2.

Stephen Stein conducted the Houston Symphony in a June 27 concert at the Miller Theatre, which included a performance of Schuman's *New England Triptych*. The reviewer praised the orchestra's string section for its excellent playing of Schuman's work. See: **W53cc**

B466 _____. "Houston Symphony Combines Irreverent Music with Sublime." *The Houston Post*, September 20, 1993, section b, p. 2.

Presents a review of the September 18 performance of the Houston Symphony at Jones Hall. Christoph Eschenbach conducted the orchestra in an "ostentatious interpretation" of the *Variations on "America."* See: **W63h**

*   Dalheim, Eric L. "Record Reviews: Rosalind Rees Sings William Schuman."

Cited as **B719**.

B467 Davis, Peter G. "New York Philharmonic." *Musical America* 84 (November 1964): 31.

A very uncomplimentary performance review of *Credendum*, performed on October 4 by the New York Philharmonic Orchestra under the direction of Josef Krips. Davis states that "William Schuman's 'Credendum' is perhaps the worst piece of music I have ever heard." See: **W49g**

B468 _____. "Concert: Plangency and Exotica." *The New York Times*, May 22, 1977, p. 52.

Concludes, in this review of the New York premiere of Schuman's *Amaryllis: Variations for String Orchestra* presented by André Kostelanetz and the New York Philharmonic, that "the piece makes its points concisely and attractively." See: **W80b**

B469 _____. "Curios for Collectors." *New York* 16 (February 7, 1983): 80, 82.

Includes a brief review of a performance of Schuman's *Symphony for Strings*, presented as a selection on a contemporary music festival at Juilliard. The Juilliard Orchestra was conducted by Jorge Mester.

B470 _____. "Looking Out for Number One." *New York* 18 (June 10, 1985): 82-83.

Sings the praises of a performance of Schuman's Piano Concerto by New York's Y Chamber Symphony and pianist Horacio Gutiérrez. Describes the concerto as "characteristically extroverted, self-confident, and optimistic" and discerns a "definite feeling of jazz" in the score. See: **W24b**

B471 Denton, David. Review of William Schuman: *Concerto for Violin and Orchestra*, recorded by the Boston Symphony Orchestra, conducted by Michael Tilson Thomas, with Paul Zukofsky, violin. *The Strad* 101 (December 1990): 1024, 1026.

An outstanding review of the Deutsche Grammophon 429860-2 recording. Maintains that Schuman's concerto "is a direct descendant of Stravinsky and Bartók" and believes that "it is one of the finest works to be composed in this format during the second half of this century." See: **D25, D27**

B472 Derhen, Andrew. "N.Y. Philharmonic: Schuman Premiere." *High Fidelity/ Musical America* 20, section 2 (April 1970): 20.

Reviews the 29 January 1970 performance of *In Praise of Shahn* by Leonard Bernstein and the New York Philharmonic. Argues that Schuman's musical style is old fashioned and out-of-date for 1970. See: **W71a**

B473 Dickinson, Peter. Review of William Schuman: *Concerto for Violin and Orchestra*, recorded by the Boston Symphony Orchestra, conducted by Michael Tilson Thomas, with Paul Zukofsky, violin. *The Gramophone* (January 1991): 1377.

Applauds, for the most part, Zukofsky's performance of Schuman's concerto on this Deutsche Grammophon CD. See: **D25, D27**

* _____. Review of William Schuman: *Night Journey*, recorded by the Atlantic Sinfonietta, conducted by Andrew Schenck.

Cited as **B799**.

B474 _____. Review of William Schuman: *New England Triptych*, *Symphony for Strings*, and *Variations on "America,"* recorded by the Seattle Symphony Orchestra, conducted by Gerard Schwarz. *The Gramophone* (July 1993): 53.

Presents Schuman's own comments, written shortly before he died, about this Delos (DE 3115) recording, which included high praise for the performance. Compares Schwarz's interpretation of the Fifth Symphony to the old Bernstein recording, preferring the work of the latter conductor for its "intense excitement." See: **D55, D88, D117**

B475 Domville, Eric. "Rare Beauty and Imagination." *Fugue* 3 (October 1978): 50-51, 54.

A record review (CBS M 35101) marked by helpful analysis and intelligent observations of the Leonard Bernstein and New York Philharmonic Orchestra performance, with the Camerata Singers and violist Donald McInnes, of the *Concerto on Old English Rounds*. After comments on each of the work's five sections, Domville evaluates the composition as "a work of rare beauty and imagination." See: **D28**

B476 Downes, Edward. "Philharmonic Plays." *The New York Times*, November 5, 1956, p. 41.

Gives an account of the New York premiere of *New England Triptych* at Carnegie Hall on November 3. While the comments about Schuman's composition are positive, the reviewer is very critical of the conducting of André Kostelanetz and the sloppy playing of the New York Philharmonic. See: **W53b**

B477 Downes, Irene, ed. *Olin Downes on Music*. New York: Simon and Schuster, 1957; reprint ed., New York: Greenwood, 1968. 473 pp. ML60 D73 1968

A collection of essays published by the famed music critic of the *Boston Post* and *The New York Times* in those newspapers from 1906 to 1955. Contains two references to performances of works by Schuman: a 20 October 1944 review of a concert in which Schuman's Third Symphony was played by the New York Philharmonic and a 9 May 1952 review of a concert by the Boston Symphony Orchestra, which also presented the Third Symphony. Both articles regard Schuman's symphony in very favorable terms. See: **W22c, W22g**

B478 Downes, Olin. "Chorus Directed by Robert Shaw: Schuman Music Played." *The New York Times*, January 14, 1943, p. 26.

Reviews the historic 13 January 1943 Town Hall Music Forum concert featuring all Schuman compositions, except for one work by J.S. Bach. The most substantial score by the young composer on the program was his Concerto for Piano and Small Orchestra, premiered by Rosalyn Tureck and the Saidenberg Little Symphony. See: **W24a, B37**

B479 _____. "Young Mr. Schuman's Third Symphony . . . Mature Mr. Menuhin's Mendelssohn." *The New York Times*, October 20, 1944.

Reviews the second New York performance of Schuman's symphony. Praises the playing of the New York Philharmonic Orchestra under Rodzinski and calls the Schuman work "brilliant and audacious." See: **W22c**

B480 _____. "Paris Cheers *Le Sacre* Thirty-nine Years Later." *The New York Times*, May 9, 1952.

Reviews an 8 May 1952 concert in Paris of the Boston Symphony Orchestra, with Pierre Monteux conducting, which included Schuman's Third Symphony. See: **W22g**

B481 Driver, Paul. "Civic Symphony Shows Fine Form." *Boston Globe*, May 1, 1984.

Reviews a 29 April 1984 concert by the Civic Symphony, conducted by Max Hobart, at Jordan Hall. Included on the program was Schuman's *New England Triptych*, described by the reviewer as a work "of raw grandeur." See: **W53k**

B482 Drobatschewsky, Dimitri. "Soloist in Perfect Tune with Elgar Cello Classic." *The Arizona Republic*, April 4, 1987, section f, p. 3.

Reviews the April 2 concert by the Phoenix Symphony Orchestra, conducted by James Sedares. The conductor gave a "precise" interpretation of Schuman's *New England Triptych*. See: **W53q**

B483 _____. "Film Composer's Piece Fails, Work's Defects Can't Be Offset by Musicians." *The Arizona Republic*, January 18, 1992, section d, p. 3.

A concert review of the January 16 and 17 performances of the Phoenix Symphony Orchestra, conducted by James Sedares. While the reviewer's opinion of Bernard Herrmann's symphony is negative, he is much more enthusiastic about the performances of Robert Schumann's Concerto for Piano and William Schuman's *New England Triptych*. See: **W53aa**

B484 Durgin, Cyrus. "Boston Symphony Introduces Three Preludes by Pfitzner." *Musical America* 70 (March 1950): 12.

Contains a review of the premiere performance of Schuman's Violin Concerto, played by the Boston Symphony Orchestra and violinist Isaac Stern. Maintains that the concerto has a "fiendishly difficult solo part" and regards the structure of the composition as somewhat unorthodox. See: **W39a**

B485 _____. "Boston: Schuman's Seventh Symphony Premiered." *Musical America* 80 (December 1960): 16, 18.

A very informative review of Schuman's Seventh Symphony, based on the world premiere performances of the work by Charles Munch and the Boston Symphony Orchestra on October 21 and 22. See: **W58a**

B486 Dyer, Richard. "'Frankenstein!!' Has U.S. Premiere." *Boston Globe*, August 15, 1980.

Reviews an August 13 concert at Tanglewood, which included works by Schuman, Copland, Luening, Gruber, and Balassa. Gunther Schuller conducted the Berkshire Music Center Orchestra in a performance of Schuman's Fourth Symphony, described as a composition with "vigor and personality." See: **W23b**

B487 _____. "BSO Brilliant with Schuman." *Boston Globe*, October 3, 1980.

A concert review of the October 2 performance of the Boston Symphony led by Seiji Ozawa. Schuman's Third Symphony was on the program. See: **W22v**

* _____. "Horblit Concert Surveys Works of William Schuman."

Cited as **B723**.

* _____. Review of William Schuman: *In Sweet Music*, *The Young Dead Soldiers*, and *Time to the Old*, recorded by Rosalind Rees and the Orpheus Trio, the White Mountains Festival Orchestra, and the pianist Thomas Muraco.

Cited as **B724**.

B488 _____. "Composer's Orchestra Debuts." *Boston Globe*, May 2, 1986, section 3, p. 36.

Gunther Schuller conducted the Boston Composer's Orchestra in a May 1 concert which included a performance of Schuman's *American Hymn*. Argues that the composition was typical of the composer's style. Schuman was present in the audience. See: **W89c**

B489 _____. "Slatkin's Virtues, Galway's Vice." *Boston Globe*, July 13, 1989, section 3, p. 69.

Reviews a concert by Leonard Slatkin and the Pittsburgh Symphony Orchestra at Great Woods on July 12 which included a performance of Schuman's *New England Triptych*. See: **W53u**

B490 _____. Review of William Schuman: *Concerto for Violin and Orchestra*, recorded by the St. Louis Symphony Orchestra, conducted by Leonard Slatkin, with Robert McDuffie, violin. *Boston Globe*, February 22, 1990, section 3, p. 7.

Reviews the EMI digital recording. Considers the concerto "a terrific piece, full of high-energy lyricism." See: **D26**

B491 _____. "Leonard Slatkin Brings Fresh Approach to the Pops." *Boston Globe*, May 23, 1990, section 3, p. 49.

A review of a May 22 Boston Pops concert which included Schuman's arrangement of Charles Ives's *Variations on "America."* Notes that the work "was highly entertaining and Slatkin encouraged the audience to laugh." See: **W63d**

B492 _____. "BSO Plays New and Old Music at Tanglewood Tribute." *Boston Globe*, August 6, 1990, section 3, p. 30.

Reviews the August 3 and 4 concerts of the Boston Symphony at Tanglewood, which were presented in honor of Schuman's eightieth birthday. Dennis Russell Davies conducted the orchestra in a performance of Schuman's Third Symphony and in the premiere of William Bolcom's *MCMXC Tanglewood*. Considers the Schuman symphony "all the exciting for being life-affirming." See: **W22cc**

B493 E., A.J.; L., M.D.; and R., S. "Juilliard School Concludes Anniversary Concert Series." *Musical America* 76 (March 1956): 37.

Deals with the Festival of American Music presented at Juilliard in honor of the institution's fiftieth anniversary. Among the numerous works presented on the series of concerts between February 10 and February 26 was the 1954 revision of Schuman's Concerto for Violin, performed on the closing concert with violinist Isaac Stern and the Juilliard Orchestra. Compares Schuman's score to the concertos of Berg, Stravinsky, and Bartók. See: **W39b**

B494 E., S.W. Review of William Schuman: *Three Colloquies for Horn and Orchestra*, recorded by the New York Philharmonic Orchestra, conducted by Zubin Mehta, with Philip Myers, horn. *Fanfare* (January-February 1988): 109.

A short recording review (New World NW 326-2) which regards Schuman's composition as "one of the best of the few American horn concertos." See: **D100**

B495 Elbert, Clarence F. "Indianapolis: Season's End." *Musical America* 82 (April 1962): 29.

Gives a report on a performance by cellist Leonard Rose and the Indianapolis Symphony of *A Song of Orpheus*. Lauds both Schuman and Rose but, at the same time, mentions the unreceptive response of the audience. See: **W59a**

B496 Elie, Rudolph, Jr. "Music: Symphony Concert." *The Boston Herald*, November 13, 1943, p. 4.

An exceedingly favorable review of a 12 November 1943 performance of Schuman's *Symphony for Strings* by the Boston Symphony Orchestra under Serge Koussevitzky. "It is evident that William Schuman is well on his way to becoming the foremost American-born composer of the day. . . . That Mr. Schuman is a master of the orchestra has long been remarked." See: **W29a**

B497 Ericson, Raymond. "Shahn's Portrait Painted in Music." *The New York Times*, January 30, 1970, p. 29.

Ericson's review of the world premiere of *In Praise of Shahn* finds the new opus to be "a hymn of praise, a celebration, somewhat noisy but impressive for all that." Commends the performance of the New York Philharmonic Orchestra and its conductor, Leonard Bernstein. See: **W71a**

B498 F., A. Review of William Schuman: *Symphony No. 3*, recorded by the New York Philharmonic Orchestra, conducted by Leonard Bernstein. *High Fidelity* (October 1961): 100-01.

In this pithy recording review of Schuman's most popular symphony, the reviewer contends that this work is one of the finest American symphonies. Provides background information about the composition and recognizes the debt owed by Schuman to Koussevitzky. Contains an analysis of the work, emphasizing that "what really sets William Schuman apart among all other composers is the overwhelming gusto, drive, and climactic yawp of his music, which the third symphony exemplifies extremely well." See: **D81**

B499 F., W. Review of William Schuman: *Symphony No.3*, recorded by the New York Philharmonic Orchestra, conducted by Leonard Bernstein. *HiFi/Stereo Review* (October 1961): 92.

Explores the influence of Roy Harris on Schuman's symphony. Praises Bernstein's interpretation of this work in this recording review (Columbia MS 6245). See: **D81**

B500 Feder, Susan. "New York." *The Musical Times* 124 (November 1983): 704-05.

Prepared as an account of the New York Philharmonic's *Horizons '83* festival, this review of the performances of numerous contemporary compositions contains a succinct, positive statement about Schuman's *Three Colloquies*. See: **W85b**

*   Fine, Irving. "Reviews of Records. Copland: *Billy the Kid* (Ballet Suite); Schuman: *Undertow, Choreographic Episodes for Orchestra*."

Cited as **B800**.

B501 Fleming, Michael. "Minnesota Orchestra Performs 2 New Pieces and an Old Favorite." *St. Paul Pioneer Press Dispatch*, September 27, 1990, section c, p. 9.

A somewhat brief review of the September 26 concert of the Minnesota Orchestra, conducted by Edo de Waart. One of the works presented on the program was Schuman's Sixth Symphony, which, according to the reviewer, was disappointing. Fleming negatively refers to Schuman's compositions "as the product of a diligent workman with a second-rate talent." See: **W41j**

B502 _____. "Seldom-Heard Britten Concerto Is a Treat." *St. Paul Pioneer Press Dispatch*, January 10, 1991, section d, p. 4.

Review of the January 9 concert of the Minnesota Orchestra at Orchestra Hall, conducted by Edo de Waart. The program opened with the Minnesota Orchestra premiere of Schuman's *Showcase: A Short Display for Orchestra*. See: **W97c**

B503 _____. "SPCO Gives Fine Preview of Upcoming Tour." *St. Paul Pioneer Press*, October 17, 1992, section b, p. 2.

Review of the October 16 performance of Schuman's Fifth Symphony, Hugh Wolff conducting the St. Paul Chamber Orchestra. Contends that Schuman's symphony "is a muscular and energetic work—by general concensus the best of Schuman's 10 symphonies. Hugh Wolff and the orchestra gave it a hearty, no-nonsense reading." See: **W29n**

B504 "Forum Series in 1942-1943 at Town Hall." *New York Herald Tribune*, February 15, 1942, section 6, p. 7.

Reveals that Schuman's Concerto for Piano and Orchestra is to be premiered on 11 November 1942 at Town Hall, performed by Daniel Saidenberg's orchestra and the pianist Rosalyn Tureck. However, according to Schreiber and Persichetti, the first performance of this work occurred at an all Schuman concert at Town Hall on 13 January 1943. See: **W24a, B328**

B505 Freed, Richard. Review of William Schuman: *Three Colloquies for Horn and Orchestra*, recorded by the New York Philharmonic, conducted by Zubin Mehta, with Philip Myers, horn. *Stereo Review* 50 (November 1985): 120-21.

An appreciative review. Compliments the composer on his use of percussion instruments and observes that Schuman prefers a tripartite structure for orchestral works. Remarks that "the work as a whole is powerful stuff." This recording also includes George Crumb's *A Haunted Landscape*. See: **D100**

B506 _____. Review of William Schuman: *In Praise of Shahn*, recorded by the Juilliard Orchestra, conducted by Otto Werner-Mueller. *Stereo Review* 54 (May 1989): 125.

Recorded as the first release of the Juilliard American Music Recording Institute. The Schuman composition appears on the New World NW 368-1 digital recording with Copland's *Connotations for Orchestra* and Sessions's *The Black Maskers* suite. Concludes that "this appealing package is musically first-rate, exciting the highest expectations for the new series." See: **D39**

B507 Frias, Leopoldo H. "Boston Symphony Premieres 7th Symphony by Schuman." *Musical Courier* 162 (December 1960): 27, 33.

Observes that the first performance of Schuman's Seventh Symphony "was worth waiting for . . . The music is both lean and lusty, altogether 'American' in its dynamism and brass component." See: **W58a**

B508 Gagnard, Frank. "Symphony Flexes Its Muscle with Style." *New Orleans Times Picayune*, January 26, 1991, section e, p. 5.

Reviews the January 23 concert by the New Orleans Symphony, which included a performance of Schuman's *New England Triptych*. Conducted by William Henry Curry, the rendition of the Schuman composition was praised as "alert and vigorous." The concert was repeated on January 26. See: **W53z**

B509 Garofalo, Robert J. "A New Plan for Concert Band." *Music Educators Journal* 67 (April 1981): 32-39.

Describes the methods and procedures involved in developing a Unit Study Composition for Schuman's *George Washington Bridge* as part of a comprehensive musicianship curriculum. Provides an analysis of the work and claims to have discovered a relationship between the structure of the composition and the architecture of the bridge.

B510 Glackin, William. "A Rousing Debut for Walnut Creek Theater." *The Sacramento Bee*, November 13, 1990, section d, p. 5.

The California Symphony opened its season on November 11 with a program which included Schuman's *New England Triptych*. The concert, which took place in the Hofmann Theatre in the new Regional Center for the Arts, was conducted by Barry Jekowsky. The reviewer describes the Schuman composition as "a beautiful, superbly well-crafted tribute to William Billings." See: **W53y**

* Goldman, Richard Franko. "Current Chronicle: New York."

Cited as **B801**.

B511 _____. "Current Chronicle: New York." *The Musical Quarterly* 42 (July 1956): 390-94.

An incomplete account of newly commissioned works, including the revised version of Schuman's Concerto for Violin, presented at Juilliard's Festival of American Music. Most of the review deals with William Bergsma's opera *The Wife of Martin Guerre*. See: **W39b**

B512 _____. "Current Chronicle: New York." *The Musical Quarterly* 49 (January 1963): 91-93.

Reports on the series of concerts presented for the grand opening of Philharmonic Hall at Lincoln Center. Among the works performed were Schuman's *A Song of Orpheus*, played for the first time in New York, and the premiere of the composer's Eighth Symphony. Devotes three paragraphs to a description of the latter composition, emphasizing the conservative nature of the symphony. See: **W59c, W60a**

B513 Griffiths, Paul. "Schuman." *The Musical Times* 114 (November 1973): 1149, 1151.

A facile review of a September 25 London performance (and English premiere) of *In Praise of Shahn*, André Previn conducting the London Symphony Orchestra. Characterizes the work as leaving "an impression of heaviness rather than depth, of self-importance and inconsequence." See: **W71b**

* Grueninger, Walter F. Review of William Schuman: *In Sweet Music, The Young Dead Soldiers*, and *Time to the Old*, recorded by Rosalind Rees and the Orpheus Trio, the White Mountains Festival Orchestra, and pianist Thomas Muraco.

Cited as **B726**.

* _____. Review of William Schuman: *Judith*, recorded by the Eastman Philharmonic Orchestra, conducted by David Effron; *Night Journey*, recorded by the Endymion Ensemble, conducted by Jon Goldberg.

Cited as **B802**.

B514 Guinn, John. "DSO, Järvi Have Some All-American Fun." *Detroit Free Press*, June 16, 1991, section g, p. 3.

Reviews the June 14 concert by the Detroit Symphony Orchestra at the Meadow Brook Music Festival. One of the compositions presented on the program by conductor Neeme Järvi and the symphony was Schuman's arrangement of Ives's *Variations on "America."* Mentions that Schuman's *American Festival Overture* will be played on the June 16 concert instead of *Variations on "America."* See: **W63e**

B515 Guregian, Elaine. "Musical Fireworks Linger at Blossom: Varied Program Brings Out the Crowd, Continues Spirit of the Fourth." *The Akron Beacon Journal*, July 7, 1991, section d, p. 5.

A review of the July 5 concert at the Blossom Music Center by the Cleveland Orchestra. Guest conductor Louis Lane led the orchestra in a performance of Schuman's orchestration of Ives's *Variations on "America."* See: **W63f**

B516 Gwiasda, Karl. "Indianapolis: Schuman's 'Orpheus.'" *The Music Magazine and Musical Courier* 164 (May 1962): 27.

An informative performance review of the Indianapolis Symphony Orchestra's world premiere of *A Song of Orpheus*. Presents background material concerning the genesis of the composition. See: **W59a**

B517 Haggin, B.H. "Music." *The Nation* 173 (November 3, 1951): 383.

Devotes the last paragraph of this article to a discussion of the Columbia recording of Schuman's Third Symphony by Eugene Ormandy and the Philadelphia Orchestra. Concludes that "its themes . . . are not expressively meaningful to my ears." See: **D80**

B518 Haines, Edmund. "Philadelphia Orchestra (Ormandy)." *High Fidelity/Musical America* 19 (April 1969): MA-22.

A very positive review of the Philadelphia Orchestra's performance of Schuman's Ninth Symphony at New York's Philharmonic Hall. "Schuman's Symphony represents an advance in his own idiomatic development . . . the total impact is compelling, the intent communicative." See: **W68b**

B519 Halbreich, Harry. Review of William Schuman: *Three Colloquies for Horn and Orchestra*, recorded by the New York Philharmonic Orchestra, conducted by Zubin Mehta, with Philip F. Myers, horn. *High Fidelity* 37 (February 1987): 62.

An enthusiastic review of the New World NW 326 recording. Asserts that Schuman's creative inspiration has not waned and describes *Three Colloquies* as a work of "genuine symphonic breadth and solidity." See: **D100**

B520 Hall, David. Review of William Schuman: *Symphony No. 3* and *Symphony No. 5*, recorded by the New York Philharmonic Orchestra, conducted by Leonard Bernstein. *Stereo Review* (November 1970): 105.

An authoritative review of the Columbia MS 7442 recording. Claims that in his best works "Schuman has produced music of towering eloquence and granitic power" and speculates that the Fifth Symphony may be the quintessential early work of the composer. Compares Bernstein's performance of the Third Symphony to earlier interpretations by Koussevitzky and Ormandy. See: **D81, D87**

* _____. Review of William Schuman: *Judith* and *Night Journey*, recorded by the Eastman Philharmonia, conducted by David Effron (*Judith*); and the Endymion Ensemble, conducted by Jon Goldberg.

Cited as **B803**.

B521 _____. Review of William Schuman: *Three Colloquies for Horn and Orchestra*, recorded by the New York Philharmonic Orchestra, conducted by Zubin Mehta. *Ovation* 6 (September 1985): 38-39.

After providing background based in part on Christopher Rouse's review of the published score of Schuman's composition, Hall presents a cursory examination of the work's three movements. Hall also praises the performance of the New York Philharmonic and the horn playing of Philip Myers in the recording (New World NW 326). See: **D100**

B522 _____. Review of William Schuman: *Symphony No. 3*, recorded by the New York Philharmonic Orchestra, conducted by Leonard Bernstein. *Stereo Review* 53 (March 1988): 99.

Hall writes that in Schuman's symphony "Everything grows out of a single melody . . . culminating in a musical statement of overwhelming power and brilliance." Deutsche Grammophon 419780-1, 419780-2. See: **D82**

B523 _____. Review of William Schuman: *Concerto for Violin and Orchestra*, recorded by the St. Louis Symphony Orchestra, conducted by Leonard Slatkin, with Robert McDuffie, violin. *Stereo Review* 55 (March 1990): 80.

This informative review of the EMI Angel CDC 49464 release states that Schuman's concerto "comes from the very top drawer of that eminent symphonist's output." See: **D26**

B524 Hamilton, David. "Carter's Concerto for Orchestra, a Gripping Musical Experience." *High Fidelity* 21 (March 1971): 82.

Reviews a recording of Carter's *Concerto for Orchestra* and Schuman's *In Praise of Shahn* (Columbia M 30112), performed by Leonard Bernstein and the New York Philharmonic. Considers Schuman's work to be "immediately accessible" and praises the composer for his "command of the orchestra." See: **D38**

B525 Harrison, Jay S. "Philharmonic Commissions." *Musical America* 84 (April 1964): 61.

Reviews a Columbia recording (MS-6512) of Schuman's Eighth Symphony. Describes each of the composition's three movements and hails the composer to be "America's greatest symphonist." See: **D93**

B526 _____. "The New York Music Scene." *Musical America* 84 (July 1964): 32-37.

In this prolonged review of concerts in New York, the author devotes a paragraph to the premiere of Schuman's orchestral version of Charles Ives's *Variations on "America."* See: **W63a**

B527 Harrison, Max. "Schuman." *The Musical Times* 110 (April 1969): 394.

Contends that the melodic writing in Schuman's Third Symphony "is not quite strong enough" to sustain the work throughout. Cites the composer's polyphonic writing, which is based primarily upon Baroque forms, as a significant compositional trait. Written after hearing a performance of the piece by André Previn and the London Symphony Orchestra. See: **W22t**

B528 _____. Review of William Schuman: *Symphony No. 7*, recorded by the Utah Symphony Orchestra, conducted by Maurice Abravanel. *The Gramophone* 51 (July 1973): 201-02.

Harrison's review of Turnabout's TVS 34447 recording of Schuman's Seventh Symphony, in which he confesses to having "underrated" the composer, is very positive. See: **D91**

B529 Heatherington, Alan. Review of William Schuman: *Violin Concerto*, recorded by the St. Louis Symphony Orchestra, conducted by Leonard Slatkin, with Robert McDuffie, violin. *The American Record Guide* 53 (March-April 1990): 104-05.

This recording review of the Angel 49464 issue praises the performance of McDuffie and the conducting of Slatkin. See: **D26**

B530 Henahan, Donal. "Birthday Concert (Not Beethoven)." *The New York Times*, December 19, 1970, p. 18.

Critically reviews a concert presented by the New York Philharmonic Orchestra in honor of the sixtieth birthdays of William Schuman and Samuel Barber, both of whom were in attendance. Although the orchestra is praised for their role in the performance of Schuman's *A Song of Orpheus*, the guest conductor, Stanislaw Skrowaczewski, is taken to task for his interpretation. See: **W59g**

B531 Henry, Derrick. "Pack a Picnic for ASO's Free Park Concerts." *Atlanta Constitution*, June 9, 1991, section n, p. 4.

Reports on a forthcoming performance of Schuman's *American Festival Overture*. The June 23 concert by the Atlanta Symphony Orchestra will be conducted by George Hanson. See: **W14q**

B532 Hertelendy, Paul. "Symphony Magic and Mozart from a Pair of Soloists." *San Jose Mercury News*, January 24, 1986, section d, p. 11.

Discusses the forthcoming January 24 and 25 performances of Schuman's *A Song of Orpheus* by the San Francisco Symphony, conducted by Stanislaw Skrowaczewski and with cello soloist Michael Grebanier. The piece was also played in San Francisco on January 22. See: **W59j**

B533 _____. "Mission Makes Magical Setting for Americana Concert." *San Jose Mercury News*, July 24, 1990, section c, p. 4.

Reports on the Cabrillo Music Festival's July 23 Americana concert at Mission San Juan Bautista. Among the works performed was Schuman's Third Symphony, judged by the reviewer to be "a meticulously crafted work of neoclassicism using even older forms such as passacaglia and toccata." The music director for the festival was Dennis Russell Davies. See: **W22bb**

B534 Humphreys, Henry S. "Cincinnati: Conductors, Critics Hold Workshops." *The Music Magazine and Musical Courier* 163 (November 1961): 61.

An account of concerts presented at the American Symphony Orchestra League Conductors Workshop and the Music Critics Association Workshop. The latter organization heard a performance of Schuman's Concerto for Violin, with violinist Joseph Fuchs. Criticizes Schuman's composition for its "jagged dissonance and non-violinistic thematic material." See: **W39d**

B535 Huning, Wilma. "Rodzinski Offers New Schuman Work." *Musical America* 62 (February 25, 1942): 21.

A perfunctory concert review of the world premiere of Schuman's Fourth Symphony on January 22 and 24, performed in Cleveland by the Cleveland Symphony Orchestra conducted by Artur Rodzinski. See: **W23a**

B536 Hurwitz, David. Review of William Schuman: *Symphony No. 7*, recorded by the Pittsburgh Symphony Orchestra, conducted by Lorin Maazel. *High Fidelity* (August 1987): 69.

Maintains that the Seventh Symphony is representative of Schuman's mature style. Criticizes Schuman's orchestration for a "general feeling of leaden dullness." A recording review of the New World NW 348-2 disc. See: **D92**

B537 Hymel, Mary Janet. "A Comparative Analysis of Three Works for Band by William Schuman." M.M.E. thesis, Lamar University, 1988. 90 pp. ML410 S386 H9258

Defines the musical style of Schuman through an examination of three band works: *George Washington Bridge*, *Chester*, and *When Jesus Wept*. After an introductory chapter dealing with purpose and organization, the second chapter presents an overview of the composer's life and career. Chapter three, the largest portion of the treatise, provides an analysis of each of the compositions. Compares these works in chapter four by means of a study of instrumentation, form, harmony, melody, and rhythm. Contains musical examples, appendixes, and an inadequate list of references.

B538 Johnson, Charles E. "Common Musical Idioms in Selected Contemporary Wind-Band Music." Ed.D. dissertation, Florida State University, 1969. 334 pp. MT73 J63 C65

Chapter four of this study presents an analysis of Schuman's *Chester Overture* for band. Contains musical examples, footnotes, and a bibliography.

B539 Johnson, Harriett. "Words and Music: Bernstein Leads Praise of 'Shahn.'" *The New York Post*, January 30, 1970, p. 52.

In this review of the premiere performance of *In Praise of Shahn*, the writer admits to being "puzzled more than excited" by the impact of the work. See: **W71a, B649**

B540 Jones, Charles. Review of William Schuman: *Symphony No. 6*. *Music Library Association Notes* 10 (June 1953): 482.

A perspicacious review of the 1952 G. Schirmer publication of the miniature score for the composer's Sixth Symphony. Acknowledges the single-movement structure of the composition and, at the same time, recognizes the work's subdivision into six sections. Argues that the piece is "full of the sort of high-powered orchestral sound that pleads its cause from the very edge of the footlights." Maintains that this difficult symphony is best suited for performance in the largest cities by the finest orchestras and conductors.

B541 Jones, Ralph E. Review of William Schuman: *Symphony No. 3*, recorded by the New York Philharmonic Orchestra, conducted by Leonard Bernstein. *The New Records* (August 1961): 3-4.

Provides brief background and discussion of the composer's score. A recording review of Columbia ML 5645/MS 6245. See: **D81**

B542 Kastendieck, Miles. "N.Y. Philharmonic: Back to Back." *Christian Science Monitor* (February 11, 1970).

Written after the world premieres of Schuman's *In Praise of Shahn* and Elliott Carter's *Concerto for Orchestra*, Kastendieck is negative about both works. Believes that Schuman's piece "reconfirms his compositional skill without further enhancing his reputation." Arrives at the conclusion that "There was a brightness of spirit that did herald praise, but somehow when everything has been stated, only a feeling of passing interest survives." See: **W71a**, **B649**

* Keats, Sheila. "William Schuman."

Cited as **B199**.

* Kennedy, Steven A. Review of William Schuman: *Night Journey*, recorded by the Atlantic Sinfonietta, conducted by Andrew Schenck.

Cited as **B807**.

B543 Kenyon, Nicholas. "Musical Events." *The New Yorker* 55 (February 11, 1980): 90-96.

Kenyon's informative account (p. 93) of the New York Philharmonic's premiere performance of Schuman's *Three Colloquies* praises the composition as "nearly perfectly constructed." See: **W85a**

B544 _____. "Musical Events." *The New Yorker* 57 (June 1, 1981): 126-31.

Contains a performance review of Schuman's Sixth Symphony (pp. 128, 131) as played on May 18 by the American Composers Orchestra under the direction of Dennis Russell Davies at Alice Tully Hall. Calls the 1948 Schuman masterpiece "accomplished." See: **W41i**

B545 Kerner, Leighton. "A Sessions Memorial Scores." *The Village Voice* 22 (November 7, 1977): 69-70.

A flattering account of the October 24 concert by the Group for Contemporary Music at the Manhattan School of Music, which highlighted a number of twentieth-century works, among them *The Young Dead Soldiers*. Characterizes Schuman's composition as "a modestly conceived, solemn, 'lamentation' for soprano, solo horn, eight winds, and nine strings, set to a poem by Archibald MacLeish." See: **W82b**

B546 _____. "New Tunes among the Old." *The Village Voice* 25 (February 25, 1980): 62-63.

Kerner's article consists of reviews of selected concerts in California and New York City. *Three Colloquies*, which was performed by Zubin Mehta and the New York Philharmonic, is portrayed as "typical of Schuman's latest products, not terribly complex or challenging, but less grayly anonymous than most of his middle-period pieces and, in sum, full of motives and colors that consistently please the ear." See: **W85a**

B547 _____. "Business Better than Usual." *The Village Voice* 26 (March 18, 1981): 70.

A critical forecast of the upcoming season of announced concerts by the New York Philharmonic Orchestra. Reflects with gratitude on recent concerts of American music featuring works by Schuman (Symphony No. 3), Aaron Copland, Ned Rorem, Lukas Foss, and Samuel Barber. Kerner acknowledges that "Schuman's symphony, in this roof-rattling performance, reasserted its claim as one of the American repertory's deservedly more enduring exhibits of neoclassical rabble-rousing."

B548 Kimmelman, Michael. "Music: Emanuel Ax Is Piano Soloist in Kapell Tribute." *The Philadelphia Inquirer*, July 23, 1986, section d, p. 4.

A review of the July 22 concert, presented in memory of the pianist William Kapell, by the Philadelphia Orchestra, with guest conductor David Zinman. Kimmelman strongly criticizes Zinman's interpretation of Schuman's *Variations on "America."* See: **W63b**

B549 Klein, Howard. "Music: Light Melodies." *The New York Times*, May 30, 1964, p. 9.

Klein's review of the 29 May 1964 performance of Schuman's *The Orchestra Song*, presented by André Kostelanetz and the New York Philharmonic as part of the "American Promenade" concert at Philharmonic Hall, emphasizes the appealing nature of the work, concluding that it is a "fine addition to orchestral literature for children's concerts or the like." See: **W62b**

B550 Kohs, Ellis B. "California: Busy Platform." *Musical America* 84 (December 1964): 48-50.

Supplies information on performances of two Schuman works, *A Song of Orpheus* and the *Symphony for Strings*, presented at U.C.L.A. during the composer's week-long visit to that campus. See: **W59e**

B551 Kolodin, Irving. Review of William Schuman: *Symphony No. 3*, recorded by the New York Philharmonic Orchestra, conducted by Leonard Bernstein. *Saturday Review* 44 (July 29, 1961): 48.

Kolodin's review of the Columbia MS 6245 recording is negative. Remarks that "it strikes me as display and nothing more." See: **D81**

B552 _____. "Music to My Ears." *Saturday Review* 51 (October 19, 1968): 50, 51, 56.

Kolodin's somewhat lengthy article includes a review of Schuman's *To Thee Old Cause*, performed by Leonard Bernstein and the New York Philharmonic. "Throughout, one is aware of a majesty of means, an absolute certainty of purpose which distributes emphasis (and the absence of it) exactly to the advancement of the composer's esthetic intent." Schuman's Third Symphony was also presented on the same program. See: **W22s, W69a**

B553 _____. "Music to My Ears." *Saturday Review* 53 (February 14, 1970): 58.

An insightful review of a performance of Schuman's *In Praise of Shahn*, conducted by Leonard Bernstein. See: **W71a, B649**

B554 _____. Review of William Schuman: *Symphony No. 3* and *Symphony No. 5*, recorded by the New York Philharmonic Orchestra, conducted by Leonard Bernstein. *Saturday Review* 53 (October 31, 1970): 54.

A generally positive, though somewhat brief, recording review (Columbia MS 7442) of both symphonies. See: **D81, D87**

B555 _____. "Music to My Ears." *Saturday Review* 59 (May 29, 1976): 48-49.

Contains a performance review of *Concerto on Old English Rounds*. "The concerto embodies a considerable creative impulse, a good deal of richly textured tonal tapestry, a sensitivity to the basic substance not unrelated to Schuman's *New England Triptych*, and a degree of elaboration that made 40 minutes' length more than a little excessive." See: **W75c**

B556 Kopetz, Barry E. "Charles Ives' *Variations on 'America.'*" *The Instrumentalist* 45 (April 1991): 20-28, 75-79.

Billed as "an interpretive analysis," this extended article is perhaps the definitive examination of William E. Rhoads's concert band version of Schuman's orchestration of the original organ composition by Ives. Following introductory comments on Ives, the author provides a section by section discussion of the work. Helpful is the list of errata (pp. 76-79) which concludes the study.

*   Kosman, Joshua. "Chamber Group's 'Night' Program."

Cited as **B808**.

B557 _____. "Nagano Squeezes the Most out of 'Oranges.'" *San Francisco Chronicle*, April 1, 1990, Sunday review section, p. 13.

Included in this article, which presents several reviews of recordings, is a review of the Angel/EMI 49464 recording of Schuman's Concerto for Violin. Though praising Robert McDuffie's performance with the St. Louis Symphony Orchestra, Kosman describes Schuman's composition as "reasonably useless." See: **D26**

B558   Kozinn, Allan. "20th-Century Symphonies Offer Riches." *The New York Times*, November 18, 1984, section 2, p. 22.

Affirms that, contrary to the opinion of some, orchestral composition continues to be a viable art form in the twentieth century. Considers examples by Arthur Honegger, Morton Gould, and William Schuman. Critiques Schuman's Sixth and Ninth Symphonies, which were paired together by Composers Recordings, Inc. (CRI SD 477) in a reissue of earlier recordings of both works by Eugene Ormandy and the Philadelphia Orchestra. Contends that "Each is a compelling score on its own terms, but the Ninth reaches more deeply into the soul." See: **D90**, **D96**

B559   Kresh, Paul. Review of William Schuman: *Concerto on Old English Rounds*, recorded by the New York Philharmonic Orchestra and the Camerata Singers, conducted by Leonard Bernstein, with Donald McInnes, viola. *Stereo Review* (December 1978): 156.

Argues, in this review of the Columbia M35101 disc, that Schuman's composition "is a piece of considerable ambition and high technical gloss that is in the end overwhelmed by the very skill that went into constructing it." See: **D28**

*   _____. Review of William Schuman: *In Sweet Music, The Young Dead Soldiers*, and *Time to the Old*, recorded by Rosalind Rees and the Orpheus Trio, White Mountains Festival Orchestra, and pianist Thomas Muraco.

Cited as **B729**.

B560   Kroeger, Karl. Review of William Schuman: *Symphony No. 7*. *Music Library Association Notes* 20 (Summer 1963): 407.

A study score (Merion Music, 1962) of Schuman's Seventh Symphony is reviewed. Even though recognizing that the work contains "some moments of brilliance, and even inspiration," Kroeger deprecates the composer for making use of "material . . . heard so many times before." Summarizes those elements found in Schuman's compositions which the reviewer finds "hackneyed."

*   _____. Review of William Schuman: *Judith, A Choreographic Poem for Orchestra*, recorded by the Eastman Philharmonia Orchestra, conducted by David Effron; *Night Journey, Choreographic Poem for 15 Instruments*, recorded by the Endymion Ensemble, conducted by Jon Goldberg.

Cited as **B809**.

B561   _____. Review of William Schuman: *Newsreel*, recorded by the Milwaukee Symphony, conducted by Lukas Foss. *The Sonneck Society Bulletin* 13 (Spring 1987): 33.

A recording review of the Pro-Arte PAD 102 disc entitled "American Festival." Schuman's *Newsreel*, one of several compositions included, is termed "thoroughly delightful." See: **D58**

B562 Kupferberg, Herbert. "N.Y. Philharmonic: Schuman Symphony No. 9." *High Fidelity/Musical America* 31 (March 1981): MA26.

Applauds the November 13 performance of this work, with Zubin Mehta conducting the New York Philharmonic. Kupferberg writes that this score is "Rich in orchestration and taut in structure, it conveys its mood in a poignant yet unsentimental manner." Notes that Schuman was present in the audience. See: **W68c**

B563 LaFave, Ken. "Little-Known Symphony Glows When PSO Plays." *The Phoenix Gazette*, January 15, 1992, Marquee section, p. 23.

Positively reviews the January 16 concert by the Phoenix Symphony Orchestra, which included Bernard Herrmann's First Symphony, Robert Schumann's Concerto for Piano, and William Schuman's *New England Triptych*. See: **W53aa**

B564 _____. "New CD Should Establish Symphony in Music World." *The Phoenix Gazette*, May 1, 1992, Marquee section, p. 10.

In this recording review of the Koch International release of the Phoenix Symphony playing Schuman's *New England Triptych* and Bernard Herrmann's First Symphony, the reviewer's advice "is to skip over the Herrmann" and listen to the Schuman first. See: **D56**

B565 Landis, John. Review of William Schuman: *New England Triptych*, recorded by the Eastman-Rochester Orchestra, conducted by Howard Hanson. *The American Record Guide* (January-February 1992): 144.

Positively reviews this Mercury reissue (Mercury 432755) of the Howard Hanson 1963 recording of *New England Triptych*. See: **D54**

* Laney, Maurice Ivan. "Thematic Material and Developmental Techniques in Selected Contemporary Compositions."

Cited as **B812**.

B566 Lengyel, Peter M. "An Analytical Study of Particular Aspects of William Schuman's *George Washington Bridge*." M.M. thesis, Indiana University, 1973. 53 pp.

Examines Schuman's *George Washington Bridge* from the standpoint of sonority, density, rhythm, and orchestration in the central portion of the study (chapters 2-5). This principal discussion is preceded by an opening chapter which, after a brief biographical sketch of less than two pages, comments on basic approach and formal structure and is concluded by a closing chapter of only one page which evaluates the work in summary style. Includes figures, footnotes, musical examples, and an extremely short bibliography.

B567 Levinger, Henry W. "New York Concert and Opera Beat: Philadelphia Orchestra." *Musical Courier* 153 (April 1956): 19.

A positive review of the March 13 New York premiere of *Credendum*, presented by Eugene Ormandy and the Philadelphia Orchestra. Contends that the work "has weight and importance" and praises the performance by Ormandy and the orchestra. See: **W49b**

B568 Lieberson, Goddard. "Over the Air." *Modern Music* 16, no. 1 (1938-39): 65-69.

After an appraisal of two Samuel Barber works performed on a concert by Arturo Toscanini and the NBC Symphony Orchestra, Lieberson focuses on various compositions presented on the Everybody's Music series heard on CBS radio, including Schuman's Second Symphony in one movement. Though critical of the work's overall formal structure, the author maintains that it represents an advance over some of the composer's earlier scores. Speculates that Schuman probably borrowed certain stylistic elements from the music of Roy Harris. See: **W13b**

B569 Linton, Michael. "Minnesota Orchestra Selection Gives Soloist Serkin a Basis for Comparison." *St. Paul Pioneer Press Dispatch*, May 12, 1990, section b, p. 6.

Linton's review of the May 9 concert by the Minnesota Orchestra, in describing the performance of Schuman's *Symphony for Strings*, observes that it "is a major work, muscular and tightly packed with focused energy." The concert was conducted by Edo de Waart. See: **W29l**

B570 Livingstone, William. "Discovering American Music." *Stereo Review* 57 (November 1992): 91-96.

Includes a short review of the Deutsche Grammophon 419780 recording of Schuman's Third Symphony. Refers to the composition as one of the "foundation blocks of the American orchestral repertoire." This disc also includes the Roy Harris Third Symphony. See: **D82**

B571 Locklair, Wriston. "Kostelanetz Opens Special Series." *Musical America* 76 (November 15, 1956): 18.

Discusses the November 3 Carnegie Hall performance by the New York Philharmonic of *New England Triptych*, conducted by André Kostelanetz. The work was commissioned by Kostelanetz. See: **W53b**

*   Lockwood, Normand. Review of William Schuman: *Undertow, Choreographic Episodes for Orchestra*.

Cited as **B813**.

* Luten, C.J. Review of William Schuman: *Judith* and *Undertow*, recorded by the Louisville Orchestra, conducted by Robert Whitney (*Judith*) and William Schuman (*Undertow*).

Cited as **B814**.

B572 _____. Review of William Schuman: *Symphony No. 3*, recorded by the New York Philharmonic Orchestra, conducted by Leonard Bernstein. *The American Record Guide* 28 (September 1961): 32-33.

A review of the Columbia (ML 5645/MS 6245) recording. Compares the new Bernstein performance to the initial recording of the symphony by Eugene Ormandy and the Philadelphia Orchestra (also recorded by Columbia). See: **D81**

B573 MacDonald, Calum. Review of William Schuman: *Symphony No. 4* and *Prayer in Time of War*, recorded by the Louisville Orchestra, conducted by Jorge Mester. *Tempo* 174 (September 1990): 53-54.

A review of the Albany Troy 027-2 reissue of an earlier recording. Argues that the Schuman symphony does not compare with the composer's more highly regarded Third and Sixth Symphonies. See: **D66**, **D84**

B574 MacDonald, Malcolm. Review of William Schuman's arrangement of Charles Ives's *Variations on "America,"* recorded by the Los Angeles Philharmonic Orchestra, conducted by Zubin Mehta. *The Gramophone* (July 1976): 176.

Though most of the discussion in this review centers on Ives's Symphony No. 2, the author does praise the "brilliant scoring" in Schuman's orchestration of Ives's *Variations on "America."* See: **D114**

* Machlis, Joseph. "William Schuman." *Introduction to Contemporary Music*.

Cited as **B230**.

B575 McKinley, Lily. "Stylistic Development in Selected Symphonies of William Schuman: A Comparison of Symphonies Numbers Three and Nine." 2 vols. Ph.D. dissertation, New York University, 1977. 203, 360 pp. UM Order No. 77-20751

A significant and comprehensive treatment of the subject. Incorporates an extensive analysis of both the Ninth Symphony (Chapter 3) and the Third Symphony (Chapter 4), concentrating on the salient elements of sound, melody, harmony, rhythm, and growth (the development of musical ideas and form). Valuable especially is the penultimate chapter (Chapter 5) entitled "Comparison of Symphonies Nos. 3 and 9," which brings into sharp focus the common elements between the two symphonies, while, at the same time, noting that the most marked differences between the two compositions are to be found in harmonic language. In addition to these three chapters which constitute the main body of the dissertation, the author also provides an "Introduction" (Chapter 1), a "Biographical Sketch" (Chapter 2), and a closing chapter entitled "Summary, Conclusions, Recommendations." Contains a selective bibliography, footnotes, musical examples, tables, and seven appendixes.

*   McLellan, Joseph. "Schuman's Flowing Talk and Music."

Cited as **B815**.

B576   _____. "Orchestral Wizardry: 'Sorcerer's Apprentice' Tops NSO Concert." *The Washington Post*, October 18, 1985, section d, p. 9.

An October 17 concert by the National Symphony Orchestra, conducted by Mstislav Rostropovich at the Kennedy Center, included Schuman's *Credendum*. McLellan notes that the work was "given an exhilarating performance in honor of the composer's 75th birthday." Schuman was present at the concert. See: **W49j**

B577   _____. "NSO's Classy Notes for Georgetown." *The Washington Post*, September 25, 1989, section b, p. 7.

Reviews a concert, presented in celebration of Georgetown University's Bicentennial celebration, given by the National Symphony Orchestra. The conductor, Mstislav Rostropovich, opened the program with Schuman's *American Festival Overture*. "The orchestra and Rostropovich gave this delightful music a performance worthy of its quality." See: **W14l**

B578   _____. "Maestro Mehta's Muscle." *The Washington Post*, August 23, 1990, section d, p. 6.

Reports on an August 22 concert at Wolf Trap by Zubin Mehta and the New York Philharmonic. Schuman's *American Festival Overture*, called "bright, energetic music" by McLellan, opened the program. See: **W14n**

B579   _____. "For NSO, A Vintage Opening." *The Washington Post*, September 14, 1990, section c, p. 1.

Reviews a September 13 concert by the National Symphony Orchestra. Mstislav Rostropovich led the orchestra in a performance of Schuman's *American Festival Overture*, described by the reviewer as a "bright, brash, vigorous" composition. See: **W14o**

B580 _____. "Hushed Beauty from the St. Louis." *The Washington Post*, February 24, 1992, section b, p. 7.

This article reviews a recent performance at the Kennedy Center by the St. Louis Symphony Orchestra, conducted by Leonard Slatkin. The concert, which took place shortly after Schuman's death, included the *American Festival Overture*. "In the bright, energetic performance, this work sounded like a celebration of life, not a lamentation of death—and that seemed fitting." See: **W14t**

B581 Masullo, Robert A. "A Gould-en Night at Symphony: Maestro Leads Stirring Concert of All-American Music." *The Sacramento Bee*, November 14, 1993, section d, p. 3.

Reports on a November 12 concert by the Sacramento Symphony under the direction of guest conductor Morton Gould. One of the compositions presented on the program was Schuman's *New England Triptych*. The concert was repeated the next evening. See: **W53ee**

B582 Mathieson, Karen. "Concert Had No Energy Shortage." *The Seattle Times*, January 21, 1991, section d, p. 3.

A concert review of the January 19 program of the Seattle Symphony Orchestra. On the concert, which was conducted by Gerard Schwarz, was Schuman's *Symphony for Strings*. See: **W29m**

B583 Mellers, Wilfrid. "New Music: Americana." *The Musical Times* 103 (November 1962): 783-84.

Compares the music of Schuman to that of his teacher Roy Harris. Evaluates Schuman as an artist who "in retrospect . . . seems a lesser composer than his master." Praises the recently published Seventh Symphony for its technical sophistication, but criticizes it for its lack of conviction. Schuman's composition is one of four American works reviewed in this essay.

B584 Milburn, Frank, Jr. "Serkin Performs Two Concertos." *Musical America* 76 (April 1956): 15.

Includes a review of a March 13 Carnegie Hall performance of *Credendum*, presented by Eugene Ormandy and the Philadelphia Orchestra. See: **W49b**

*   Miller, Karl F. Review of William Schuman: *Night Journey*, recorded by the Atlantic Sinfonietta, conducted by Andrew Schenck.

Cited as **B816**.

B585 _____. Review of William Schuman: *Symphony No. 10, American Festival Overture*, *New England Triptych*, and *Variations on "America,"* recorded by the St. Louis Symphony, conducted by Leonard Slatkin; *Symphony for Strings, Judith, New England Triptych*, and *Variations on "America,"* recorded by the Seattle Symphony, conducted by Gerard Schwarz; *New England Triptych*, recorded by the Phoenix Symphony, conducted by James Sedares. *The American Record Guide* (September-October 1992): 159-60.

Miller reviews three new recordings in this article: RCA 61282, Delos 3115, and Koch 7135. The reviewer's fondness for the composer's music is evident throughout. After an opening paragraph which praises Schuman's musical style, Miller then provides a thorough and enthusiastic discussion of each disc. See: **D6, D44, D55, D56, D57, D88, D97, D117, D118**

* Miller, Philip L. Review of William Schuman: *Judith* and *Undertow*, recorded by the Louisville Orchestra, conducted by Robert Whitney and William Schuman; *Symphony No. 3*, recorded by the Philadelphia Orchestra, conducted by Eugene Ormandy.

Cited as **B817**.

* Monson, Karen. Review of William Schuman: *In Sweet Music, The Young Dead Soldiers*, and *Time to the Old*, recorded by Rosalind Rees and the Orpheus Trio, the White Mountains Festival Orchestra, and pianist Thomas Muraco.

Cited as **B733**.

B586 Moor, Paul. Review of William Schuman: *Symphony No. 3*, recorded by the New York Philharmonic Orchestra, conducted by Leonard Bernstein. *High Fidelity* 38 (May 1988): 57.

Takes Bernstein to task for cuts made in the Harris symphony, but believes that Schuman's "impressive work fares considerably better." Finds fault with the orchestra's string section in the final movement of the Schuman work. Deutsche Grammophon 419780-2. See: **D82**

B587 Morton, Lawrence. Review of William Schuman: *Concerto for Violin and Orchestra*. *Music Library Association Notes* 20 (Winter 1962-63): 125.

A negative review of both the study score and piano reduction score published by Merion Music in 1960. Predicts that the concerto's extinction is "inevitable and imminent."

B588 "Music: Bread & Butter." *Time* 55 (February 20, 1950): 46-47.

Comments on a rehearsal of Schuman's Concerto for Violin in Boston and reviews the first performance of the work, with Charles Munch conducting the Boston Symphony Orchestra and Isaac Stern on violin. See: **W39a**

B589 "National Symphony in Rhapsodic Control." *The Washington Post*, November 15, 1985, section b, p. 6.

A concert review of the November 14 program of the National Symphony, conducted by Rafael Frühbeck de Burgos. Schuman's *New England Triptych* "got the evening off to a brash start." See: **W53o**

B590 "New England Triptych Sets Record." *The Musical Leader* 98 (August 1966): 9.

A short, yet very informative, news item about the composition. Believes that the work, which was commissioned and first conducted by André Kostelanetz, has received "a record number of performances for a contemporary American Symphony work." Observes that *New England Triptych* has been programmed by numerous orchestras in the United States and by several orchestras abroad.

B591 "New Music: A 'Newsreel in Five Shots' by Schuman for School Band." *Musical America* 64 (April 10, 1944): 28.

An enthusiastic review of the newly published G. Schirmer band score of *Newsreel in Five Shots*. According to the reviewer, "This is a capital work for school bands . . . published . . . for symphonic band and for standard band."

B592 "New Publications in Review." *Musical Courier* 142 (December 1, 1950): 42.

This review, which discusses new publications by several composers, mentions the G. Schirmer editions of Schuman's *Prayer in Time of War* and Fourth Symphony.

B593 "New Publications in Review: New Music." *Musical Courier* 146 (November 1, 1952): 29.

Announces a new study score edition of Schuman's Sixth Symphony and offers an abbreviated description of the work.

B594 North, James H. Review of William Schuman: *Concerto for Violin and Orchestra*, recorded by the Boston Symphony Orchestra, conducted by Michael Tilson Thomas, with Paul Zukofsky, violin. *Fanfare* (July-August 1991): 271-72.

A recording review (Deutsche Grammophon 429860 2) which notes that the Schuman concerto "combines the rock-em-sock-em style of his early symphonies with some of his most lyrical writing." Contends that the composition is "a unified work which could not part with a single note." See: **D25, D27**

*   _____. Review of William Schuman: *Night Journey*, recorded by The Atlantic Sinfonietta, conducted by Andrew Schenck.

Cited as **B818**.

B595 "Notes and Comment." *The Juilliard Review* (Winter 1955-56): 52.

Includes a review of the 4 November 1955 premiere performance of *Credendum* by the Cincinnati Symphony Orchestra. Provides information about forthcoming performances of the work. See: **W49a**

B596 "N.Y. Philharmonic: Summer Park Concert Series." *Variety* 239 (August 18, 1965): 56.

Concert review of a New York Philharmonic summer performance in Central Park. The program, conducted by William Steinberg, included the premiere of Schuman's *Philharmonic Fanfare*. See: **W65a**

B597 O., M.E. Review of William Schuman: *Symphony No. 3*, recorded by the New York Philharmonic Orchestra, conducted by Leonard Bernstein. *The Gramophone* (November 1987): 737.

Praises the new Deutsche Grammophon issue of Schuman's Third Symphony, observing that "it is one of the most natural-sounding live recordings I have ever heard." Relates Schuman's musical style and technique to that of his mentor, Roy Harris. See: **D82**

B598 Page, Tim. "Music: Schuman Concerto and 10th Symphony." *The New York Times*, December 16, 1985, section 3, p. 16.

Extols Schuman's achievements in American music and praises his compositions in general, commenting that his "music may stand on its own merits." However, this article, a review of the Juilliard Orchestra's Friday 13 performance of the *Concerto on Old English Rounds* and the Tenth Symphony, also argues that "One occasionally senses the presence of a superb craftsman going about his business, rather than a composer with an urgent message to convey." Furnishes brief but perceptive opinions about both works. See: **W75e, W79b**

B599 Paris, Robert. "National Sym: Schuman Prems." *High Fidelity/Musical America* 26 (August 1976): MA-30.

Critically reviews three compositions written by Schuman for the Bicentennial which were premiered at the Kennedy Center on April 6 and 7 by the National Symphony Orchestra: *The Young Dead Soldiers, Symphony No. 10,* and *Casey at the Bat*. See: **W79a, W81a, W82a**

B600 Parker, Craig B. Review of William Schuman: *Symphony No. 7*, recorded by the Pittsburgh Symphony Orchestra, conducted by Lorin Maazel. *American Music* 6 (Fall 1988): 352-53.

A substantial review of the New World Records (NW 348) recording of Schuman's Seventh Symphony, which is coupled with Leonardo Balada's *Steel Symphony* on this issue. Comments on the significance of Schuman's ten symphonies, arguing that they "form the core of his creative output," and notes the abundance of recordings, including a prior performance of the Seventh Symphony by the Utah Symphony Orchestra on Turnabout (TVS-34447). Following background material on the genesis of the symphony, the author presents an examination of the composition's four movements, which, though only a paragraph in length, is quite informative. Praises the "exciting interpretation" of conductor Lorin Maazel and the bass clarinet solos by Richard Page. Refers to the notes provided by Leonard Burkat. See: **D92**

*   Parmenter, Ross. "First Winner of Critics Circle Prize."

Cited as **B275**.

B601   _____. "Season Is Opened by Philharmonic." *The New York Times*, October 5, 1962, p. 29.

Discusses the first concert given by the New York Philharmonic in Lincoln Center's new Philharmonic Hall. One of the works played and commissioned for this event was Schuman's Eighth Symphony. Describes the three-movement symphony as "unfailingly expressive." See: **W60a**

B602   Perkins, James Robert. "Characteristics of Nationalistic Style in Three Folk Song Settings for Band." M.A. thesis, Western State College of Colorado, 1983. 51 pp.

A comparative study of the following twentieth-century compositions for band: William Schuman's *Chester Overture*, Ralph Vaughan Williams's *Folk Song Suite*, and Darius Milhaud's *Suite française*. Chapter three (pp. 15-26) presents a superficial investigation of the Schuman work. The representation of literature on Schuman included in the bibliography is woefully inadequate.

B603   Pernick, Ben. "Superb Schuman." *Fanfare* (September-October 1978): 105.

The reviewer praises the Columbia M35101 recording of *Concerto on Old English Rounds*, noting the superb performances by Leonard Bernstein and the New York Philharmonic, the violist Donald McInnes, and the Camerata Singers. See: **D28**

B604   Persichetti, Vincent. "Current Chronicle: Philadelphia." *The Musical Quarterly* 38 (April 1952): 298-301.

Evaluates Schuman's Sixth Symphony in light of a recent performance by Eugene Ormandy and the Philadelphia Orchestra. Asserts that the symphony is comparable in stature to the composer's best works. Briefly analyzes the single-movement composition and includes excerpts from the musical score. See: **W41d**

B605   Peterson, Melody. "Los Angeles: Los Angeles Chamber Orchestra (Schwarz)." *High Fidelity/Musical America (1980)* 31 (June 1981): MA 26.

A performance review of Schuman's Fifth Symphony and works by Mozart, Rossini, and Haydn.

B606 "Philharmonic, Capital Church Join Voices." *The Sacramento Bee*, May 27, 1993, section f, p. 3.

Notes that the Sacramento Philharmonic Orchestra and the Capital Christian Center Sanctuary Choir will present two concerts entitled "Portraits of America" on May 29 and 30. Schuman's *New England Triptych* was scheduled to be played on the program.

B607 Pincus, Andrew L. Review of William Schuman: *In Praise of Shahn*, recorded by the Juilliard Orchestra, conducted by Otto Werner-Mueller. *The New York Times*, August 20, 1989, section h, p. 29.

Contains a review of the New World 368 issue. See: **D39**

B608 _____. "Tanglewood Honors Composer Schuman." *(Pittsfield, Massachusetts) Berkshire Eagle*, August 6, 1990.

Reviews an August 4 Tanglewood performance of Schuman's Third Symphony by the Boston Symphony Orchestra, conducted by Dennis Russell Davies in celebration of the composer's eightieth birthday. Contends that the work is "rock-solid music." Indicates that Schuman, who was present in the audience, received tremendous applause at the conclusion of the performance. See: **W22cc**

B609 Porter, Andrew. "Musical Events." *The New Yorker* 52 (May 3, 1976): 114, 117.

A generally favorable performance review of Schuman's *Concerto on Old English Rounds*, conducted by Leonard Bernstein. Praises the solo viola playing of Donald McInnes and the singing of the Abraham Kaplan Camerata Singers. See: **W75b**

B610 _____. *Music of Three Seasons: 1974-1977*. New York: Farrar Straus Giroux, 1978. 668 pp. ISBN 0 374 21646 0 ML60 P895 M88

Another collection of essays written by the music critic of *The New Yorker*. Contains performance reviews of *Concerto on Old English Rounds* (3 May 1976) and the Seventh Symphony (29 March 1976). See: **W75c**

B611 _____. "Musical Events." *The New Yorker* 61 (December 2, 1985): 131-36.

A report (pp. 133-34) from New York's Carnegie Hall on a November 1985 performance of Schuman's *Symphony for Strings*. Criticizes the rendition of the work by the American Composers Orchestra for being "uninspired." Remarks that the concert also included the presentation of the William Schuman Award to David Diamond. See: **W29j**

B612 "Premieres: William Schuman's *In Praise of Shahn*." *BMI: The Many Worlds of Music* (April 1970): 10-11.

Makes reference to the world premiere performance of *In Praise of Shahn* on January 29, presented by Leonard Bernstein and the New York Philharmonic. Quotations about the work are provided by the composer, by a reviewer from *The New York Times*, and from Irving Kolodin's review in *Saturday Review*. Includes a photograph of the composer. See: **W71a**

B613 Prindl, Frank Joseph. "A Study of Ten Original Compositions for Band Published in America since 1946." Ed.D. dissertation, Florida State University, 1956. 121 pp. UM Order No. 00-17029 MT125 P75 1956a

Schuman's *George Washington Bridge* is examined in Chapter 10 (pp. 93-102) of this treatise. A brief biographical sketch of the composer is followed by an overview of Schuman's style, which then leads to an analysis of the work. The ten compositions discussed in this dissertation were chosen on the basis of a survey sent by the author to six university band directors who were asked to select ten works which represented significant contributions to band literature. Includes an appendix, bibliography, footnotes, and musical examples.

B614 Protzman, Bob. "Recording Review." *St. Paul Pioneer Press Dispatch*, June 7, 1992, section d, p. 5.

Review of the recording (Delos DE 3115) by Gerard Schwarz and the Seattle Symphony entitled "A Tribute to William Schuman." See: **D44, D55, D88, D117**

B615 Rabinowitz, Peter J. Review of William Schuman: *In Praise of Shahn*, recorded by the Juilliard Orchestra, conducted by Otto Werner-Mueller. *Fanfare* 12 (March-April 1989): 268-69.

Depicts Schuman's music as "grimly insistent" and "imperious." Characterizes the peroration as "pain which turns to anguish as the music rises to its climax." Copland's *Connotations* and Sessions's *The Black Masters Suite* are combined with *In Praise of Shahn* on this New World CD (NW 368-2). See: **D39**

B616 Reich, Howard. "Arts Festivals Stage Everything from Goofy to Gershwin." *Chicago Tribune*, June 9, 1985, Travel section, p. 9.

Mentions that Leonard Slatkin is scheduled to conduct the Boston Symphony Orchestra in a performance of Schuman's *Credendum* at the Tanglewood Festival on July 6. See: **W49h**

B617 _____. "Heroic Sounds Spring from Our Darkest Era." *Chicago Tribune*, September 3, 1989, Arts section, p. 12.

This discussion of American music in the 1930s and 1940s contains several references to Schuman. Believes that Schuman's Third Symphony "was music with a clear agenda: to express the hopes of the common man in a forceful, unflinching way."

B618 Review of William Schuman: *Symphony No. 3*, recorded by the Philadelphia Orchestra, conducted by Eugene Ormandy. *The New Records* (October 1951): 6.

This recording review (Columbia ML 4413) begins with the pronouncement that Schuman's symphony is "a major contribution to the symphonic literature." See: **D80**

B619 Review of William Schuman: *To Thee Old Cause*. *Variety* 252 (October 9, 1968): 54.

B620 Review of William Schuman: *Symphony No. 3*. *Neue Zeitschrift für Musik* 129 (November 1968): 462.

B621 Review of William Schuman: *To Thee Old Cause*. *Neue Zeitschrift für Musik* 130 (January 1969): 11.

B622 Rhodes, Stephen L. "A Comparative Analysis of the Band Compositions of William Schuman." D.A. dissertation, University of Northern Colorado, 1987. 131 pp. UM Order No. 87-21960 MT130 S335 R56x 1987

The major portion of this study is devoted to an examination of five original works for band by Schuman in order of chronological appearance. Framing the principal discussion is an opening chapter which presents background material and a concluding chapter which provides a synthesis for the monograph. Bibliography, footnotes, and copious musical examples.

B623 _____. "William Schuman: Chester Overture for Band." *BDGuide* 3 (March-April 1989): 32, 35-38.

Studies this work chiefly by means of a stylistic analysis emphasizing harmonic and melodic elements. Compares the band version to the original orchestra score, observing that the adaptation for concert band "is more than a transcription" and concluding that "Schuman's composition is truly one of the significant works of the 20th century written for band." Also provides helpful rehearsal suggestions and a "time line" chart. Regards Schuman as one of the important twentieth-century American composers for band.

B624 Rich, Alan. "2 Premieres at Lincoln Center Offered by Juilliard Orchestra." *The New York Times*, September 29, 1962, p. 14.

Reports on the first New York performance of *A Song of Orpheus*. Believes the composition to be a "beautiful work" and one that "really sings." This Philharmonic Hall rendition on 28 September 1962 was by the Juilliard Orchestra, conducted by Jean Morel, with cellist Leonard Rose. See: **W59c**

B625 _____. "Band of Angels." *New West* (November 17, 1980): 130.

Reflects upon a recent performance of Schuman's Third Symphony by Carlo Maria Giulini and the Los Angeles Philharmonic Orchestra. Finds Giulini's interpretation of this well-known score "not only knowledgeable but profound" and extols the work as "a strong and original piece." Suggests that Schuman's composition reveals influences from other composers, most notably Vaughan Williams, Sibelius, and Roy Harris. See: **W22u**

B626 Rivers, Kate. "Taiwan Academy and Brooklyn College Orchestras." *The Washington Post*, March 8, 1989, section d, p. 11.

Notes a concert at the Kennedy Center by the combined forces of the Symphony Orchestra of the National Taiwan Academy of Arts and the Conservatory Orchestra of Brooklyn College. Dorothy Klotzman led the combined orchestras in "a thorough reading" of Schuman's *New England Triptych*. See: **W53s**

B627 Rockwell, John. "Bolcom Piece Honors William Schuman at 80." *The New York Times*, August 8, 1990, section c, p. 10.

A performance review of two compositions, William Bolcom's *MCMXC Tanglewood* (written as a tribute to Schuman and for Tanglewood's fiftieth anniversary) and Schuman's Third Symphony, featured at Tanglewood's 1990 Festival of Contemporary Music in honor of Schuman's eightieth birthday. In writing about Schuman's best-known symphony, Rockwell asserts that "its neo-Baroque aspects seemed to clash with its vigorous symphonic Americana, lending the enterprise a slightly stuffy, fustian quality." See: **W22cc**

B628 Roos, James. "Peter Zazofsky Solos with Philharmonic." *The Miami Herald*, November 28, 1985, section d, p. 20.

Reports on a November 26 performance of Schuman's *New England Triptych* in Fort Lauderdale. The rendition, by the Philharmonic Orchestra of Florida under Emerson Buckley, was in honor of the composer's seventy-fifth birthday. See: **W53p**

B629 _____. "Philharmonic Stirring with Yaffe at Helm." *The Miami Herald*, March 28, 1990, section d, p. 7.

A review of the March 27 concert in Fort Lauderdale presented by the Philharmonic Orchestra of Florida, John Yaffe conductor. Lauds the conducting of Yaffe in a performance of Schuman's *American Festival Overture*. See: **W14m**

B630 _____. "St. Louis Symphony Was Superb." *The Miami Herald*, February 17, 1992, section c, p. 4.

A concert review of a February 13 performance at the Broward Center for the Performing Arts by the St. Louis Symphony. Leonard Slatkin's conducting of Schuman's *American Festival Overture* was praised. The work was also presented on February 12 at the West Palm Beach Auditorium. See: **W14s**

B631 Rosenfeld, Paul. "Current Chronicle: Copland-Harris-Schuman." *The Musical Quarterly* 25 (July 1939): 372-81.

Presents illuminating discussion on recently performed compositions by each of the three composers. The Schuman works included are the Second Symphony and the *Prologue* for orchestra and chorus. See: **W13a, W17a**

B632 Rothweiler, Kyle. Review of William Schuman: *Prayer in Time of War* and *Symphony No. 4*, recorded by the Louisville Orchestra, conducted by Jorge Mester. *The American Record Guide* (November-December 1990): 66.

A negative recording review of the Albany reissue of these works. See: **D66, D84**

B633 Rouse, Christopher. "Expansion of Material in the Seventh Symphony of William Schuman." M.F.A. thesis, Cornell University, 1977. ML30 1977 R863

The fundamental study of Schuman's Seventh Symphony by one of the outstanding authorities on the composer. Presented as a concomitant monograph (Part II) to Rouse's original composition (Part I, *Gacela del Amor Imprevisto*) for the master's thesis, the author provides a definitive explication of the symphony. Prior to his discussion of the work, Rouse gives a biographical sketch of the composer and a comprehensive discussion of Schuman's musical style, emphasizing the areas of orchestration, melody, harmony, rhythm, form and structure, and the composer's use of borrowings from earlier works. Divides Schuman's compositions into two stylistic periods, regarding the Sixth Symphony as a watershed work. According to the author's stated purpose, as it appears in the abstract, the thesis considers "an examination of the composer's *Symphony No. 7* (1960), particularly as it relates to the second of his *Three Piano Moods* (1958). Special attention is paid to the symphony's third movement, which constitutes an orchestration and expansion of material from the piano piece." Contains endnotes and copious musical examples.

B634 Sabin, Robert. Review of William Schuman: *Symphony No. 4* and *Prayer in Time of War*. *Music Library Association Notes* 8 (December 1950): 129-30.

An appreciative review of 1950 study scores published by G. Schirmer. Characterizes Schuman's symphony as music "which is as functional, and as beautiful, in its way, as a skyscraper or an ocean liner. Yet it is neither inhuman nor unfeeling. On the contrary, it is a direct expression of the spirit of its time in art." Provides a helpful movement by movement examination of the work. Interprets *Prayer in Time of War* as "dignified music," though not as profound as the symphony. See: **B635**.

B635 _____. "Two Schuman Works in Study Score Form." *Musical America* 71 (February 1951): 232.

Another review by Sabin of these Schuman compositions published by G. Schirmer in study score form. Gives opinions and information about both works, especially praising the Fourth Symphony as "one of the best of contemporary American symphonies." Compares the symphony to the composer's Third Symphony, contending that the Fourth "is more contained, more disciplined, more economical in style, yet equally strong in texture and convincing in development." Contains an informative discussion of each of the symphony's movements. See: **B634**.

B636 _____. "Schuman's Symphony No. 6 Issued in Study Score." *Musical America* 72 (December 1, 1952): 28.

Sabin's article, which recognizes the publication of a new study score (G. Schirmer's Edition of Study Scores, No. 60) for Schuman's Sixth Symphony, lauds the composition as "one of Schuman's most intellectually impressive and emotionally inspired works" and argues that the symphony should frequently appear on orchestral concerts.

B637 _____. "William Schuman Pays Tribute to Billings." *Musical America* 78 (February 1958): 212.

Compares Schuman to William Billings in this review of *New England Triptych*. Observes that "Like Billings, Schuman is a bold thinker . . . he keeps the salt and sting of life itself in his art."

B638 _____. "William Schuman's Violin Concerto." *Musical America* 80 (August 1960): 33.

Supplies information on a newly published piano reduction of the orchestral score to Schuman's Concerto for Violin. Documents the history of performances of the work, as well as its various versions, and presents a superficial analysis.

B639 _____. "Schuman Seventh in New York Premiere." *Musical America* 81 (January 1961): 244.

A less than enthusiastic review of Schuman's Seventh Symphony, on the occasion of its New York premiere by the Boston Symphony Orchestra, with Charles Munch conducting. See: **W58b**

B640 Sádlo, Karel Pravoslav. "Soucasná americká symfonie." *Hudebn i rozhledy* 12, no. 4 (1959): 162. In Czech.

A performance review of Schuman's Third Symphony.

B641 Salzman, Eric. "As American as Pittsburgh." *Stereo Review* 52 (September 1987): 118.

In this recording review of Schuman's Seventh Symphony, Salzman reflects upon the quest for the "Great American symphony," citing examples by Copland, Harris, and Schuman. Considers Schuman's contributions to the symphonic genre generally more contemporary in outlook than the works of his counterparts. Leonardo Balada's *Steel Symphony* also appears on this recording (New World NW 348-1, NW 348-4, and NW 348-2). See: **D92**

B642 Sargeant, Winthrop. "The Inside Track." *The New Yorker* 36 (December 10, 1960): 231-33.

A critical commentary of Schuman's Seventh Symphony, written in review of a performance of the work by the Boston Symphony in Carnegie Hall. Berates the composer for not composing music intended to appeal to the general public. Accuses the Koussevitzky Foundation, which commissioned the work, and other such organizations of an unfair selection process. See: **W58b, B313**

B643 Schneider, John. "Atlanta Sym.: Schuman Concerto." *High Fidelity/Musical America* 29 (June 1979): MA 27.

Schneider engagingly reviews a performance of the *Concerto on Old English Rounds*, presented on February 8 by the Atlanta Symphony under Robert Shaw, with Donald McInnes as viola soloist. Acclaims the performance of the soloist and notes that the composer was present in the audience. See: **W75d**

B644 Schneider, Richard. Review of William Schuman: *Concerto for Violin and Orchestra*, recorded by the St. Louis Symphony Orchestra, conducted by Leonard Slatkin, with Robert McDuffie, violin. *Stereophile* 13 (May 1990): 181-82.

Schneider's review of the EMI CDC 7 49464 2 compact disc praises the performance of Robert McDuffie and considers Schuman's concerto "a nervous, agitated, anxious work, filled with nuclear jitters and cold-war paranoia, and yet there are moments of lyric repose and consolation, even the naive euphoria which Schuman finds so irresistible as an expression of ultimate optimism." See: **D26**

B645 _____. Review of William Schuman: *Symphony No. 10, American Festival Overture, New England Triptych*, and *Variations on "America,"* recorded by the St. Louis Symphony, conducted by Leonard Slatkin; *New England Triptych, Symphony for Strings, Judith*, and *Variations on "America,"* recorded by the Seattle Symphony, conducted by Gerard Schwarz. *Stereophile* (March 1993): 187.

A fairly extensive review of two recordings: RCA 61282 and Delos 3115. Concludes with the opinion that these performances "make each of these recordings worth owning, despite the duplications in the other works." See: **D6, D44, D55, D57, D88, D97, D117, D118**

B646 Schonberg, Harold C. "Music: Philharmonic at Home Base." *The New York Times*, October 4, 1968, p. 35.

Reviews the 3 October 1968 concert of the New York Philharmonic Orchestra, which included both Schuman's Third Symphony and the premiere performance of his *To Thee Old Cause*, a work commissioned by the Philharmonic. Praises the playing of the orchestra led by Leonard Bernstein and characterizes the composer's newest composition as "an ingenious piece of writing that seems to metamorphosize a chord." See: **W22s, W69a**

B647 _____. "Music: Philadelphia with Johansen." *The New York Times*, January 15, 1969, p. 37.

Writes, in this review of the 14 January 1969 concert in New York's Philharmonic Hall by the Philadelphia Orchestra, that Schuman's Ninth Symphony "is a serious work written in his sharp, clear, busy style." Yet the reviewer goes on to admit that he is not that enamored with the work. See: **W68b**

B648 _____. "Music: A New Schuman." *The New York Times*, January 25, 1980, section 3, p. 10.

Claims, in this rather pessimistic review of the world premiere of Schuman's *Three Colloquies*, that the work is essentially a "color piece," noting that the composer's primary concern is in dissimilar sonorities. Though the reviewer compliments Schuman's compositional skill and craftsmanship, he observes that the music "does not really have much nourishment" and concludes that "The gestures sound a bit tired and routine." See: **W85a**

B649 "Schuman and Carter." *American Musical Digest* 1, no. 5 (1970): 23-26.

Reprints excerpts of articles or entire articles dealing with Schuman's *In Praise of Shahn* which originally appeared in other publications: "N.Y. Philharmonic: Back to Back," 11 February 1970, *Christian Science Monitor*, by Miles Kastendieck; "Schuman's 'In Praise of Shahn,'" 14 February 1970, *Saturday Review*, by Irving Kolodin; and "Words and Music: Bernstein Leads Praise of 'Shahn,'" 30 January 1970, *New York Post*, by Harriett Johnson. Also prints a one-page excerpt from the score of the composition. See: **W71a, B539, B542, B553**

B650 "Schuman Is Honored by Westchester Unit." *The New York Times*, April 26, 1962, p. 24.

Discusses a concert by the Orchestral Society of Westchester given in honor of Schuman. In addition to a presentation to the composer made by Aaron Copland, the concert featured Schuman's *A Song of Orpheus* and *New England Triptych*.

B651 Schwarz, K. Robert. "Debuts & Reappearances: New York." *High Fidelity/Musical America* 36 (March 1986): 14-16.

An articulate review of a New York performance by the American Composers Orchestra on November 17 offered in celebration of the birthdays of three composers: Aaron Copland, William Schuman, and David Diamond. The program included Copland's *Statements*, Schuman's *Symphony for Strings*, and Diamond's Ninth Symphony. Schwarz infers that "Schuman seems to have been particularly taken with the possibilities of polytonality; triads are layered by means of both skillful counterpoint and simple homophony." See: **W29j**

B652 _____. "Recordings in Review: Bernstein, *Serenade*; Schuman, Concerto for Violin and Orchestra." *Musical America* 110 (January 1990): 61.

Lavishes praise on Schuman's Concerto for Violin in this enthusiastic review of the recording (Angel EMI CD: CDC 49464) by the St. Louis Symphony Orchestra, conducted by Leonard Slatkin, and with violinist Robert McDuffie. See: **D26**

B653 Seckerson, Edward. Review of William Schuman: *Concerto for Violin and Orchestra*, recorded by the St. Louis Symphony Orchestra, conducted by Leonard Slatkin, with Robert McDuffie, violin. *The Gramophone* 67 (December 1989): 1127-28.

A thoroughly positive review of the compact disc recording (EMI Angel CDC 49464 2). See: **D26**

B654 _____. Review of William Schuman: *New England Triptych*, recorded by the Phoenix Symphony Orchestra, conducted by James Sedares. *The Gramophone* (September 1992): 71.

A recording review (Koch International 3 7135-2) which, though noting the accuracy of the rendition, believes that the end result is somewhat lacking in intensity. See: **D56**

B655 _____. Review of William Schuman: *American Festival Overture, New England Triptych, Symphony No. 10*, and *Variations on "America,"* recorded by the St. Louis Symphony Orchestra, conducted by Leonard Slatkin. *The Gramophone* (May 1993): 51.

This recording review delivers high praise for both the composer and the performers. In commenting on the works, the reviewer offers the following assessment: "Schuman's is both music of the land—gritty, pioneering, open—and of the first cityscapes: iron and steel, always reaching outwards and upwards." This RCA Victor Red Seal (09026 61282-2) presents the first recording of the composer's Tenth Symphony. See: **D6, D57, D97, D118**

B656 "76 Bicentennial Report." *BMI: The Many Worlds of Music* (Spring 1976): 32-35.

In this discussion of works composed for the Bicentennial by several American composers, three Schuman compositions are included: *The Young Dead Soldiers* (incorrectly given here as *The Dead Young Soldiers*), the Tenth Symphony, and the cantata *Casey at the Bat*. The first two works were commissioned specifically for the Bicentennial season by the National Symphony Orchestra. All three of these pieces received their world premieres at a concert given by the orchestra on April 6. See: **W79a, W81a, W82a**

B657 Shen, Ted. "Grant Park Symphony Makes Summer Fare a Hit Again." *Chicago Tribune*, August 7, 1992, News section, p. 14.

Enthusiastically reports on an August 5 concert which included two of the fanfares commissioned for the 1986 Texas Sesquicentennial. Schuman's *Showcase: A Short Display for Orchestra* was conducted by Jahja Ling. See: **W97d**

B658 Shepard, Richard F. "Schuman Finishes His 9th Symphony." *The New York Times*, April 9, 1968, p. 57.

An informative article which deals with the genesis of Schuman's Ninth Symphony. Points out that this composition, which was commissioned by the Philadelphia Orchestra, is the composer's first programmatic symphony. Notes that the score was finished by Schuman in Rome, the site of the World War II atrocity which inspired the program.

B659 Shulgold, Marc. "Symphony Performs; Audience Stays Home." *Rocky Mountain News*, November 22, 1989, Entertainment section, p. 46.

Murry Sidlin conducted a Thanksgiving concert of the Colorado Symphony Orchestra in Boettcher Hall on November 21. Schuman's *New England Triptych* was one of the works on the program. See: **W53v**

B660 Shupp, E.E., Jr. Review of William Schuman: *Symphony No. 3* and *Symphony No. 5*, recorded by the New York Philharmonic Orchestra, conducted by Leonard Bernstein. *The New Records* (October 1970): 4-5.

Shupp's succinct recording review (Columbia MS 7442) remarks that Bernstein's rendition of the Fifth Symphony is characterized by "remarkable vigor and insight" and summarizes the conductor's interpretation of the Third Symphony as "pointed and searching." See: **D81, D87**

B661 Sigmon, Carl. "Orchestras in New York: A Debut and a Legend." *Musical America* 82 (December 1962): 25-28.

An extended review of orchestral activity in New York City during the month of October, which included a performance on October 7 of Schuman's Eighth Symphony by Leonard Bernstein and the New York Philharmonic. See: **W60a**

B662 _____. "New Music: Short, Dark and Handsome." *Musical America* 83 (December 1963): 288.

In this review of several compositions by twentieth-century composers, Schuman's *A Song of Orpheus* is examined.

B663 Simmons, Walter. Review of William Schuman: *Symphony No. 3*, recorded by the New York Philharmonic Orchestra, conducted by Leonard Bernstein. *Fanfare* (March-April 1988): 195-96.

An informative review of the Deutsche Grammophon 419780-2 compact disc. Compares Schuman's Third Symphony to the Roy Harris Third Symphony, which is paired with the Schuman on this recording. Calls the Schuman composition a "wholly satisfying work" and observes that it "exudes a brisk self-confidence and vigorous sense of purpose." Lauds the conducting of Bernstein. See: **D82**

B664 _____. Review of William Schuman: *Concerto for Violin and Orchestra*, recorded by the St. Louis Symphony Orchestra, conducted by Leonard Slatkin, with Robert McDuffie, violin. *Fanfare* 13 (March-April 1990): 288-89.

Compares the violin concerto to *Judith*, *Credendum*, and the Sixth Symphony. Claims that "this is an arresting, emotionally exciting, and intellectually stimulating work, rewarding attentive, repeated listening." Compliments the interpretation of McDuffie on this recording (EMI Angel CDC 49464). See: **D26**

B665 _____. Review of William Schuman: *New England Triptych*, recorded by the Eastman-Rochester Orchestra, conducted by Howard Hanson. *Fanfare* (July-August 1992): 219-20.

Refers to the reissue on CD of this 1963 performance of Schuman's work as "a stunning performance." See: **D54**

B666 _____. Review of William Schuman: *Symphony No. 5*, *Judith*, *New England Triptych*, and *Variations on "America,"* recorded by the Seattle Symphony Orchestra, conducted by Gerard Schwartz; *Symphony No. 10*, *New England Triptych*, *American Festival Overture*, and *Variations on "America,"* recorded by the St. Louis Symphony Orchestra, conducted by Leonard Slatkin. *Fanfare* (September-October 1992): 347-49.

A substantial and important recording review of two new all-Schuman releases: Delos DE 3115 and RCA Victor Red Seal 09026-61282-2. Upholds Schuman's position as a significant figure in American music and as a major composer. Provides an informative discussion of the works on these recordings, especially *Judith*, the Fifth Symphony, and the Tenth Symphony. See: **D6**, **D44**, **D55**, **D57**, **D88**, **D97**, **D117**, **D118**

B667 Smith, Dean. "Musical Pictures Grace Symphony Show." *The Charlotte Observer*, November 14, 1993, section f, p. 1.

Reports that the Charlotte Repertory Orchestra, conducted by Stephen Platte, will perform Schuman's *American Festival Overture*. See: **W14v**

B668 Smith, Patrick J. "New York Philharmonic, Bernstein: Britten, Schuman." *High Fidelity/Musical America* 26 (August 1976): MA-26.

Reviews an April 15 concert by Leonard Bernstein and the New York Philharmonic, which included a performance of Schuman's *Concerto on Old English Rounds*. See: **W75b**

B669 Smith, Tim. "Philharmonic Orchestra Offering 'Eroica,' Prokofiev." *Fort Lauderdale Sun-Sentinel*, March 28, 1990, section e, p. 3.

Discusses a performance of Schuman's *American Festival Overture* by conductor John Yaffe and the Philharmonic Orchestra of Florida on March 26. See: **W14m**

B670 Smoley, Lewis M. Review of William Schuman: *Newsreel*, recorded by the Milwaukee Symphony Orchestra, conducted by Lukas Foss. *The American Record Guide* 47 (May 1984): 58-59.

Newsreel is one of several twentieth-century American compositions to appear on this Pro Arte release (Pro Arte, digital; PAD-102, LP; PCD-102, cassette) entitled "American Festival." The reviewer states: "William Schuman's somewhat urbane treatment of presumably newsworthy events might have been the subject of a Movietone release in the 1940s. . . . The music is cosmopolitan in approach and conservative in style." See: **D58**

B671 Snook, Paul A. Review of William Schuman: *Prayer in Time of War* and *Symphony No. 4*, recorded by the Louisville Orchestra, conducted by Jorge Mester. *Fanfare* (November-December 1990): 348-50.

A fine recording review of the Albany reissue of two Schuman works. Snook writes: "In many ways, if America has had a musical conscience over the past several decades, William Schuman, in his reaction to and remembrance of this primordial confrontation between good and evil, has embodied many of its important dimensions, and the 'Prayer' marks a major stage in this evolution." Provides good discussion of both compositions. See: **D66**, **D84**

B672 Stacy, William B. Review of William Schuman: *In Praise of Shahn*, recorded by the Juilliard Orchestra, conducted by Otto Werner-Mueller. *The Sonneck Society Bulletin* 16 (Summer 1990): 89.

Considers the score to be representative of Schuman's style and compares some aspects of the work to the Roy Harris Third Symphony. Compliments the superb performance of the orchestra and, for the most part, the 1988 New World recording (New World Records NW 368-1). Copland's *Connotations* and Sessions's *Black Maskers Suite* also appear on this offering, though in each case the Juilliard Orchestra is led by a different conductor, in the Copland by Sixten Ehrling and in the Sessions by Paul Zukofsky. See: **D39**

B673 Stedman, Preston. *The Symphony*. Englewood Cliffs, NJ: Prentice-Hall, 1979. 429 pp. ISBN 0 138 80062 6 ML1255 S83

Investigates Schuman's symphonic style (pp. 353-66) in a chapter entitled "The Twentieth Century Symphony in America." Following a brief essay on the composer's music in general, the author provides comments on each of Schuman's nine symphonies (the Tenth Symphony had not been composed at the time of this publication). Analyzes in some detail (pp. 358-66), complete with musical examples, the Third Symphony. Concludes with a summary.

B674 Stevens, Denis. "Notes from Abroad: New York." *The Musical Times* 97 (May 1956): 268-69.

Although principally a report of the musical activities surrounding the celebration of the Juilliard School's fiftieth anniversary, Stevens presents an outstanding review of Schuman's *Credendum*. The author concludes his comments on the work with the following evaluation: "The signs of weakness often inherent in a commissioned work are reassuringly absent here. It is as if Schuman had warmed spontaneously to his task, creating a deeply felt work of original cast and powerful design." See: **W49b**

B675 Stutsman, Grace May. "Native Work Played by Koussevitzky." *Musical America* 64 (October 1944): 5.

The first Boston performance of Schuman's *Prayer in Time of War*, presented by Serge Koussevitzky and the Boston Symphony Orchestra, is reviewed in this article. Stutsman writes that "the 'Prayer' . . . contains many moving measures." See: **W28d**

B676 Swift, Richard. Review of William Schuman: *In Praise of Shahn*. *Music Library Association Notes* 29 (December 1972): 320.

A generally favorable review of the orchestral score published by Merion Music in 1971. After a cursory description of the work, the reviewer considers that "Admirers of Mr. Schuman's music will find all the familiar traits . . . For others, the work will seem thin, one-dimensional, and more than a little gaudy."

B677 Teachout, Terry. "Six Composers in Search of an Audience." *Musical America* 109 (July 1989): 68-70.

Primarily a discussion of recently released recordings containing works by the following composers: Elliott Carter, Roger Sessions, Harold Shapero, Samuel Barber, Aaron Copland, and William Schuman. Evaluates a New World issue (NW 368-2) of *In Praise of Shahn* and a Deutsche Grammophon recording (DG 419780-2) of the Third Symphony. See: **D39, D82**

B678 Tiedman, Richard E. Review of William Schuman: *Symphony No. 3*, recorded by the New York Philharmonic Orchestra, conducted by Leonard Bernstein. *The American Record Guide* 51 (May-June 1988): 34-35.

An admirable review replete with information about Schuman's symphony. Expresses disappointment in the sound quality of this digital recording. Roy Harris's Third Symphony also appears on this recording (DG 419780-2). See: **D82**

B679   Tircuit, Heuwell. "A Brahms Collection among the New Albums." *San Francisco Chronicle*, March 11, 1973, p. 30.

Contains a short recording review of the Turnabout (TVS 34447) issue of Schuman's Seventh Symphony, performed by Maurice Abravanel and the Utah Symphony Orchestra. See: **D91**

B680   Trimble, Lester. "Two Ninths by Two Contemporary Americans." *Stereo Review* 28 (April 1972): 70-71.

Compares, in this perceptive record review (RCA LSC 3212), the Ninth Symphony of Schuman to the Ninth Symphony of Vincent Persichetti. Draws attention to the expansive style common to Schuman's orchestral music in general and to the Ninth Symphony in particular. Asserts, in conclusion, that the work displays "a conception of musical time that is unique to Schuman, expressively powerful, and . . . utterly American." See: **D95**

B681   _____. Review of William Schuman: *Symphony No. 7*, recorded by the Utah Symphony Orchestra, conducted by Maurice Abravanel. *Stereo Review* 28 (June 1972): 89.

Reviews the first recording (Turnabout TVS 34447) of Schuman's Seventh Symphony. Affirms the kinship between the composer's Seventh, Eighth, and Ninth Symphonies and considers the Seventh to be one of Schuman's finest achievements. See: **D91**

B682   Trootstwyk, Arthur. "Miami Orchestra in Schuman Premiere." *Musical America* 76 (November 15, 1956): 10.

Contains a complimentary review of the world premiere performance of Schuman's *New England Triptych* by André Kostelanetz and the University of Miami Symphony Orchestra. Argues that the composer's work is one "of thorough craftsmanship and richness of musical invention." See: **W53a**

B683   Tucker, Marilyn. "Youthful Conservatory Orchestra Plays the Herbst." *San Francisco Chronicle*, April 25, 1990, section e, p. 2.

Reports on an April 23 performance of Schuman's *Circus Overture* by the San Francisco Conservatory of Music orchestra, conducted by Denis de Coteau. See: **W32f**

*   "The Two Schumans."

Cited as **B386**.

B684   Ulrich, Allen. "Schuman Concerto a Rare Beauty." *The San Francisco Examiner*, November 13, 1992.

Considers Schuman's violin concerto to be one of the outstanding American works in that genre. This concert review of a performance by the San Francisco Symphony and violinist Robert McDuffie comments that Schuman's composition "spotlights much of what has made the concerto form endure." Takes American orchestras to task for not programming more literature by American composers. See: **W39g**

B685   Valdes, Lesley. "Conductor Litton Makes Debut with Phila. Orchestra at the Mann." *The Philadelphia Inquirer*, June 25, 1992, section d, p. 3.

A fairly substantial review of the Philadelphia Orchestra's June 24 concert, conducted by Andrew Litton. The first selection presented on the program was Schuman's *New England Triptych*. See: **W53bb**

B686   von Rhein, John. "De Waart Concert a Tale of 2 Nations." *Chicago Tribune*, March 14, 1987, Tempo section, p. 13.

An affirmative review of the March 12 concert presented by the Chicago Symphony Orchestra. The program, conducted by Edo de Waart, featured Schuman's Tenth Symphony. Describes the work as characteristic of the composer's mature style. See: **W79c**

B687   _____. "Recordings." *Chicago Tribune*, February 7, 1988, Arts section, p. 22.

A brief but excellent review of the Deutsche Grammophon release of the third symphonies of Roy Harris and William Schuman. See: **D82**

B688   _____. "Recordings." *Chicago Tribune*, October 15, 1989, Arts section, p. 25.

A perceptive and informative recording review of the EMI Angel issue of Schuman's Concerto for Violin and Bernstein's Serenade for Violin, Strings and Percussion. Proclaims Schuman's concerto "a masterpiece" and believes that this recording "should bring it the wide recognition it deserves." See: **D26**

B689   _____. "Basically the Best; An Accessible Guide to Music of the 20th Century." *Chicago Tribune*, October 29, 1989, Arts section, p. 10.

This list of recommended recordings includes the Deutsche Grammophon release (DG 419780-2) of the third symphonies of Roy Harris and William Schuman. "No collection of 20th Century American music should be without these archetypal symphonies; strong, stirring performances." See: **D82**

B690   _____. "Kiri Te Kanawa Shines in Her Auditorium Recital." *Chicago Tribune*, March 12, 1990, p. 16.

The second part of this review discusses a concert by the Chicago String Ensemble, conducted by Alan Heatherington. Schuman's *Symphony for Strings* was one of the featured works on the program. See: **W29k**

B691   _____. "Music — American Voices: New CDs Venture Beyond Tired
Symphonic Programs." *Chicago Tribune*, July 19, 1992, Arts section, p. 12.

This article, which reviews several new recordings, favorably describes three new
Schuman discs: RCA 61282, Delos 3115, and Koch 7135. See: **D6, D44, D56**

B692   Walsh, Michael. Review of William Schuman: *Three Colloquies for Horn and
Orchestra*, recorded by the New York Philharmonic, conducted by Zubin Mehta, with
Philip Myers, horn. *Time* 125 (June 24, 1985): 82.

This review is strongly critical of Schuman's composition, arguing that the work is a
rehash of the composer's musical style of the 1950s. Also takes Mehta to task for an
ineffectual interpretation. The New World Records recording is coupled with George
Crumb's *A Haunted Landscape*. New World NW 326. See: **D100**

B693   Webster, Daniel. "Music: The Opening Program by Frühbeck at the Academy." *The
Philadelphia Inquirer*, November 16, 1984, section d, p. 3.

Reviews the November 15 concert of the Philadelphia Orchestra, conducted by Rafael
Frühbeck de Burgos. Criticizes the conductor's interpretation of Schuman's *New
England Triptych*. See: **W531**

B694   _____. "Music: Artymiw, Two Composers Brighten Program." *The
Philadelphia Inquirer*, December 22, 1984, section c, p. 3.

Presents a review of the first Philadelphia performance of William Schuman's Eighth
Symphony on December 21, played by the Philadelphia Orchestra, conducted by
William Smith. "Smith led a firm reading of the Schuman symphony, a 20-year-old
work that sounds somber and insistent. . . . The orchestra was not on its best mettle in
this piece, blurring entrances and missing expressive markings in pursuit of broad
outline." Also on the program was the Chopin First Piano Concerto, played by Lydia
Artymiw, and Handel's Concerto Grosso (Op. 3, No. 5). See: **W60c**

B695   _____. "2 Contribute Music Written in the '80s." *The Philadelphia Inquirer*,
May 26, 1985, section h, p. 8.

In reviewing the New World NW 326 recording of Schuman's *Three Colloquies for
Horn*, Webster says, "The soloist is not presented as virtuoso, but (despite the
obvious difficulties of the writing) as thoughtful collaborator given to roaming in the
instrument's low and middle range with dramatic outbursts in the highest range."
See: **D100**

B696   _____. "A Return to the City for Slatkin." *The Philadelphia Inquirer*, July 8,
1987, section c, p. 4.

A very positive review of *New England Triptych* presented on the July 7 concert at the Mann Music Center by the Philadelphia Orchestra, with guest conductor Leonard Slatkin. Observes that "Schuman's music bursts with an invigorated optimism that may be inherent in Billings' hymn tunes, and the playing reinforced that affirmation." See: **W53r**

B697 _____. "A Piece by a Winning Composer." *The Philadelphia Inquirer*, April 28, 1990, section d, p. 3.

A review of the April 27 concert of the Philadelphia Orchestra, which included a work entitled *Island Prelude* by the prize winning composer Joan Tower. Also presented on the program, conducted by Leonard Slatkin, was Schuman's Third Symphony. See: **W22aa**

B698 _____. Review of William Schuman: *Prayer in Time of War* and *Symphony No. 4*, recorded by the Louisville Orchestra, conducted by Robert Whitney and Jorge Mester. *The Philadelphia Inquirer*, July 1, 1990, section h, p. 12.

A brief review of the Albany TROY 027-2 recording. Also contains Roy Harris's *When Johnny Comes Marching Home* and *Epilogue to Profiles in Courage: JFK* and John J. Becker's *Symphonia Brevis*. See: **D66**, **D84**

B699 _____. Review of William Schuman: *New England Triptych*, *Judith*, and *Symphony for Strings*, recorded by the Seattle Symphony Orchestra, conducted by Gerard Schwarz. *The Philadelphia Inquirer*, June 14, 1992, section g, p. 10.

Includes a review of the Delos 3115 compact disc recording entitled "Tribute to William Schuman." Argues that the *New England Triptych* performance is first rate and contends that *Judith* is an intensely emotional composition. See: **D44**, **D55**, **D88**

B700 _____. "A Rainy Season-Opener at the Mann." *The Philadelphia Inquirer*, June 23, 1993, section f, p. 2.

Reviews the June 21 concert by the Philadelphia Orchestra at the Mann Music Center. Schuman's arrangement of Ives's *Variations on "America"* was the opening selection of the evening. The conductor was Lawrence Foster. See: **W63g**

B701 Widder, Milton. "Cleveland." *The Musical Leader* 96 (March 1964): 10.

This report of musical activities in Cleveland contains a negative review of a Cleveland Orchestra performance of *A Song of Orpheus*, with cellist Leonard Rose. See: **W59d**

B702 Widder, Rose. "Cleveland." *Musical Courier* 155 (May 1957): 29.

Reviews a Cleveland Orchestra performance of *New England Triptych*. Following a short description of the work, Widder writes: "This is music of great appeal and fascinating construction. It was heartily applauded by the audience." See: **W53c**

B703 Wierzbicki, James. "St. Louis Symphony: Schuman 'American Hymn' [premiere]."
High Fidelity/Musical America 33 (February 1983): MA 31.

Presents a knowledgeable though generally unfavorable review of the 24 September
1982 premiere performance of *American Hymn: Orchestral Variations on an
Original Melody* by conductor Leonard Slatkin and the St. Louis Symphony
Orchestra. Argues that despite "evidence of the craftsmanship that has characterized
the music of the seventy-two year old Schuman," the composition is "not compelling
music." See: **W89a**

B704 _____. "St. Louis Symphony Gives Festive Bash at Powell." *St. Louis Post
Dispatch*, January 2, 1990, section a, p. 4.

Offers a review of the New Year's Eve Powell Hall performance, with Leonard
Slatkin conducting the St. Louis Symphony. Wierzbicki briefly mentions that the
orchestra played "William Schuman's richly comic 1963 arrangement of Charles Ives'
Variations on 'America.'" See: **W63c**

B705 _____. "Grand Opening . . . Symphony Shows No Hesitation on First Night."
St. Louis Post Dispatch, September 15, 1991, section b, p. 2.

This review of the September 13 concert by conductor Leonard Slatkin and the St.
Louis Symphony praises the orchestra's playing and notes that Schuman's *American
Festival Overture* opened the program. See: **W14r**

B706 _____. "Aimless Bluster in Schuman's Symphony." *St. Louis Post Dispatch*,
November 4, 1991, section a, p. 4.

Wierzbicki, in reviewing the November 2 concert of the St. Louis Symphony in
Powell Hall, takes exception to the St. Louis Symphony's program booklet naming
William Schuman "the Great American Symphonist." Calls Schuman's Tenth
Symphony, presented on the program, "bottom-of-the-barrel stuff" and goes on to
suggest that the composer's best works are his songs, choral works, and concert
overtures. Argues that one should look for "the Great American Symphonist" in the
works of Howard Hanson, Roy Harris, Roger Sessions, or Walter Piston. The concert
was conducted by Leonard Slatkin. See: **W79d**

B707 Williams, Arthur L. "The Band Stand . . . " *The School Musician* 28 (June 1957):
10, 52.

Reviews the first performance of the *Chester Overture* for band. See: **W50a**

B708 Wolffers, Jules. "Bostonians Premiere New Schuman Violin Concerto." *Musical
Courier* 141 (March 1, 1950): 22-23.

Provides a review of the premiere of Schuman's Concerto for Violin, played by
violinist Isaac Stern and the Boston Symphony Orchestra under Charles Munch.
Comments on the difficulty of the work and praises the virtuoso playing of Stern.
See: **W39a**

B709 Wolter, Richard Arthur. "A Description and Analysis of Selected Music Written for the Concert Band Performable by American High School Bands." M.A. thesis, Washington University, 1959. 130 pp.

Examines two of Schuman's compositions for band: *When Jesus Wept* (pp. 84-89) and *Chester* (pp. 90-92). After a rather superficial, descriptive analysis of the music, complete with musical examples, Wolter provides information on time of performance, level of difficulty, and instrumentation. Contains footnotes and a bibliography.

Works: Chamber Music

B710 Adam, Claus. Review of William Schuman: *String Quartet No. 4*. *Music Library Association Notes* 12 (March 1955): 324-25.

G. Schirmer's 1953 issue of the miniature score of this quartet receives a positive review in this article. Briefly relates the details concerning the commissioning of the work by the Elizabeth Sprague Coolidge Foundation and comments on performances and the Juilliard String Quartet recording. Touches upon an examination of the composition's four movements, remarking, for example, that the first movement contains "rhythm and melodic patterns [that] are unmistakably American."

B711 Bargreen, Melinda. "New & Notable." *The Seattle Times*, June 23, 1994, section e, p. 3.

Mentions a new Crystal Records release of Schuman's *Dances*, performed by the Westwood Wind Quintet and percussionist Matthew Kocmieroski. The disc also contains William Bergsma's Concerto for Wind Quintet and other selections. See: **D30**

B712 Bassett, Leslie. Review of William Schuman: *Quartettino for Four Bassoons*. *Music Library Association Notes* 15 (September 1958): 649.

Reviews a 1956 publication of the *Quartettino for Four Bassoons* score by Peer International. Questions whether the work will appeal to a broad range of musicians, yet remarks that teachers of bassoon will view it as a welcome addition to the literature.

B713 Blechner, Mark. "Chamber Music Society: Schuman Premiere." *High Fidelity/Musical America* 29 (March 1979): MA 20.

Begins by tracing the history of Schuman's usage of Shakespeare's poem "Orpheus with His Lute" in three compositions: the original song from the 1940s, *A Song of Orpheus* for cello and orchestra written in 1962, and its recent treatment by the composer in *In Sweet Music*. This article evaluates the premiere performance of *In Sweet Music* by the Chamber Music Society of Lincoln Center, the ensemble for which the work was composed. See: **W83a**

B714 Chase, William W. Review of William Schuman: *In Sweet Music, The Young Dead Soldiers*, and *Time to the Old*, recorded by Rosalind Rees and the Orpheus Trio, the White Mountains Festival Orchestra, and pianist Thomas Muraco. *The New Records* (August 1981): 10-11.

Considers the compositions on this CRI SD 439 recording "not on a par with Schuman's best work." Believes that *The Young Dead Soldiers* and *Time to the Old* are "well crafted," though "predictable," and observes the relationship between *In Sweet Music* and the composer's *A Song of Orpheus*. See: **D40, D105, D124**

B715 Chertok, Pearl. "Let Us Get Acquainted with Our Composers: Schuman and Mennin Write for Harp." *The American Harp Journal* 7, no. 1 (Summer 1979): 19.

Mentions that *In Sweet Music* was one of "two important new works" premiered at Lincoln Center. Furnishes information about the performance and remarks that "The work received excellent reviews." See: **W83a**

B716 Copland, Aaron. "Current Chronicle: New York." *The Musical Quarterly* 37 (July 1951): 394-96.

An influential and thorough review of Schuman's Fourth String Quartet written following the first New York performance of the work at a League of Composers concert. Claims that this composition is a watershed work for the composer and alludes to a possible influence stemming from the music of Roger Sessions. Examines the chamber piece from the standpoint of harmony, the composer's use of the instruments, and structure. See: **W44c, B717**

B717 _____. *Copland on Music*. Garden City, NY: Doubleday, 1960; reprint ed., New York: Da Capo, 1976. 285 pp. ISBN 0 306 70775 6 ML63 C48 1976

Includes a reprint (pp. 233-36) of Copland's well-known article on Schuman's Fourth String Quartet first published in the July 1951 issue of *The Musical Quarterly*. See: **B716**

B718 Creditor, Bruce. "Quintessence, The Wind Quintet Informant: No. 7." *The Clarinet* 16 (May-June 1989): 10.

A favorable and informative review of Schuman's *Dances*. Provides excellent background material and concludes that "Schuman's typical sweeping melodic lines and individual harmonic motion and voicings as well as a good measure of his 'brashness' are all present in this 'thank-you' piece."

B719 Dalheim, Eric L. "Record Reviews: Rosalind Rees Sings William Schuman." *American Music* (Spring 1983): 99-101.

A thoughtful review of the Composers Recording, Inc. (CRI SD 439) 1980 release of Rosalind Rees's performance of *In Sweet Music*, with the Orpheus Trio; *The Young Dead Soldiers*, with Robin Graham, french horn, and the White Mountains Festival Orchestra, conducted by Gerard Schwarz; and *Time to the Old*, with Thomas Muraco, piano. Dalheim argues that "*In Sweet Music* establishes for Schuman a firm position in the mainstream of twentieth-century vocal chamber music." He then goes on to say, about *The Young Dead Soldiers*, that "Schuman's individual way with expressive atonality and a lyrical vocal line thoroughly captures the elegiac essence of the poetry." Regarding *Time to the Old*, the reviewer observes that "Schuman's atonal writing is even more angular, but effectively appropriate for words that comment on the passage of time, the meaning of time, and living with the imminence of death. I find this intimate, short cycle a bit less ingratiating and less moving than the other pieces, though it does contain passages of ineffable beauty." See: **D40**, **D105**, **D124**

B720 Deane, James G. "Mrs. Coolidge Honored at Capital Festival." *Musical Courier* 142 (November 15, 1950): 3.

An account of performances associated with the chamber music series held at the Library of Congress observing the twenty-fifth anniversary of the Elizabeth Sprague Coolidge Foundation. Schuman's Fourth String Quartet was one of four works commissioned for the occasion. Deane believes the quartet to be "expertly fashioned" and "serious in vein." See: **W44a**

B721 Dickinson, Peter. Review of William Schuman: *String Quartet No. 2*, *String Quartet No. 3*, and *String Quartet No. 5*, recorded by the Lydian String Quartet. *The Gramophone* (August 1994): 70.

An informative recording review (Harmonia Mundi HMU 907114) which centers on the Fifth String Quartet. See: **D73**, **D77**, **D79**

B722 Downes, Olin. "Coolidge Quartet of Strings Heard." *The New York Times*, February 28, 1940, p. 16.

Reviews the 27 February 1940 Town Hall concert which introduced Schuman's Third String Quartet to the public for the first time. Believes that an accurate evaluation of the music can only be made in the future after further hearings of the work. See: **W19a**

B723 Dyer, Richard. "Horblit Concert Surveys Works of William Schuman." *Boston Globe*, October 7, 1980.

Reports on the 5 October Horblit Award Concert presented in honor of Schuman. Several compositions by the composer, including *In Sweet Music*, *The Young Dead Soldiers*, and *Time to the Old*, were performed. See: **W82c**, **W83b**, **W86b**

B724 _____. Review of William Schuman: *In Sweet Music*, *The Young Dead Soldiers*, and *Time to the Old*, recorded by Rosalind Rees and the Orpheus Trio, the White Mountains Festival Orchestra, and pianist Thomas Muraco. *Fanfare* (November-December 1981): 236-37.

The reviewer of this CRI SD 439 recording refers to Schuman as "arguably our most distinguished composer—in any event among the three or four most distinguished." Provides an insightful discussion of each of these works. See: **D40, D105, D124**

B725 Evett, Robert. "Current Chronicle: Washington, D.C." *The Musical Quarterly* 51 (April 1965): 406-09.

Reports on a performance of Schuman's *Amaryllis*, which was presented as part of the Coolidge Festival. Criticizes the composition for "the juxtaposition of tonal and nontonal materials" and applauds, however, "the seriousness of the piece and the brilliance of the string writing." See: **W64a**

B726 Grueninger, Walter F. Review of William Schuman: *In Sweet Music, The Young Dead Soldiers*, and *Time to the Old*, recorded by Rosalind Rees and the Orpheus Trio, the White Mountains Festival Orchestra, and pianist Thomas Muraco. *Consumers' Research Magazine* 64 (November 1981): 43.

Praises Schuman as one of America's best composers and commends Rees and the instrumentalists for their performances. Review of the CRI 439 recording. See: **D40, D105, D124**

* Henahan, Donal. "Chamber: Center Society."

Cited as **B168**.

* Holland, Bernard. "The Bottom Line in Tune."

Cited as **B177**.

B727 Ienni, Philip C. "Schuman Writes Bassoon Quartet." *Musical America* 77 (October 1957): 26.

Advertizes the publication of the *Quartettino for Four Bassoons* by Southern Music. Observes that the composition should be useful in the teaching of bassoon.

* Kingman, Daniel. *American Music: A Panorama*.

Cited as **B202**.

B728 Kolodin, Irving. "Quartet Gives Work by Schuman." *The New York Sun*, February 28, 1940, p. 25.

A negative review of the February 27 performance of Schuman's Third String Quartet given by the Coolidge Quartet at New York's Town Hall. See: **W19a**

B729 Kresh, Paul. Review of William Schuman: *In Sweet Music, The Young Dead Soldiers*, and *Time to the Old*, recorded by Rosalind Rees and the Orpheus Trio, White Mountains Festival Orchestra, and pianist Thomas Muraco. *Stereo Review* 46 (August 1981): 97-98.

Regards these three vocal compositions as among the composer's best works. Praises the sound quality of this CRI SD 439 recording. See: **D40, D105, D124**

B730 Lehman, Mark L. Review of William Schuman: *String Quartet No. 2, String Quartet No. 3*, and *String Quartet No. 5*, recorded by the Lydian Quartet. *The American Record Guide* (November-December 1994): 187-88.

An outstanding review of the recent Harmonia Mundi recording of these quartets. Offers an excellent discussion of these compositions and contends that the composer's "mature quartets are almost symphonic in their richness of sonority and breadth of statement." See: **D73, D77, D79**

B731 Lewando, Ralph. "New Works: William Schuman's Amarylis [*sic*]: Variations for String Trio." *Music Journal* 23 (September 1965): 88-89.

A short, descriptive account of the initial New York performance of Schuman's *Amaryllis*. The reviewer reports that Schuman's writing for each instrument is outstanding. See: **W64b**

B732 Lewis, Richard. "Composer's Showcase: William Schuman." *Musical America* 80 (March 1960): 33.

A performance review of a Composer's Showcase concert on February 1 featuring Schuman's Fourth String Quartet and choral selections by the composer presented by the Camerata Singers. According to the reviewer, Schuman's string quartet, played by the Lenox Quartet, "demands a great deal of its listeners, but gives much that is evocative and moving." See: **W44d**

* McLellan, Joseph. "Schuman's Flowing Talk and Music."

Cited as **B815**.

B733 Monson, Karen. Review of William Schuman: *In Sweet Music, The Young Dead Soldiers*, and *Time to the Old*, recorded by Rosalind Rees and the Orpheus Trio, the White Mountains Festival Orchestra, and pianist Thomas Muraco. *High Fidelity/Musical America (1980)* 31 (November 1981): 96-97.

Strongly criticizes Schuman's skill as a song composer. Argues that these works fail to achieve the kind of communication that one expects in the art song. Considers *Time to the Old* the best of the three, primarily praising the union of text and music. A review of the Composers Recording, Inc. issue, CRI SD 439. See: **D40, D105, D124**

B734 Page, Tim. "Chamber Music Society in Schuman Premiere." *The New York Times*, November 4, 1986, section 3, p. 14.

A somewhat cynical performance review of *Dances: Divertimento for Wind Quintet and Percussion*. Page begins his remarks with a statement which notes Schuman's skill as a composer, but he then goes on to conclude the statement with the opinion that "even when he seems to have nothing to say, he says it adeptly." See: **W94a**

B735 Persichetti, Vincent. "Modern American Music Series, Columbia Masterworks." *The Musical Quarterly* 40 (July 1954): 471-76.

An extended review of a number of significant recordings of chamber music by several American composers. Included is Schuman's String Quartet No. 4 performed by the Juilliard String Quartet on Columbia LP ML 4493. Persichetti states that the "String Quartet No. 4 is mature Schuman, exciting, fresh, and ingenious. It is a landmark both in his musical development and in contemporary chamber literature. This is Schuman of a wider harmonic palette and unfailing urgency." See: **D78**

B736 Porter, Andrew. "Musical Events." *The New Yorker* 63 (March 30, 1987): 104, 109-110.

Includes a brief mention (p. 110) of an Alice Tully Hall performance of Schuman's *Awake, Thou Wintry Earth*. Portrays this chamber work for clarinet and violin as being comprised of "two slight, agreeable movements." See: **W96a**

B737 Roos, James. "Composers Quartet Delivers Compelling World Premiere." *The Miami Herald*, September 20, 1986, section c, p. 4.

Reviews the September 19 performance of Schuman's Third String Quartet at the University of Miami by the Composers Quartet. See: **W19b**

B738 Schonberg, Harold C. "Concert Review." *The New York Times*, October 31, 1978, p. 49.

Reviews the Alice Tully Hall concert presented in celebration of the tenth anniversary of the Chamber Music Society of Lincoln Center. Comments on Schuman's *In Sweet Music*, which was played for the first time on this concert. See: **W83a**

B739 _____. "Chamber Music Society." *The New York Times*, November 6, 1978, p. 55.

Reports on the 29 October 1978 concert presented in honor of the tenth season of the Chamber Music Society of Lincoln Center. Schuman's *In Sweet Music*, one of several works played on this occasion, received its world premiere. Schonberg's response to the composer's new composition is generally negative, contending that Schuman's "inspiration seemed to give out after a short while." See: **W83a**

B740 Schultz, Herbert L. "William Schuman's 'In Sweet Music' (Serenade on a Setting of Shakespeare)." *Woodwind, Brass and Percussion* 20 (May-June 1981): 19.

Describes *In Sweet Music* as "a delightful chamber work of truly varied musical timbres." Discusses the scoring of the composition and the composer's directions given in the score.

B741 Silliman, A. Cutler. "A Study of Musical Practices in Selected American String Quartets, 1930-1950." Ph.D. dissertation, University of Rochester, 1954. 215 pp. ML95.3 S584

Investigates in depth the musical language demonstrated in nineteen American string quartets written between 1930 and 1950, analyzing various structural devices and procedures having to do with harmony, cadences, texture, counterpoint, and form. This study is replete with musical examples from quartets by Samuel Barber, William Bergsma, Ross Lee Finney, Roy Harris, Walter Piston, Quincy Porter, Wallingford Riegger, Roger Sessions, Randall Thompson, and William Schuman (String Quartets 2 and 3).

B742 Simmons, Walter. Review of William Schuman: *String Quartet No. 2*, *String Quartet No. 3*, and *String Quartet No. 5*, recorded by the Lydian String Quartet. *Fanfare* (July 1994): 234-36.

Simmons expresses the view that Schuman's string quartets are representative of each of the composer's different style periods. Presents substantial background information related to the five string quartets and argues that the Fourth String Quartet, not presented on this Harmonia Mundi disc, is the most distinguished of Schuman's quartets. See: **D73, D77, D79**

B743 Slonimsky, Nicolas. "Chamber Music in America." *Cobbett's Cyclopedic Survey of Chamber Music*, edited by Walter Willson Cobbett. 2nd ed. London: Oxford University Press, 1963. Vol. 3, pp. 152-93.

Slonimsky's essay contains discussion (pp. 157-58) of Schuman's second and fourth string quartets.

B744 Smith, Cecil. "Coolidge Festival Silver Anniversary Honors Benefactor." *Musical America* 70 (November 15, 1950): 3, 6, 37.

A substantial review of the Coolidge Festival held on October 28, 29, and 30 in Washington, D.C. Schuman's Fourth String Quartet was one of the works commissioned for the festival. In discussing the performance of the composition by the Hungarian String Quartet, Smith states that "The new quartet is one of the strongest and most consistently wrought of Schuman's recent works." See: **W44a**

B745 Sparber, Gordon. "Charming Winds of Expertise." *The Washington Post*, May 1, 1990, section d, p. 10.

Reviews a concert by the Capitol Woodwind Quintet, which presented a performance of Schuman's *Dances*. See: **W94b**

B746   Thorpe, Day. "Washington, D.C./Coolidge Festival." *Musical America* 84 (December 1964): 64.

In this review of a Washington performance of Schuman's *Amaryllis* for string trio, Thorpe states that "The writing for strings is extraordinarily sensitive, the whole piece is very moving, and Mr. Schuman has provided ambitious string trios with what they have heretofore lacked—a companion piece for the Mozart Divertimento in E flat." See: **W64a**

Works: Choral Music

B747   Armstrong, Donald Jan. "A Study of Some Important Twentieth Century Secular Compositions for Women's Chorus with a Preliminary Discussion of Secular Choral Music from a Historical and Philosophical Viewpoint." D.M.A. dissertation, University of Texas at Austin, 1969. 215 pp. UM Order No. 69-15776 ML1506 A75 1987

Following an introduction, this study consists of three parts (each with several chapters): I. "A Preliminary Discussion of Secular Choral Music with Specific Attention to Composition for the Women's Chorus;" II. "A Discussion of Some Important Twentieth Century Compositions for Women's Chorus;" and III. "A Discussion of the Preparation and Performance of the Foregoing Compositions." Analyzes Schuman's *Prelude* (1939) in Chapter 7 (pp. 85-89), located in Part II. Contains a summation, bibliography, footnotes, and musical examples.

B748   Bialosky, Marshall. Review of William Schuman: *Carols of Death*, *Perceptions*, and *Te Deum*. *The Sonneck Society Bulletin* 18 (Spring 1992): 38-39.

Compares the choral writing of Schuman to that of Leo Sowerby and criticizes Schuman's choral style for being more orchestral than choral. Suggests that *Carols of Death* "does have a certain scope and breadth and modern tautness absent in Sowerby's music." This compact disc (Bay Cities BCD 1022, 1990) contains choral selections, all performed by the Chorale of Roberts Wesleyan College, by three American composers: Leo Sowerby, William Schuman, and Stephen Shewan. See: **D11**, **D64**, **D99**

B749   Boyer, D. Royce. Review of William Schuman: *Carols of Death*, recorded by The New York Virtuoso Singers, conducted by Harold Rosenbaum. *The Sonneck Society Bulletin* 19 (Summer 1993): 41.

Favorably reports on a 1992 compact disc recording (CRI 615) of choral works by American and European twentieth-century composers. Included is Schuman's *Carols of Death*, which is considered by the reviewer to be a pivotal composition in the composer's career. See: **D12**

B750   Carrington, Mark. "King's College's Heavenly Airs." *The Washington Post*, September 18, 1991, section b, p. 2.

Reviews a performance at the Washington Cathedral by the Choir of King's College, Cambridge, directed by Stephen Cleobury, which included Schuman's *Carols of Death*. See: **W54g**

*   Carter, Elliott. "Coolidge Crusade; WPA; New York Season."

Cited as **B450**.

B751   Copland, Aaron. "Scores and Records." *Modern Music* 15, no. 4 (1937-38): 244-48.

A valuable early review in which Copland investigates a large collection of musical scores and recordings, ranging from such well-known composers as Roger Sessions, Roy Harris, and Ralph Vaughan Williams to less-recognized composers like Nicholas Nabokoff and Robert McBride. In discussing Schuman's choral work *Pioneers*, Copland lavishes great praise on its composer. "Schuman is, so far as I am concerned, the musical find of the year. There is nothing puny or miniature about this young man's talent. If he fails he will fail on a grand scale. . . . From the testimony of this piece alone, it seems to me that Schuman is a composer who is going places."

B752   Davis, Peter G. "Music: The American Way." *New York* 19 (17 November 1986): 90-91.

Following a spate of compliments, this fairly substantial performance review of *On Freedom's Ground* judges Schuman's cantata to be devoid of communication. The author defers to Virgil Thomson's opinion of Schuman's music, which was published in a 1945 *New York Herald Tribune* article. See: **W95a**

B753   Dickinson, Peter. Review of William Schuman: *Carols of Death*, recorded by the Choir of King's College, Cambridge, conducted by Stephen Cleobury. *The Gramophone* (October 1991): 182.

Compares Schuman's settings of Whitman's text to settings by Vaughan Williams and Holst. A recording review of an EMI disc. See: **D14**

B754   Gresham, Mark. "The Choral Legacy of William Schuman." *Chorus* 4 (July 1992): 3.

Surveys the choral music of Schuman from 1933 to *On Freedom's Ground* of 1985. Argues that two of the composer's choral compositions stand as watershed works in his career: *A Free Song* of 1942 and *Carols of Death* of 1958. Observes the predominance of English texts in Schuman's catalog. Valuable for a chronological listing of Schuman's choral works which concludes the article.

B755   Griffin, Malcolm Joseph. "Style and Dimension in the Choral Works of William Schuman." D.M.A. dissertation, University of Illinois, 1972. 191 pp. UM Order No. 72-19835

A thorough examination of Schuman's choral music. The first chapter presents pertinent biographical information related to the choral works. The second chapter, which is the heart of the study, analyzes twenty of the composer's compositions for chorus. The final chapter offers the author's conclusions. Contains musical examples, footnotes, bibliography, and an appendix.

B756 _____. "William Schuman's *Carols of Death*: An Analysis." *The Choral Journal* 17 (February 1977): 17-18.

Stresses the relationship between text and music in Schuman's choral music. Studies two of the three *Carols of Death*: "The Last Invocation" and "To All, to Each." Identifies five idiosyncrasies found in the former composition, ranging from the designation of characteristic motives to the recognition by measures of counterpoint in contrary motion. Divides the examination of the latter composition into two parts, each emphasizing different aspects of the piece.

B757 Guregian, Elaine. "Orchestra Plays Winning Ballgame." *The Akron Beacon Journal*, August 12, 1991, section c, p. 4.

Guregian reviews an August 10 concert by the Cleveland Orchestra at the Blossom Music Center. According to the reviewer, Schuman's *Casey at the Bat*, conducted by Leonard Slatkin, "was the big piece of the evening." See: **W81d**

B758 _____. "King's College Choir Performance: Solid, But Too Stolid." *The Akron Beacon Journal*, September 7, 1991, section c, p. 4.

Reports on a September 5 performance at the College of Wooster of Schuman's *Carols of Death*. The work was presented as part of a concert by the King's College Choir, conducted by Stephen Cleobury. See: **W54f**

* Holland, Bernard. "The Bottom Line in Tune."

Cited as **B177**.

B759 Johnson, Bret. Review of William Schuman: *Carols of Death*, *Te Deum*, and *Perceptions*, recorded by the Roberts Wesleyan College Chorale, conducted by Robert Shewan. *Tempo* 178 (September 1991): 57, 59.

Johnson contends, in this compact disc (Bay Cities BCD 1022) review, that the *Carols of Death* are "deservedly famous." See: **D11**, **D64**, **D99**

B760 Kleiman, Dena. "A Final Concert Is Set for Liberty Centennial." *The New York Times*, September 18, 1986, section 3, p. 20.

An announcement of the forthcoming October 28 concert at Avery Fisher Hall to be presented in honor of the one hundredth anniversary of the Statue of Liberty. Notes that Schuman's new cantata, *On Freedom's Ground*, will be premiered on this occasion and provides brief information about the work. See: **W95a**

B761 Kosman, Joshua. "Choral Artists' 20th Century Highs and Lows." *San Francisco Chronicle*, January 15, 1990, section f, p. 4.

Reviews a performance of Schuman's *Carols of Death* by the San Francisco Choral Artists.

* Kresh, Paul. Review of William Schuman: *Concerto on Old English Rounds*, recorded by the New York Philharmonic Orchestra and the Camerata Singers, conducted by Leonard Bernstein, with Donald McInnes, viola.

Cited as **B559**.

B762 McCurdy, Charles. "Music: Concert by Choir." *The Philadelphia Inquirer*, March 5, 1984, section e, p. 3.

Notes a March 4 performance of Schuman's *A Free Song*, presented by Singing City and conductor Elaine Brown. See: **W25e**

B763 MacDonald, Calum. "Recordings." *Tempo* 101 (July 1972): 56.

An unenthusiastic review of a recording (Everest SDBR 3129) of Schuman's *Carols of Death*, performed by the Gregg Smith Singers. The disc also includes Copland's *In the Beginning* and Barber's *Reincarnation*. See: **D10**

* McLellan, Joseph. "William Schuman's Vivid Vocal Works."

Cited as **B846**.

B764 _____. "The NSO, All American; An Admirable Season Opener." *The Washington Post*, September 18, 1987, section d, p. 1.

Contains a review of the Washington premiere of Schuman's cantata *On Freedom's Ground*, presented by the National Symphony Orchestra under Mstislav Rostropovich. Regards the work as "nearly the ideal celebratory cantata . . . instantly comprehensible and enjoyable." See: **W95b**

B765 Mize, Lou Stem. "A Study of Selected Choral Settings of Walt Whitman Poems." Ph.D. dissertation, Florida State University, 1967. 165 pp. UM Order No. 68-369 ML80 W48 M6

Investigates the choral settings of Whitman's poems by four American composers: Norman Dello Joio, Howard Hanson, Roy Harris, and William Schuman. The sixth chapter (pp. 114-39), devoted to a discussion of Schuman, is divided into five sections: Schuman and Whitman, *Pioneers*, *A Free Song*, *Carols of Death*, and a summary. Includes numerous musical examples, footnotes, and a bibliography.

B766 Moremen, Ray; Pooler, Frank; Rubsamen, Walter; Salamunovich, Paul; and Zearott, Michael. "In Quest of Answers: An Interview with William Schuman." *The Choral Journal* 13 (February 1973): 5-15.

A thought-provoking interview, conducted by a panel of five distinguished choral musicians, from the point of view of choral music in general and Schuman's choral music specifically. See: **B767**

B767 _____. "In Quest of Answers: An Interview with William Schuman." *The Choral Journal* 33 (February 1993): 52-53.

Reprints a portion of the interview originally published by *The Choral Journal* twenty years earlier. See: **B766**

B768 "New Composition for Statue of Liberty Rededication." *The Sonneck Society Newsletter* 12 (Spring 1986): 32.

Reports that Schuman's *On Freedom's Ground*, composed for the centennial celebration of the Statue of Liberty, will be presented for the first time on October 28. Provides brief comments about the cantata by the composer. See: **W95a**

* Paris, Robert. "National Sym: Schuman Prems."

Cited as **B599**.

B769 Pisciotta, Louis Vincent. "Texture in the Choral Works of Selected Contemporary American Composers." Ph.D. dissertation, Indiana University, 1967. 411 pp. UM Order No. 68-7253 ML 1511 P572

Divided into twelve chapters, this dissertation presents a thorough examination of musical texture in the choral works of ten composers. Chapter ten (pp. 311-42), devoted entirely to William Schuman, analyzes eight choral works composed between 1937 and 1959. Framing the principal body of the work is an opening chapter on the objectives, scope, and procedures of the study and a concluding chapter on a summary of the investigation. Footnotes, bibliography, appendix, and numerous musical examples.

B770 "Premieres: *On Freedom's Ground*." *The American Organist* 20 (November 1986): 47.

On October 28, the premiere performance of *On Freedom's Ground*, written for the centennial celebration of the Statue of Liberty, was presented featuring baritone Sherrill Milnes, the Crane Chorus, and Zubin Mehta conducting the New York Philharmonic Orchestra. This review records that the work was commissioned jointly by several orchestras, among them the New York Philharmonic and the Crane School of Music of Potsdam College. See: **W95a**

B771 Reiter, Susan. "Music for Miss Liberty." *Ovation* 7 (June 1986): 28-29, 31.

Describes the musical events planned for the celebration of the Statue of Liberty's centennial. Offers fairly extensive discussion about Schuman's cantata *On Freedom's Ground*, planned for a premiere performance on 28 October 1986, exactly one hundred years after the dedication of the statue. Prints several quotations by the composer about the genesis of the work. See: **W95a**

B772 Renzelman, Gary Eugene. "A Stylistic Analysis and Comparison of the A Cappella Choral Music for Mixed Voices by Three Contemporary American Composers: Aaron Copland, William Schuman, Randall Thompson." M.A. thesis, University of California at Los Angeles, 1960.

B773 Robertson, Nan. "Nixons Attend Concert at Kennedy Hall." *The New York Times*, September 10, 1971, p. 40.

Reports on a gala National Symphony Orchestra concert celebrating the opening of the Kennedy Center Concert Hall, at which Schuman's cantata *A Free Song* was performed. The composer and his wife joined the president's party in the presidential box. See: **W25d**

B774 _____. "A Musical Collaboration in Homage to America." *The New York Times*, January 2, 1986, section 3, p. 16.

Written in advance of the forthcoming premiere performance of *On Freedom's Ground* on 28 October 1986, this article carefully looks at Schuman's new cantata composed in honor of the centennial celebration of the Statue of Liberty. Suggests that the consortium of musical institutions to sponsor this work represents "the largest group of musical organizations ever to participate in such a commission." Comments on the composition's individual movements and devotes a substantial portion of the article to the working relationship between the composer and the poet, Richard Wilbur. See: **W95a**

B775 Robison, Richard W. "Reading Contemporary Choral Literature: An Analytical Study of Selected Contemporary Choral Compositions with Recommendations for the Improvement of Choral Reading Skills." Ph.D. dissertation, Brigham Young University, 1969. 363 pp. UM Order No. 70-4721 MT870 R62 1987

Schuman's "The Last Invocation," from *Carols of Death*, is one of several compositions examined in this treatise. Discussion of the work is found in Chapter 4 (pp. 203-13) and Chapter 5 (pp. 307-20). Seven tables helpfully present the following aspects of analysis: Form, Rhythmic Features and Related Skills, Melodic-Pitch Features and Related Skills, Harmonic Features and Related Skills, Rhythmic Skills and Related Learning Procedures, Melodic-Pitch Skills and Related Learning Procedures, and Harmonic Skills and Related Learning Procedures. Provides footnotes, musical examples, bibliography, appendixes, tables, and plates.

B776 Rockwell, John. "Music: Liberty Potpourri." *The New York Times*, November 2, 1986, p. 78.

Pans Schuman's new cantata, *On Freedom's Ground*, as a work generally devoid of meaningful musical ideas. Believes that the composition achieves its finest moments in the instrumental interludes. See: **W95a**

B777 Rogers, Emmy Brady. "New Works: Colorado." *Music Journal* 24 (June 1966): 63.

A performance review of Jerald Lepinski's Classic Chorale concert at the Colorado Women's College on April 20. Schuman's *Carols of Death* were presented on this program. See: **W54b**

* Rosenfeld, Paul. "Current Chronicle: Copland-Harris-Schuman."

Cited as **B631**.

B778 Sabin, Robert. "Twentieth-Century Americans." *Choral Music*, edited by Arthur Jacobs. Baltimore: Penguin, 1963; reprint ed., New York: Penguin, 1978, pp. 370-86. ISBN 0 140 20533 0 ML1500

Credits Schuman as being "the most original and forceful of twentieth-century American choral composers thus far." Explores the "many seemingly contradictory qualities" of the composer's musical style. Furnishes a brief but provocative discussion of several of Schuman's choral compositions, particularly the cantata *A Free Song*.

* "76 Bicentennial Report."

Cited as **B656**.

B779 Siebert, F. Mark. Review of William Schuman: *The Lord Has a Child*. *Music Library Association Notes* 17 (June 1960): 474-75.

In this review of several recently published sacred choral works, Siebert refers to Schuman's atypical harmonic progressions in *The Lord Has a Child*.

B780 Slonimsky, Nicolas. "Composers' Forum Opens Music Week." *The New York Times*, May 8, 1939, p. 20.

Review of a concert, featuring Alexander Smallens and Alexander Richter conducting the Federal Symphony Orchestra of New York, presented under the auspices of the Composers Forum Laboratory, in which five compositions were performed: Paul Nordoff's *Concerto for Two Pianos*, Walter Piston's *Concertino for Piano and Chamber Orchestra*, Roy Harris's Second Symphony, Aaron Copland's *An Outdoor Overture*, and William Schuman's *Prologue* for chorus and orchestra. Considers the Schuman and Harris works the most important and, in discussing the Schuman composition, remarks that "Mr. Schuman is forging to the front among native composers of the day." See: **W17a**

B781 Spaeth, Jeanne. "Gregg Smith Singers." *The Washington Post*, December 7, 1992, section b, p. 2.

Notes a performance of Schuman's *Orpheus with His Lute* by the Gregg Smith Singers at George Mason University. Observes that the work was "performed with precision and impressive vocal blending."

B782 "Stadium Launches Its Twenty-Third Outdoor Season." *Musical America* 60 (July 1940): 3, 6, 27.

Alexander Smallens conducted the People's Philharmonic Choral Society and the New York Philharmonic in the premiere performance at Lewisohn Stadium on July 4 of Schuman's cantata *This Is Our Time*. In addition to including remarks concerning the performers, the reviewer provides a cursory analysis of the composition. See: **W20a**

B783 Straus, Noel. "Composers' Forum Opens Music Week." *The New York Times*, May 8, 1939, p. 20.

Discusses the notable 7 May 1939 Composers Forum Laboratory concert at Carnegie Hall which presented works by five American composers, all Guggenheim Fellows in Composition. Contends that the premiere of Schuman's *Prologue* for chorus and orchestra was extremely successful. Argues that "There was a clarity of line, a transparency in every phrase of this richly promising piece of writing that showed how rapidly Mr. Schuman is forging to the front among native composers of the day." See: **W17a**

B784 Thomson, Virgil. "Superficially Warlike." *New York Herald Tribune*, April 4, 1943.

A performance review of a Boston Symphony Orchestra concert which included the first New York performance of Schuman's *A Free Song*. See: **W25b**

B785 _____. "University Festival." *New York Herald Tribune*, May 4, 1947.

Reports on a music festival, which included a performance of Schuman's *Requiescat,* at Fisk University, held in honor of the acquisition by that institution of the George Gershwin Memorial Collection of Music and Musical Literature. See: **W27b**

B786 Valdes, Lesley. "New York Philharmonic: Schuman 'On Freedom's Ground' [premiere]." *Musical America* 107 (May 1987): 49-50.

A sententious review of a 28 October 1986 performance of Schuman's cantata *On Freedom's Ground*, written for the centennial celebration of the Statue of Liberty. After thoughtful remarks on Richard Wilbur's text, Valdes praises the work of the composer, remarking that "it is honest music that the distinguished Schuman, now 75, has composed." See: **W95a**

B787 von Rhein, John. "Slatkin, CSO Team Up to Give All-American Salute to Music." *Chicago Tribune*, November 13, 1987, Chicagoland section, p. 10.

Contends, in this review of the first Chicago performance of *On Freedom's Ground*, that Schuman's composition "is in many ways a musical embodiment of that same American vigor and optimism, a spirit that seems to burn almost as brightly in the recent works of our musical elder statesman as in the works he composed in his younger years." See: **W95c**

B788 _____. "Chorale Celebrates with Custom-Tailored Flourishes." *Chicago Tribune*, March 29, 1992, Tempo section, p. 4.

A positive review of a March 27 concert by the William Ferris Chorale, which included "William Schuman's stirring Te Deum Laudamus." See: **W35b**

B789 _____. "William Ferris Chorale Heads to Ballpark with a Concert Dedicated to Bill Veeck." *Chicago Tribune*, February 13, 1994, Tempo section, p. 5.

Reviews a February 11 concert, which included a performance of Schuman's cantata *Casey at the Bat,* of the William Ferris Chorale. See: **W81e**

B790 Webster, Albert K. "Schuman's Latest Commission: Amending the Record." *Symphony Magazine* 36, no. 4 (1985): 14.

A response in the form of a letter to the editor to a letter published in the October/November issue in this same journal by Lisa M. Cania regarding Schuman's *On Freedom's Ground*. Corrects Cania in terms of the institutions involved in the commissioning of the work. Notes the forthcoming performance of the composition on 28 October 1986 in Avery Fisher Hall. See: **W95a**

B791 Wierzbicki, James. "Review: Classical Music, Beautiful Sounds Soar Forth from Two Choruses." *St. Louis Post Dispatch*, March 15, 1988, section d, p. 5.

Reviews a performance of Schuman's *Carols of Death* on March 13 in Powell Hall, with Thomas Peck conducting the St. Louis Symphony Chorus. See: **W54d**

Works: Ballet

B792 Belfy, Jeanne Marie. "The Commissioning Project of the Louisville Orchestra, 1948-1958: A Study of the History and Music." Ph.D. dissertation, The University of Kentucky, 1986. 266 pp. UM Order No. 8801958

The definitive account of the Louisville commissioning project. Clarification of the significance of Schuman's *Judith* to the project is advanced in this dissertation. Divides, in chapter two, the discussion of *Judith* into three subsections: "The *Judith* Episode," "Description of *Judith: A Choreographic Poem*," and "Conclusions Regarding the Impact of *Judith*." Contains a bibliography and a large supplement of appendixes. See: **B793**

B793 _____. "*Judith* and the Louisville Orchestra: The Rest of the Story." *College Music Symposium* 31 (1991): 36-48.

Sheds light on the polemic surrounding the importance of the first performances of *Judith* in Louisville and in New York City to the financial and artistic stability of the Louisville Orchestra. Maintains, predicated on well-documented events prior to the 1949-50 season, that *Judith*, while a pivotal work in the orchestra's history, was not the reason the orchestra was saved. Based upon the author's 1986 University of Kentucky Ph.D. dissertation. See: **W42a, W42b, B792**

B794 Berger, Arthur. "Spotlight on the Moderns." *Saturday Review* 34 (September 29, 1951): 60-61.

Discusses new recordings of compositions by several important twentieth-century composers. Two recordings of Schuman works are considered: *Judith* and *Undertow* (Mercury MG 10088) and the Third Symphony (Columbia LP 4413). Describes, partly in a derogatory fashion, the serious tone present in much of Schuman's music and observes a new musical style in *Judith*. See: **D41, D80, D107**

B795 Bergsma, William. Review of William Schuman: *Judith*. *Music Library Association Notes* 8 (June 1951): 564.

Views *Judith* as a watershed composition in Schuman's career, interpreting it as "a rhetorical work, in which formal interest is greater than the musical communication," yet, at the same time, finding that it conveys restrained emotion. Provides a succinct, though valuable, analysis which concludes that the work is very accessible. Ranks *Judith* among the finest of contemporary scores. This perceptive review was written in response to the 1950 G. Schirmer publication of the study score.

B796 Birkhead, Carole C. "The History of the Orchestra in Louisville." M.A. thesis, University of Louisville, 1977. 184 pp. ML200.8 L82 O7 1977

Traces the history of orchestras in Louisville, Kentucky, from the early 1840s to 1977. Chapter seven discusses Schuman's *Judith*.

* Broder, Nathan. "Reviews of Records."

Cited as **B436**.

B797 Canby, Edward Tatnall. Review of William Schuman: *Judith* and *Undertow*, recorded by the Louisville Orchestra, conducted by Robert Whitney. *Saturday Review* (December 8, 1951): 45.

A short recording review of the Mercury LP. Considers both Schuman scores "intense" and "dramatically violent." See: **D41, D107**

B798 Croan, Robert. "Rhythm Strength: Maazel's Mastery Ties Three Pieces into One Package." *Pittsburgh Post-Gazette*, October 1, 1993, Entertainment section, p. 20.

Discusses the September 31 Pittsburgh premiere of Schuman's *Judith* by the Pittsburgh Symphony. Praises the conducting of Lorin Maazel and lauds the music of the ballet score. See: **W42d**

B799 Dickinson, Peter. Review of William Schuman: *Night Journey*, recorded by the Atlantic Sinfonietta, conducted by Andrew Schenck. *The Gramophone* 69 (April 1992): 43.

Dickinson's recording review (Koch International 37051-2) argues that *Night Journey* "was a breakthrough work for Schuman" and concludes by noting that Schuman was an important American composer who deserves to be remembered. Speculates that Schuman's ballet was composed as a reaction to Copland's *Appalachian Spring*. See: **D60**

B800 Fine, Irving. "Reviews of Records. Copland: *Billy the Kid* (Ballet Suite); Schuman: *Undertow, Choreographic Episodes for Orchestra.*" *The Musical Quarterly* 40 (October 1954): 622-24.

Review of a recording of the symphonic version of *Undertow* (Capitol P-8238), with Joseph Levine conducting the Ballet Theatre Orchestra. Despite admitting to an unpleasant initial experience with the work, Fine now praises the composition as "a very exciting piece, remarkably successful in form and far more symphonic in character than is usual with ballet scores." See: **D108**

B801 Goldman, Richard Franko. "Current Chronicle: New York." *The Musical Quarterly* 37 (April 1951): 254-60.

Concert review of a New York performance of newly commissioned works by the Louisville Orchestra, which included Schuman's *Judith*. Examines the musical style of *Judith* in some detail. Concludes "that *Judith* seems one of the most wholly satisfactory of Schuman's scores." See: **W42b**

B802 Grueninger, Walter F. Review of William Schuman: *Judith*, recorded by the Eastman Philharmonic Orchestra, conducted by David Effron; *Night Journey*, recorded by the Endymion Ensemble, conducted by Jon Goldberg. *Consumers' Research Magazine* 68 (September 1985): 43.

A briefly stated review of the CRI 500 issue on compact disc. Characterizes Schuman's music as "cosmopolitan" and "well-crafted." See: **D43**, **D59**

B803 Hall, David. Review of William Schuman: *Judith* and *Night Journey*, recorded by the Eastman Philharmonia, conducted by David Effron (*Judith*); and the Endymion Ensemble, conducted by Jon Goldberg. *Ovation* 6 (August 1985): 35.

An informative and complimentary review (CRI SD 500). Discusses and compares the two scores prepared for Martha Graham; reports on the history of recordings for both works. Hall convincingly argues that "*Judith* is by far the most impressive of the two scores, not only by virtue of its sheer brilliance and drama, but because . . . it finds Schuman adding to his already impressive orchestral and rhythmic prowess an element of harmonic flexibility that has remained an integral part of his musical language." See: **D43, D59**

B804 Hart, Philip. *Orpheus in the New World.* New York: W.W. Norton, 1973. 562 pp. ISBN 0 393 02169 6 ML1211 H3

A valuable study of the symphony orchestra in the United States. Includes, in the chapter on the Louisville Orchestra, discussion (pp. 192-93) of Schuman's *Judith.*

B805 Joiner, Thomas Witherington. "A History and Analysis of the Repertoire of the Louisville Orchestra Seasons 1937-38 to 1977-78." Master's thesis, Southern Baptist Theological Seminary, 1978.

B806 Kay, Alfred. "New 'Peter and Wolf' a Visual Delight: ABT Unveils Enchanted Premiere of Classic Tale During Abbreviated Season in S.F." *The Sacramento Bee*, January 20, 1992, section d, p. 8.

Negatively reviews a January 18 San Francisco performance of Schuman's *Undertow* by the American Ballet Theatre. See: **W37f**

B807 Kennedy, Steven A. Review of William Schuman: *Night Journey*, recorded by The Atlantic Sinfonietta, conducted by Andrew Schenck. *The Sonneck Society Bulletin* 18 (Summer 1992): 85-86.

The reviewer criticizes Schuman's *Night Journey* for its undue length, recorded here using the original ballet score rather than the briefer 1980 concert version. Contends that the "neo-Baroque orchestral choir writing, typical of Schuman's style, does not come across well with chamber forces." This 1991 compact disc also includes Menotti's *Errand into the Maze* and Hindemith's *Hérodiade*. See: **D60**

B808 Kosman, Joshua. "Chamber Group's 'Night' Program." *San Francisco Chronicle*, January 23, 1988, section c, p. 8.

Reviews the January 21 concert of the San Francisco Chamber Orchestra, conducted by William McGlaughlin. Included on the program was Schuman's *Night Journey*, which, according to Kosman, was in Schuman's "characteristically bland, unobjectionable style." See: **W90c**

B809 Kroeger, Karl. Review of William Schuman: *Judith, A Choreographic Poem for Orchestra*, recorded by the Eastman Philharmonia Orchestra, conducted by David Effron; *Night Journey, Choreographic Poem for 15 Instruments*, recorded by the Endymion Ensemble, conducted by Jon Goldberg. *The Sonneck Society Bulletin* 13 (Spring 1987): 32.

Considers these performances on CRI SD 500 "definitive." Contends that "Schuman's music has maintained over the years a remarkable (some might say distressing) stability of sound and utterance." See: **D43**, **D59**

B810 Krokover, Rosalyn. "Martha Graham—Indomitable." *High Fidelity/Musical America* 16 (January 1966): 142.

Contains a derogatory discussion of *The Witch of Endor*. Declares that Schuman's music for the ballet does not enhance the production. Reflects that the composition "moved relentlessly along in a narrow dynamic range, desperately avoiding anything resembling a melodic line." See: **W66a**

B811 Kuppenheim, Hans F. "Martha Graham Dances in Louisville Premiere." *Musical Courier* 141 (February 15, 1950): 35.

Extols the dancing of Martha Graham and the music of Schuman's *Judith* in this review of the January 4 world premiere by the Louisville Orchestra. "The music is tragic, somber, highly emotional, full of tension and of beautiful melodies, and abounds in technical difficulties." See: **W42a**

B812 Laney, Maurice Ivan. "Thematic Material and Developmental Techniques in Selected Contemporary Compositions." Ph.D. dissertation, Indiana University, 1964. 211 pp. UM Order No. 64-12050

This study includes an examination of Schuman's *Judith: A Choreographic Poem* (pp. 27-43).

B813 Lockwood, Normand. Review of William Schuman: *Undertow, Choreographic Episodes for Orchestra*. *Music Library Association Notes* 4 (June 1947): 362.

A lucid review of Schuman's concert version of the ballet score, published by G. Schirmer in 1946. Argues that Schuman's work is "positive and exciting" and applauds the composer for his skill in orchestration.

B814 Luten, C.J. Review of William Schuman: *Judith* and *Undertow*, recorded by the Louisville Orchestra, conducted by Robert Whitney (*Judith*) and William Schuman (*Undertow*). *The American Record Guide* (September 1951): 16.

Argues that violence is a salient feature of the composer's ballets. Believes that "Both scores . . . are made well, sound well, and are wholly suited to their purposes." A recording review of Mercury's MG 10088 disc. See: **D41**, **D107**

B815 McLellan, Joseph. "Schuman's Flowing Talk and Music." *The Washington Post*, May 19, 1983, section o, p. 1.

"After a superb concert of his music last night, William Schuman relaxed and chatted with his audience in the Terrace Theater." Among several compositions presented on the program were *Night Journey*, performed by the Peabody Contemporary Music Ensemble, conducted by Frederik Prausnitz, and *In Sweet Music*, performed by soprano Rosalind Rees, flutist Carol Wincenc, violist Donald McInnes, and harpist Susan Jolles. See: **W83c, W90b**

B816 Miller, Karl F. Review of William Schuman: *Night Journey*, recorded by the Atlantic Sinfonietta, conducted by Andrew Schenck. *The American Record Guide* (January-February 1992): 144.

Regards *Night Journey* as one of Schuman's "most introspective works" and reflects that the composer "produced a stark score of unnerving intensity." Highly recommends this Koch 37051 disc. See: **D60**

B817 Miller, Philip L. Review of William Schuman: *Judith* and *Undertow*, recorded by the Louisville Orchestra, conducted by Robert Whitney and William Schuman; *Symphony No. 3*, recorded by the Philadelphia Orchestra, conducted by Eugene Ormandy. *Library Journal* 77 (April 1, 1952): 585.

Contains a recording review of Mercury MG 10088 and Columbia ML 4413. See: **D41, D80, D107**

B818 North, James H. Review of William Schuman: *Night Journey*, recorded by The Atlantic Sinfonietta, conducted by Andrew Schenck. *Fanfare* (September-October 1991): 444-45.

Believes, in this recording review (Koch 37051), that Schuman's ballet contains "strong doses of neoclassicism and of lyricism." See: **D60**

B819 Redlich, Hans F. Review of William Schuman: *Judith*, published by G. Schirmer. *The Music Review* 12 (August 1951): 241.

A perfunctory evaluation which finds fault with the work for being "too self-assured and thematically too little distinguished to capture the imagination of the more sophisticated listener."

B820 "Reviews of New Music: Scores." *Musical Opinion* 74 (February 1951): 217.

Brief review of the G. Schirmer miniature score of *Judith*. Praises the composition for its brilliant orchestration and regards Schuman as a first-rate composer.

B821 Sabin, Robert. "Martha Graham Creates Dance with Louisville Orchestra." *Musical America* 70 (January 15, 1950): 67, 87.

The January 4 and 5 premiere performances in Louisville, Kentucky, of *Judith* are thoroughly reviewed here with great approbation. In praising the interpretation of dancer Martha Graham and the music of Schuman, Sabin claims that their collaboration results in a new genre, the "dance concerto," later pointing out that such disparate components as "movement, music, costume, setting—as separate entities . . . were fused in a true concerted form." The author's discussion of the music includes the following evaluation: "It is music in blacks and greys, music of understatement and tremendous restrained power." Compliments the orchestra, led by Robert Whitney, for its intelligent and capable rendition. See: **W42a**

*   Simmons, Walter. Review of William Schuman: *Symphony No. 5*, *Judith*, *New England Triptych*, and *Variations on "America,"* recorded by the Seattle Symphony Orchestra, conducted by Gerard Schwartz; *Symphony No. 10*, *New England Triptych*, *American Festival Overture*, and *Variations on "America,"* recorded by the St. Louis Symphony Orchestra, conducted by Leonard Slatkin.

Cited as **B666**.

B822 Stewart, Louis C. "Music Composed for Martha Graham: A Discussion of Musical and Choreographic Collaborations." D.M.A. dissertation, The Peabody Institute of The Johns Hopkins University, 1991. 325 pp. UM Order No. 9125560

A careful, well-researched explication of the topic. Analyzes Schuman's music for *Night Journey* (pp. 85-93) in chapter three, highlighting the numerous parallels between the composer's music and the ballet's dramatic structure. Chapter four examines *Judith* (pp. 132-38), describing the highly organized structure of the work, and *The Witch of Endor* (pp. 150-53), emphasizing its polytonal harmonies. Briefly looks at *Voyage* (p.283) in chapter eight, a work the composer orchestrated for Graham from his recently completed *Voyage* for piano. This dissertation is replete with musical examples and contains a good bibliography.

B823 Thomson, Virgil. "Schuman's *Undertow*." *New York Herald Tribune*, April 29, 1945.

Published on the same day as the 29 April 1945 production at New York's Ballet Theater, this article, for the most part, offers a favorable assessment of Schuman's ballet. See: **W37c**

B824 Tucker, Marilyn. "ABT Revives a Mythic 'Undertow.'" *San Francisco Chronicle*, January 21, 1992, section e, p. 2.

A review of the January 19 San Francisco production of Schuman's *Undertow* by the American Ballet Theatre. The conductor of "Schuman's flashy music" was Emil De Cou. See: **W37f**

Works: Opera

B825 "Baseball in Cold Blood." *Time* 61 (May 18, 1953): 60.

Discusses the Hartford, Connecticut, world premiere of Schuman's opera *The Mighty Casey*. See: **W45a**

B826 Berges, Ruth. "John Brownlee Opera Theater: Juilliard Opera Center." *Opera Canada* 32 (1991): 36.

Reviews the Juilliard School's productions of Schuman's *A Question of Taste* and *The Mighty Casey*. Both operas were presented in honor of the composer's eightieth birthday. See: **W45i, W102b**

* Haskell, Harry. "William (Howard) Schuman."

Cited as **B162**.

B827 Holland, Bernard. "'Casey,' New Schuman Work, as Glimmerglass Opens." *The New York Times*, June 26, 1989, section 3, p. 14.

A major review of the Glimmerglass Opera's productions of Schuman's *The Mighty Casey* and *A Question of Taste*. Holland finds fault with both operas, but believes the former work to be "a stronger piece." See: **W45h, W102a**

B828 Hughes, Allen. "Opera: 'Mighty Casey.'" *The New York Times*, August 31, 1967, p. 28.

Makes known the New York premiere of *The Mighty Casey* on 30 August 1967. The enthusiastic production was mounted by the pupils of the Theater Workshop for Students at the East River Amphitheater. Three additional performances were scheduled to be given through September 2. See: **W45e**

B829 Hume, Paul. Review of William Schuman: *The Mighty Casey*. *Music Library Association Notes* 12 (June 1955): 485-86.

A review of the 1954 G. Schirmer vocal score to *The Mighty Casey*. Contends that the opera is difficult and too long. See: **W45**

B830 Kandell, Leslie. "Glimmerglass Opera: Schuman 'A Question of Taste'[premiere], 'The Mighty Casey.'" *Musical America* 109 (November 1989): 36.

Compliments the Glimmerglass Opera summer production of Schuman's *The Mighty Casey*, presented in Cooperstown, New York, as part of the festivities surrounding the celebration of the fiftieth anniversary of the baseball Hall of Fame. Coupled with the composer's baseball opera was the premiere performance of his new opera, *A Question of Taste*. Reports that during the intermission between the two works, the composer offered remarks about his music. See: **W45h, W102a**

B831 Kolodin, Irving. "'Casey' Strikes Out—Again." *Saturday Review* 38 (March 19, 1955): 26.

A carping review of *The Mighty Casey*. The performance reviewed was presented on the television program Omnibus. See: **W45b**

* Kornick, Rebecca Hodell. *Recent American Opera: A Production Guide.*

Cited as **B28**.

B832 McClatchy, J.D. "William Schuman: A Reminiscence." *The Opera Quarterly* 10, no. 4 (1994): 21-37.

Based on a diary written by the author, the librettist of *A Question of Taste*, this article provides a record of the year-long collaboration between McClatchy and Schuman and the subsequent revisions and rehearsals which led to the first performance of the opera. McClatchy's conclusion is especially moving: "He was a man almost *driven* to happiness: an outsize life and career, the innovations and institutions he started, the buoyant optimism of his personality and convictions, the dramatic flair of his music. Underneath it all—and this is true of every great artist— was a strong, serious, stubborn streak that knew what he wanted, that listened to the voice he'd had in his mind's ear since childhood, and that time and again cannily found ways to let that voice sing out. It will have been one of the rare privileges of my life to have once given him words for that voice."

B833 Nilsson, B.A. "In Review: Cooperstown, New York." *Opera News* 51 (November 1986): 57.

Nilsson reviews an exceedingly successful performance, at which the composer was in attendance, of Schuman's *The Mighty Casey* at Cooperstown. See: **W45g**

B834 _____. "Cooperstown, N.Y." *Opera News* 52 (November 1987): 55.

An account of the concert celebrating the opening of the Glimmerglass Opera's new Alice Busch Theater, at which a variety of operatic selections were performed, including a piece from *The Mighty Casey*.

B835 Parmenter, Ross. "The World of Music." *The New York Times*, May 13, 1951, section 2, p. 7.

Briefly discusses the genesis of Schuman's forthcoming opera based on "Casey at the Bat."

B836 RePass, Richard. "New American Opera." *The Music Review* 14 (August 1953): 224-27.

Questions, in this tepidly-written review of the 4 May 1953 premiere performance of *The Mighty Casey* in Hartford, Connecticut, the dramatic effect of the opera. Believes that "despite some clever scoring and a few interesting harmonic and rhythmic ideas *The Mighty Casey* never really came to life until the game—and the opera—were nearly over." Closes with the following statement: "In its 75 minutes, however, this opera introduces almost as many characters (all of them deliberate caricatures) as Charpentier's *Louise*, which gives some idea of its fragmentary and, I'm afraid, rather superficial nature." Schuman's work is one of eight operas discussed in this article. See: **W45a**

B837 "Reviews of New Music: Scores." *Musical Opinion* 78 (April 1955): 415.

The vocal score (G. Schirmer) of *The Mighty Casey* is examined in this review. The author contends that Schuman's music is exciting and dramatic. See: **W45**

B838 Schonberg, Harold C. "Casey Bats Again with same Result." *The New York Times*, May 5, 1953, p. 34.

A somewhat pessimistic review of the world premiere production of *The Mighty Casey* in Hartford, Connecticut. See: **W45a**

B839 _____. "There Is No Joy in 'Casey' Opera." *The New York Times*, March 7, 1955, p. 21.

In this review of the 6 March 1955 presentation of *The Mighty Casey* on CBS television, the reviewer is strongly critical of the opera, charging that the setting of Thayer's text is "essentially unvocal" and that the music is in "a quasi-modern style that is lacking in charm." See: **W45b**

B840 Simmons, Walter. Review of William Schuman: *The Mighty Casey* (excerpts), recorded by the Gregg Smith Singers, Long Island Symphonic Choral Association, and Adirondack Chamber Orchestra, conducted by Gregg Smith, with vocal soloists. *Fanfare* (September-October 1991): 350-51.

An enlightening recording review (Premiere PRCD 1009) of Schuman's first opera. Argues that the composer's music, in general, "reveals an inner spirit that is probably more deeply 'American' than that of any other American composer who does not borrow from vernacular idioms." Predicts that *The Mighty Casey* may become one of Schuman's works which will stand the test of time. See: **D47**

B841 Smith, Patrick J. "Gregg Smith Singers: 'Casey.'" *High Fidelity/Musical America* 26 (September 1976): MA-20.

Strongly criticizes Jeremy Gury's libretto for *The Mighty Casey* in this review of an Alice Tully Hall performance. See: **W45f**

B842 Sullivan, Dan. "Composer Wields Bat on 'Mighty Casey' Opera." *The New York Times*, August 16, 1967, p. 35.

Reports on a rehearsal of *The Mighty Casey* by students of the Theater Workshop for Students. Schuman, who was in attendance by invitation, consented to rehearse the chorus. See: **W45e**

B843 Vance, W.Y. "Hartford Premieres The Mighty Casey, Baseball Opera by William Schuman." *Musical Courier* 147 (June 1953): 12.

An informative, enthusiastic review of the first performance of Schuman's opera sponsored by the Hartt Opera Guild in Hartford, Connecticut. Performances were given over three successive evenings (May 4, 5, and 6) to "delighted jam-packed Hartford audiences." Discusses the style of the opera, commenting particularly on the importance of the chorus and the composer's use of the orchestra. See: **W45a**

B844 Waleson, Heidi. "Filling a Twin Operatic Bill from Out of Left Field." *The New York Times*, June 11, 1989, section 2, pp. 27-28.

Discusses the forthcoming performance at the Glimmerglass Opera of an operatic twin bill: *The Mighty Casey* and *A Question of Taste*, both by Schuman. Recalls the success of the Glimmerglass production in 1986 of *The Mighty Casey* and declares that *A Question of Taste* will receive its world premiere in the approaching June 24 engagement. Traces the genesis of the composer's new opera, which is the first commissioned work by the Glimmerglass company, and provides substantive information about the collaboration between the librettist J.D. McClatchy and Schuman. See: **W45h, W102a**

Works: Songs

* Chase, William W. Review of William Schuman: *In Sweet Music*, *The Young Dead Soldiers*, and *Time to the Old*, recorded by Rosalind Rees and the Orpheus Trio, the White Mountains Festival Orchestra, and pianist Thomas Muraco.

Cited as **B714**.

* Dalheim, Eric L. "Record Reviews: Rosalind Rees Sings William Schuman."

Cited as **B719**.

* Dyer, Richard. "Horblit Concert Surveys Works of William Schuman."

Cited as **B723**.

* _____. Review of William Schuman: *In Sweet Music*, *The Young Dead Soldiers*, and *Time to the Old*, recorded by Rosalind Rees and the Orpheus Trio, the White Mountains Festival Orchestra, and pianist Thomas Muraco.

Cited as **B724**.

*   Grueninger, Walter F. Review of William Schuman: *In Sweet Music*, *The Young Dead Soldiers*, and *Time to the Old*, recorded by Rosalind Rees and the Orpheus Trio, the White Mountains Festival Orchestra, and pianist Thomas Muraco.

Cited as **B726**.

B845 Henahan, Donal. "Concert: Gregg Smith Singers Present Four World Premieres." *The New York Times*, May 21, 1980, section 3, p. 25.

Publicizes the first performance of Schuman's *Time to the Old*, performed by Rosalind Rees. Refers to the composition as "an unrelentingly somber setting of three Archibald MacLeish poems about death and dying." In addition, several other vocal and choral works by the composer were presented on the program. See: **W86a**

*   Kresh, Paul. Review of William Schuman: *In Sweet Music*, *The Young Dead Soldiers*, and *Time to the Old*, recorded by Rosalind Rees and the Orpheus Trio, the White Mountains Festival Orchestra, and pianist Thomas Muraco.

Cited as **B729**.

B846 McLellan, Joseph. "William Schuman's Vivid Vocal Works." *The Washington Post*, May 8, 1986, section c, p. 13.

Reports on a concert of Schuman's vocal and choral works at the Library of Congress presented in celebration of the composer's seventy-fifth birthday. Schuman, who was in attendance, heard performances of *Time to the Old*, presented by soprano Rosalind Rees and pianist Gary Steigerwalt, and of choral works (*Prelude for Voices*, *Perceptions*, *Carols of Death*, and *Five Rounds on Famous Words*) sung by the University of Maryland Chorus Chamber Singers, conducted by Paul Traver. In addition, Steigerwalt played the piano cycle *Voyage*. According to the reviewer, "Schuman's choral writing is brilliant." See: **W16b**, **W47b**, **W51a**, **W54c**, **W86c**, **W92b**

*   Monson, Karen. Review of William Schuman: *In Sweet Music*, *The Young Dead Soldiers*, and *Time to the Old*, recorded by Rosalind Rees and the Orpheus Trio, the White Mountains Festival Orchestra, and pianist Thomas Muraco.

Cited as **B733**.

*   Paris, Robert. "National Sym: Schuman Prems."

Cited as **B599**.

B847 Webster, Daniel. "Moving the Horn into New Roles." *The Philadelphia Inquirer*, February 1, 1987, section i, p. 3.

Contains a recording review of the MusicMasters MMD 20115L release, which contains a song by Schuman.

Works: Keyboard Music

B848 Deimler, Kathryn George. "Quartal Harmony: An Analysis of Twelve Piano Compositions by Twentieth Century Composers." Ph.D. dissertation, New York University, 1981. 230 pp. UM Order No. 81-15483

An in-depth study of the use of quartal harmony in twentieth-century piano works. According to the author, "The aim of the study was to find and analyze extended passages of quartal harmony in piano compositions by twentieth-century composers in order to validate the use of quartal harmony for extended composition." The heart of the study (chapter 3) presents an analytical examination in chronological order of twelve compositions composed between 1908 and 1958. This principal discussion is preceded by two background chapters and is concluded by a closing chapter which contains a summary and recommendations. An analysis of Schuman's *Three-Score Set*, divided into three subsections entitled "Inverted Quartal Chords," "Linear Rise and Fall," and "Rhythmic Variety," occurs in chapter 3 (pp. 184-88). Includes musical examples, a bibliography, and two appendixes.

B849 Dillon, Frances. Review of William Schuman: *Three Piano Moods*. *Music Library Association Notes* 18 (June 1961): 489.

Reviewed as part of a series entitled "Piano Music for Children: A Survey," the *Three Piano Moods* are cited as "little masterpieces of our time." Following an introductory paragraph, the individual pieces are discussed. Suggests a relationship between these works and contemporary dance rhythms.

B850 Gano, Peter. Review of William Schuman: *When Jesus Wept* (arranged for organ by Samuel Adler), performed by Barbara Harbach. *The Sonneck Society Bulletin* 14 (Spring 1988): 47.

Reviews a compact disc (Gasparo GS 258) issued in 1985 entitled *American Hymn Preludes* which contains Samuel Adler's organ transcription of Schuman's "When Jesus Wept," the second movement of *New England Triptych*. Also presented on the disc are Adler's *Hymnset for Organ Solo* and Gardner Read's *Preludes on Old Southern Hymns*. Each of the sixteen hymns performed on organ is also sung by the Rochester Singers. See: **D123**

B851 Hansen, G. Review of William Schuman: *When Jesus Wept* (arranged for organ by Samuel Adler), performed by Barbara Harbach. *The American Record Guide* (March-April 1991): 156.

Reviews the first recording (Gasparo GS 258) of Samuel Adler's arrangement for organ of *When Jesus Wept*. See: **D123**

* Holland, Bernard. "The Bottom Line in Tune."

Cited as **B177**.

B852 Lee, Douglas A. "Record Reviews: A Crazy Quilt of American Piano Music." *American Music* 6 (Fall 1988): 359-61.

A noteworthy review of the Musical Heritage Society (MHS 7534) 1986 recording of representative piano works by a diverse group of American composers, ranging from Louis Moreau Gottschalk to John Cage. "William Schuman is represented by 'Dynamics,' the third of *Three Piano Moods* (1958); the sparse texture, dissonant harmony, and pointillistic lines typical of him work toward an accumulated sonority appropriate for the conclusion of a set of three pieces or, as here, the conclusion of the album." See: **D101**

* McLellan, Joseph. "William Schuman's Vivid Vocal Works."

Cited as **B846**.

B853 Sabin, Robert. "William Schuman Cycle for Piano Published." *Musical America* 75 (March 1955): 34.

Included in this announcement of the publication of the piano cycle *Voyage* by G. Schirmer is a very helpful review of the composition. Reconstructs the rather unusual and complicated history of the work, especially highlighting the dance version prepared by the composer for Martha Graham. Attempts to relate the meaning of the drama associated with the dance form of *Voyage*. Concerning the piano work, the author asserts that "It is music of great integrity, expressive power, and economy of means."

B854 Sternfeld, Frederick W. Review of William Schuman: *Voyage*, a cycle of five pieces for piano. *Music Library Association Notes* 12 (March 1955): 329-30.

After discussing the original dance setting of the composition, Sternfeld observes that the "keyboard version has not lost its pungency or evocativeness as a 'cycle of piano pieces.'"

B855 Wheeler, Scott. Review of William Schuman: *When Jesus Wept* (arranged for organ by Samuel Adler), performed by Barbara Harbach. *Fanfare* (January-February 1991): 128.

Wheeler's recording review (Gasparo GS 258) of Samuel Adler's arrangement for organ of Schuman's *When Jesus Wept* is positive. See: **D123**

Bibliography of Writings
by Schuman

S1   Schuman, William. "A Novel One-Volume Encyclopedia." *Modern Music* 15 (1937-38): 128-30.

Favorably reviews Nicolas Slonimsky's *Music Since 1900*, published by W.W. Norton in 1937. Contains a general description of the contents of the volume. Questions the omission of any reference to the Composers Forum Laboratory of the Federal Music Project.

S2   _____. "Unconventional Case History." *Modern Music* 15 (1937-38): 222-27.

Traces the progress of a Sarah Lawrence College student involved in a nontraditional approach to the study of music composition.

S3   _____. "Layman's Guide and Student Opera." *Modern Music* 16 (1938-39): 135-37.

Review of Aaron Copland's book *What to Listen for in Music* and his opera *The Second Hurricane*.

S4   _____. "From the Mail Pouch: Roy Harris's Symphony." *The New York Times*, March 19, 1939, section 2, p. 6.

A response to a review by Olin Downes of a performance of Roy Harris's Third Symphony by Koussevitzky and the Boston Symphony Orchestra. Schuman writes that "the symphony has dramatic fire and a definite sense of direction, which gives it great power."

S5   _____. "Taylor-Made Topics." *Modern Music* 17 (1939-40): 197-99.

This review of Deems Taylor's book *The Well-Tempered Listener* takes the author to task for a superficial treatment of American music and modern music.

S6 _____. "Writing for Amateurs and Pros." *The New York Times*, June 30, 1940, section 9, p. 5.

Anticipates the impending performance of his new cantata, *This Is Our Time*, to be performed by the People's Philharmonic Choral Society, an amateur chorus directed by Max Helfman, and the New York Philharmonic Orchestra. Discusses the format of the composition and remarks on problems encountered when writing for amateur singers, specifically commenting on the fugue at the end of the third movement. Embraces the concept of *Gebrauchsmusik* for American composers. See: **W20a**

S7 _____. "A Brief Study of Music Organizations Founded in the Interest of the Living Composer." *Twice a Year 1940-1941*, edited by Dorothy Norman. New York: Twice a Year Press, 1941, pp. 361-67. AP2 T94

Surveys organizations active at that time in promoting the music of American composers. Offers the opinion that the Composers Forum Laboratory is the most significant of the groups discussed.

S8 _____. "From the Mail Pouch." *The New York Times*, April 5, 1942, section 8, p. 6.

Schuman's letter to the music editor voices his opposition to a composition contest for a new opera sponsored by the New Opera Company. States reasons supporting his position and concludes that "the New Opera Company, while obviously motivated by high ideals, would do well to reconsider its action." See: **B228, S9**

S9 _____. "From the Mail Pouch: Prizes and Pay for Composers." *The New York Times*, April 19, 1942, section 8, p. 6.

A response, in the form of a letter to the music editor of *The New York Times*, taking Irving Lowens to task for misinterpreting remarks made by Schuman in a previous letter about a composition contest held by the New Opera Company. In the following excerpt from this letter, Schuman writes: "In his letter Mr. Lowens finds that my reasoning implies a contempt for the younger composers and a feeling that only established composers are writing worth-while music. Nothing could be further from the truth than such an assertion." See: **B228, S8**

S10 _____. "Songs America Has Sung." *The New York Times*, June 13, 1943, section 7, p. 8.

A favorable review of *A Treasury of American Song* (New York: Alfred A. Knopf) by Olin Downes and Elie Siegmeister. "In short, this collection is indispensable for any song-minded gathering of Americans."

S11 _____. "Music Master." *The New York Times*, June 27, 1943, section 7, p. 8.

Schuman's review of John N. Burk's *The Life and Works of Beethoven* (New York: Random House) is most complimentary. Particularly praises the author's skill in writing for the general reader.

S12 _____. "A Symphonic Composer Comments on Some Current Problems." *Music Publishers Journal* (September-October 1943): 5, 39.

Reveals Schuman's opinions on four questions, each about American composers, posed by the editor of this journal. Especially illuminating is the composer's response to the query "What is American music?": "My own observation has been that those who holler the loudest about what American music should be are often those who are least acquainted with the music that our American composers have already produced. *Any* composer must of necessity write out of his total life experience."

S13 _____. "Opportunities for Music Workers." *The Etude* 64 (September 1946): 500.

Originally part of a commencement address given by Schuman at the Institute of Musical Art. Urges excellence on the part of musicians preparing for careers as performers, teachers, orchestral musicians, conductors, and composers. Points out the need in the world of music for an enlightened audience.

S14 _____. "A Composer Looks at Critics." *Musical America* (November 15, 1948): 8, 31.

Based upon a speech previously given to the Hartford Symposium of Musical Criticism, Schuman's pithy article addresses the issue of relations between the contemporary composer and the music critic. Recognizes the importance of the critic's role to musical life in the twentieth century. Takes music critics and musicologists to task for failing to take an active interest in new music.

S15 _____. "The Final Triumph." *Stravinsky in the Theatre*, edited by Minna Lederman. New York: Pellegrini & Cudahy, 1948; reprint ed., New York: Da Capo, 1975, pp. 134-35. ISBN 0 306 70665 2 ML410 S932 L4 1975

Attests to the power and influence of Stravinsky's music.

S16 _____. "On Teaching the Literature and Materials of Music." *The Musical Quarterly* 34 (1948): 155-68.

Thoroughly explains the newly implemented Literature and Materials of Music curriculum at the Juilliard School. Concerning the training of young musicians, Schuman contends that "it is essential that their education lead them beyond mere technical proficiency and insure intelligent and musicianly comprehension." Stresses the importance of designing curriculum appropriate for the individual student. Emphasizes "that the primary goal of education in music theory is to achieve a meaningful transfer of theoretical knowledge into practical performance." Outlines the basic framework of the literature and materials courses for the undergraduate years and lists the requirements of an examination given at the end of two years of study. Briefly concludes with a description of the other divisions in the school.

S17 _____. "Virtuosity in Discernment." *Paul Rosenfeld, Voyager in the Arts*, edited by Jerome Mellquist and Lucie Wiese. New York: Creative Age Press, 1948; reprint ed., New York: Octagon, 1977, pp. 105-08. ISBN 0 374 95561 1 ML55 R65 M4 1977

Characterizes the critic Paul Rosenfeld as "a virtuoso listener." Recounts the details of an interview Rosenfeld had with the author in 1938.

S18 _____. "Louisville Policy." *The New York Times*, December 24, 1950, section 2, p. 9.

Praises the Louisville Orchestra for that organization's devotion to the performance of contemporary music. Observes that this emphasis upon twentieth-century compositions has been achieved together with an increase in the total number of subscribers. Recalls his own association with Louisville, which resulted in *Judith*, and notes the recording of that work. See: **D41**

S19 _____. "The Side of the Angels." *Etude* 69 (June 1951): 9-10, 50.

Explores the desired balance between economic success and musical development necessary for every professional musician in order to truly achieve a fulfilled career. Stresses the importance for each musician to understand the language and literature of music. Argues that "the true musician will never lose sight of the values in which he believes and he will bring to any task, however modest, an intensity of expressive purpose." Contends that "A true musician is one who remains faithful to his own highest artistic standards despite the practical compromises he may be obliged to make." Observes that the assiduous musician can serve the art of music at many different levels and in a wide variety of careers.

S20 _____. "On Freedom in Music." *The Arts in Renewal*, introduction by Sculley Bradley. Philadelphia: University of Pennsylvania Press, 1951; reprint ed., Freeport, NY: Books for Libraries Press, 1969, pp. 67-106. ISBN 0 836 91121 0 CB425 A75 1969

One of a collection of lectures originally given in 1950 as part of the Benjamin Franklin Lectures at the University of Pennsylvania, this valuable essay is written primarily from the viewpoint of the composer. Contemplates the role of music in the United States and its impact on contemporary society. Surveys twentieth-century compositional techniques available to the modern composer in terms of harmony, melody, orchestration, and counterpoint. Points out the difficulty a composer of new music has in earning a living wage from his works. Examines the impact of music education, orchestras, chamber groups, opera, ballet, and other media upon performances of contemporary music, as well as the role of the critic and listener.

S21 _____. "Importance of Recording to Contemporary Music." *Review of Recorded Music.* (July 1952).

S22 _____. "The Place of Composer Copland." *The New York Times*, November 8, 1953, section 7, pp. 3, 49.

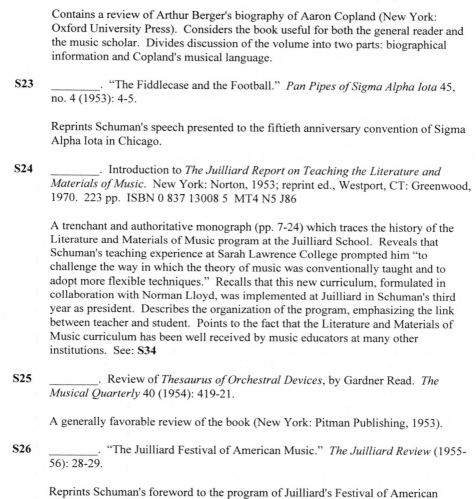

Contains a review of Arthur Berger's biography of Aaron Copland (New York: Oxford University Press). Considers the book useful for both the general reader and the music scholar. Divides discussion of the volume into two parts: biographical information and Copland's musical language.

S23   _____. "The Fiddlecase and the Football." *Pan Pipes of Sigma Alpha Iota* 45, no. 4 (1953): 4-5.

Reprints Schuman's speech presented to the fiftieth anniversary convention of Sigma Alpha Iota in Chicago.

S24   _____. Introduction to *The Juilliard Report on Teaching the Literature and Materials of Music*. New York: Norton, 1953; reprint ed., Westport, CT: Greenwood, 1970. 223 pp. ISBN 0 837 13008 5 MT4 N5 J86

A trenchant and authoritative monograph (pp. 7-24) which traces the history of the Literature and Materials of Music program at the Juilliard School. Reveals that Schuman's teaching experience at Sarah Lawrence College prompted him "to challenge the way in which the theory of music was conventionally taught and to adopt more flexible techniques." Recalls that this new curriculum, formulated in collaboration with Norman Lloyd, was implemented at Juilliard in Schuman's third year as president. Describes the organization of the program, emphasizing the link between teacher and student. Points to the fact that the Literature and Materials of Music curriculum has been well received by music educators at many other institutions. See: **S34**

S25   _____. Review of *Thesaurus of Orchestral Devices*, by Gardner Read. *The Musical Quarterly* 40 (1954): 419-21.

A generally favorable review of the book (New York: Pitman Publishing, 1953).

S26   _____. "The Juilliard Festival of American Music." *The Juilliard Review* (1955-56): 28-29.

Reprints Schuman's foreword to the program of Juilliard's Festival of American Music, held in honor of the school's fiftieth anniversary.

S27   _____. "The Responsibility of Music Education to Music." *Music Educators Journal* 42 (June-July 1956): 17-19.

Originally given as a speech at the 1956 Music Educators National Conference meeting in St. Louis, Schuman states as the basic premise for this paper that "The quality of performance in school music is in direct proportion to the musical skills of the teacher," and he then goes on to say that "A music teacher who is generally interested in music will be able to answer 'yes' to each of the following questions: 1. Do you have an interest in the art of music beyond the immediate concern of your school position and, if so, what evidence can you supply to prove this interest? 2. Are you making a continuing effort to perfect your equipment in music either as a performer or composer?" Observes that most music teachers appear to have little interest in contemporary music. Also published in *Etude* 74 (Sept. 1956), 11-12.

S28 _____. Review of *Orchestration*, by Walter Piston. *The Musical Quarterly* 42 (1956): 103-05.

A very informative review which highly praises Piston's publication (New York: Norton, 1955). "While this book could not have been written without Piston's enviable scholarly attainments or the organization and presentation of its materials attained without his seasoned teacher's grasp, the emphasis throughout is on creativity in study, which stems directly from Piston the composer."

S29 _____. "Teaching Our Youth." *The New York Times*, March 15, 1959, section 2, p. 9.

This cogent argument is based on an address first given by Schuman in Kansas City at a meeting of the Music Teachers National Association. Opposes the practice of using banal entertainment music in the public schools. Upholds, though not without criticism, the significance of the private teacher for music education. Comments on the importance of providing the student with a thorough grounding in sight singing. Questions "whether there has not been an overemphasis on group performance at the expense of the study of music as literature."

S30 _____. "Music as Usual." *The Music Journal* 17 (April 1959): 12-13, 70-71.

Stresses the need for a reassessment of music education in America and deplores the overuse of "entertainment music" in our schools. Recognizes the significant role of the private music teacher in music education. Calls for the elimination from music education of "those activities which cannot be defended as educationally significant." This article was originally presented as an address to the Biennial Convention of the Music Teachers National Association held in Kansas City, Missouri. Also published in *The American Music Teacher* 8 (May-June 1959): 6-7, 16-19, and in *The Juilliard Review* 6 (Spring 1959): 3-4,22-224.

S31 _____. "From the Mail Pouch: Aim of Naumburg Competition to Be a 'Constructive Force' in Music." *The New York Times*, November 13, 1960, section 2, p. 11.

A thoughtful letter to the editor written in response to Ross Parmenter's article on competitions. At the outset, Schuman declares that he hopes "to clarify the picture, at least as far as the Board of Directors of the Naumburg Foundation sees it." Schuman was president of the Naumburg Foundation at the time.

S32   _____. "A Birthday Salute to Aaron Copland." [Program: Juilliard School of Music] (November 14 and 15, 1960): 6-7.

Program notes, actually reprinted from the 30 October 1960 *New York Herald Tribune*, honoring Copland on the composer's sixtieth birthday. Schuman concludes that "Copland is very much the American composer. His works have their roots here—in the sights and sounds of our land and in the writings of American authors. While it is a verity that the composer of major stature writes music for the large arena and that his local origin is of small significance, it is, nonetheless, a joy to know that here is an authentic American voice."

S33   _____. "Introduction." *Songs of the Gilded Age*, edited by Margaret Bradford Boni. New York: Golden Press, 1960. 156 pp. M1630.18 B647

This collection of popular American songs, arranged by Norman Lloyd, contains a brief introduction by Schuman.

S34   _____. "William Schuman Summarizes Juilliard Objectives." *Musical America* (February 1961): 18-19.

Explains the objectives and organization of Juilliard's Literature and Materials of Music curriculum. Criticizes the traditional ways to teach music appreciation and music theory. Stresses the "lack of uniformity" in this curriculum and contends that it "can be applied to the teaching of music anywhere." This article is a reprint of excerpts from Schuman's Introduction to the Juilliard Report. See: S24

S35   _____. "The Compleat Musician: Vincent Persichetti and Twentieth-Century Harmony." *The Musical Quarterly* 47 (July 1961): 379-85.

An extended, enthusiastic review of Persichetti's book *Twentieth-Century Harmony: Creative Aspects and Practice*, published in 1961 by W.W. Norton. After introductory remarks praising Persichetti as a musician, composer, and teacher, Schuman focuses on the organization and content of the book. Points out that the author composed his own musical examples for the text rather than relying upon the more traditional practice of utilizing excerpts from compositions by other composers. Concludes that "In the scope of its imagination, creative scholarship, and objective distillations, Vincent Persichetti's *Twentieth-Century Harmony* is in and of itself a work of art."

S36   _____. "Civic Values in the Arts." *Music Journal* 20 (March 1962): 37.

Calls for widespread support of the arts in all communities.

S37   _____. "The Lincoln Center: Vivendi Causa." *County Government* (July 1962): 36-40.

In this article, written while Lincoln Center was under construction, Schuman provides an overview of the arts institution. Describes the events planned for the opening of Philharmonic Hall in September and stresses that the first week will focus on three commissioned works for the hall's organ by Henry Cowell, Vincent Persichetti, and Virgil Thomson, as well as orchestral music by other American composers. Discusses forthcoming plans for all the constituent members of the Center.

S38   _____. "The Idea: 'A Creative, Dynamic Force.'" *The New York Times Magazine*, September 23, 1962, section 2, pp. 11, 34, 35, 38.

Delineates the philosophy which guided the creation of Lincoln Center. Describes the physical plant and overall organization of the institution, with separate discussion of each of the constituent members. Refers to forthcoming projects such as the Lincoln Center Teachers Institute and the Lincoln Center "Festival 66." Considers the question of government support for the arts and addresses the issue of the importance of culture in contemporary society.

S39   _____. "The Responsibility of Lincoln Center to Education." *Music Educators Journal* 49 (September-October 1962): 35-38.

After a rather lengthy description of plans projected for the new Lincoln Center, including a discussion of the extensive inaugural concerts on September 23 proposed for the opening of Philharmonic Hall, the article focuses on a special project identified as the Lincoln Center Teacher's Institute. Schuman advocates "that teacher training in the field of music education more often than not places far too much emphasis on courses which are not really germane to the development of the musician." He goes on to suggest that "The Lincoln Center Teacher's Institute would concern itself solely with the thing itself; that is with the art of music, or dance or drama." States that the ultimate goal of the institute would be to "raise the level of music teaching for thousands of teachers, and for literally millions of students." Originally presented at the March 1962 convention of the Music Educators National Conference held in Chicago.

S40   _____. "An American Partnership." *Cincinnati Symphony Orchestra Program Notes* (October 11, 1962): 60-62.

S41   _____. "The Arts in Our Colleges." *Musical America* 83 (June 1963): 5.

Written in the form of an editorial, Schuman's essay postulates that colleges and universities should take an active role in fostering the arts "as part of the grand design of artistic enrichment for the creator, performer and observer." Also published in the *Dartmouth College Alumni Magazine* (January 1963).

S42   _____. "Have We 'Culture'? Yes—and No." *The New York Times Magazine*, September 22, 1963, pp. 21, 82-84.

The efficacy of Schuman's argument is propelled by his adept prose in this significant article. Addresses the issue of the position of the arts in American society, observing that "The creative aspect of our artistic life, despite many problems, is one of health. In music, the theater, the dance, the film, we have our high-level creators who can take their places with the most gifted of the world and, what is more, whose diversity of styles, techniques, esthetics are paralleled in no other country." Cites as evidence the mastery of our composers, the strength of our educational institutions, and the skill of our performers. Nevertheless, Schuman tempers his praise with the recognition that "we still reveal feelings of inferiority in the discrimination we often practice in this country against our own artists." Compares the freedom enjoyed by the arts in this country with the restrictions placed upon the arts in the Soviet Union. Contends that the arts must "supply more than entertainment, more than mere pleasure. The stuff of the performing arts, at their highest level, involves artists and works dedicated to nothing less than the exploration of every conceivable nuance of man's capacity for revelation through the unique worlds of music, theater, and dance: worlds which cannot be geared solely to the values of show-business entertainment, for they encompass far more." Concludes that "no form of societal organization relies more heavily on the full development of the talents of its citizens than democracy."

S43   _____. "Fritz Reiner . . . " *Musical America* 83 (December 1963): 283.

This encomium, presented by Schuman on November 18 at the funeral of Fritz Reiner and reprinted here, panegyrizes the conductor as "the virtuoso performer" and "ever the teacher." Briefly discusses Reiner's conducting technique and mentions his devotion to contemporary music.

S44   _____. "The Case for a Center." *Opera News* 29 (September 26, 1964): 6-11.

Presented in the format of an interview, Schuman addresses questions from *Opera News* regarding the purpose and function of the new Lincoln Center. Includes several photographs of the center in various stages of construction.

S45   _____. "The Prejudice of Conformity." *Music Journal* 23 (September 1965): 44, 76-77.

A commencement address delivered at Brandeis University's fourteenth graduation exercises. Cautions against narrow attitudes in evaluating and judging new works of art. Chastises the Pulitzer Prize Advisory Board for their failure to award the Pulitzer Prize in music two years in a row. Declares to the graduating class that "Art has a far deeper meaning than mere delight—than mere entertainment. It is a transforming experience . . . The degree to which you have become and will become susceptible to this special world—a world which transcends understanding—to that extent you will have riches unavailable through any other means."

S46   _____. "The Heart of an Arts Center." *Music Educators Journal* 53 (November 1966): 34-36.

Description of the basic mission of a center for the performing arts: "it is heart that gives the arts center its reason for being and makes it more, rather than less, practical . . . . The heart of an arts center is its mission, its sense of mission, its desire for mission, and its belief in the necessity of having a mission." First presented as a speech to the Arts Council of America in New York City on 20 May 1966.

S47 _____. "The New Establishment." Published by Lincoln Center, 1966.

Publishes a speech given by the composer at Princeton University on 8 December 1966.

S48 _____. "Center No Sponsor of Mall." *The New York Times*, January 13, 1967, p. 22.

In this letter to the editor, Schuman denies a report that the leadership of the Lincoln Center wanted to build a mall between Central Park and the performing arts complex.

S49 _____. "The Role of Lincoln Center." *Music Journal* (March 1967): 23-24, 71-75.

Summarizes the purpose of Lincoln Center, chiefly with regard to the Center's organization and, most significantly, artistic programs.

S50 _____. "The Arts in America." *Music Journal Annual* 25 (1967): 23, 50, 52.

Upholds America as a nation of the arts. Points to the newly opened John F. Kennedy Center for the Performing Arts as perhaps positive appreciation for the arts on the part of the government. Accuses Congress of failing to realize the role of the arts to the nation.

S51 _____. "The Arts: A New Priority." *Vital Speeches of the Day* (February 15, 1968): 281-83.

In this reprint of an important address given to the Economic Club of New York on 17 January 1968, Schuman argues for financial support of the arts in this country. He notes "that the arts are crucial to our automated age" and that "Our obligation, therefore, in a democratic society is to make the arts available to the many without compromising the standards set by the few." Also reprinted in *The Composer* 1 (1969): 8-13.

S52 _____. "Cultivating Student Taste; Excerpts from Address." *Today's Education* 57 (November 1968): 10-13.

Asserts that the performing arts should hold a position of prominence in the American public education system. Considers it erroneous to assume that students involved in school performing groups are receiving a first-rate education in the arts and takes music appreciation classes to task in general for their failure to cultivate artistic insight. Identifies "the fundamental problem: the lack of understanding that the arts are as basic to the development of an educated person as mathematics, history, English, or any other subject." Urges that the performing arts be presented to students for intellectual growth and development rather than for entertainment. Notes the efforts of the Lincoln Center to reach out to students, both at Lincoln Center and through performances presented in the schools. This article was extracted from an address made by Schuman to the Association for Supervision and Curriculum Development of the NEA.

S53   _____. "The Contribution of Koussevitzky." *Lincoln Center Program Book* (1968).

S54   _____. "The Performing Arts and the Curriculum." *New York State Education Department Journal* (1968).

Prints a speech given to an education conference in Atlantic City on 10 March 1968.

S55   _____. "A Special Editorial." *Music and Artists* 1, no. 2 (1968): 1.

S56   _____. "Music Mailbag: William Schuman Protests a Completely False History." *The New York Times*, October 26, 1969, section 2, p. 29.

A scathing response in the form of a letter to the editor answering criticism previously published in an article by Martin Mayer, "Are the Trying Times Just Beginning." Argues that "The article presents a completely false history in which I as president of the Juilliard School persuaded its board of directors to move the school to Lincoln Center . . . In short, a complete criminal history—fraud, assault and, finally, attempted larceny." See: **B240**

S57   _____. "Introduction." *The Orchestral Composer's Point of View*, edited by Robert Stephan Hines. Norman: University of Oklahoma Press, 1970, pp. 3-10. ISBN 0 806 10862 2 ML55 H53

A collection of essays, written by twelve prominent composers, on twentieth-century orchestral music. The thought-provoking introduction is by Schuman.

S58   _____. "The Malady Lingers On." *They Talk about Music*, preface by Robert Cumming. New York: Music Journal, 1971. Vol. 2, pp. 92-102. ML60 C95

Argues that the arts are relegated to a secondary position in the American educational system and offers the opinion that educators have generally misunderstood the nature of the arts and their role in the curriculum. Contends, when compared with other disciplines, that the study of the arts is just as valuable and educational. Concludes that the arts are fundamental to any first-rate educational program and that, without question, the arts better society and enhance the quality of life. Also published in the *Music Journal Annual* 26 (1968), 30-32, and *Musart* 21, No. 1 (1968), 10.

S59 _____. "Why the Arts?" *NAHO* (Fall 1974): 14-15.

Presents excerpts of a speech given on 20 September 1974 at the Convocation of the Regents of the University of the State of New York.

S60 _____. "Needed: More Arts in Education." *Inside Education* (November 1974): 12-13.

A charge to the state of New York proposing that gifted students in the arts receive specialized instruction throughout their public school experience. This article was extracted from a speech given to the New York State Board of Regents Convention.

S61 _____. "Coalition for Education and the Arts." *New York State Education Department Journal*, 1974.

Publishes an address presented by the composer to the regents of the University of the State of New York on 20 September 1974.

S62 _____. "Semper Fidelis." *The School Musician* 48 (October 1976): 42-44.

This article, first delivered as a speech on 23 August 1976 at the Kennedy Center for the Performing Arts as part of the ceremony honoring the induction of John Philip Sousa into the Hall of Fame for Great Americans, considers the question of which characteristics constitute American music. Observes the polarity between the only other composers elected to the Hall of Fame, Stephen Foster and Edward MacDowell. Praises Sousa as a "superb composer . . . who knew precisely what his principal matier [*sic*] was." See also, *Perspectives on John Philip Sousa*, Washington: Library of Congress, 1981.

S63 _____. "Presentation to Samuel Barber of the Gold Medal for Music." *Proceedings of the American Academy and Institute of Arts and Letters*, 2nd series, 27 (1976): 26.

Portrays Barber as a traditionalist and praises him for his outstanding accomplishments. Claims that the art of Barber is, in a word, "impeccable."

S64 _____. "Americanism in Music: A Composer's View." *Music in American Society 1776-1976*, edited by George McCue. New Brunswick: Transaction Books, 1977, pp. 15-25. ISBN 0 878 55209 X ML200.1 M9

Schuman's article, published as the introductory essay in a book inspired by the symposium held in connection with the 1976 festival—the Bicentennial Horizons of American Music and the Performing Arts—which took place in St. Louis, contains a perceptive perspective on American music from the viewpoint of an American composer. Attempts to identify the characteristics fundamental to American music by posing several questions which are then addressed by the author. Confines discussion to a consideration of serious music, particularly symphonic music. Contends that "one of the common threads running through all American music is the nature of its orchestration." Concludes with an appeal to orchestras in the United States to program American symphonic works with regularity.

S65   _____. "Establishment of the Richard Rodgers Production Award for the Musical Theatre." *Proceedings of the American Academy and Institute of Arts and Letters*, 2nd series, No. 27 (1977).

S66   _____. "Introduction." *Composers in America*, by Claire R. Reis. New York: Da Capo, 1977. ISBN 0 306 70893 0 ML390 R38 1977

Schuman's introduction to a reprint edition of this well-known collection of information about twentieth-century American composers praises the achievement of the volume and its compiler. Each composer entry (Schuman, pp. 319-20) features a biographical survey as well as a listing of works by genre.

S67   _____. "The Esthetic Imperative." *Economic Pressures and the Future of the Arts*. New York: The Free Press, 1979, pp. 31-60. ISBN 0 029 28120 2 NX705.5 U6 S38

First presented at the College of Business and Public Administration at New York University as a lecture in the Charles C. Moskowitz Memorial Lectures series. Posits that "there can be no dichotomy between economics and esthetics: They are interdependent." Cites three important publications dealing with the economics of the arts, especially recommending a 1978 book by Dick Netzer entitled *The Subsidized Muse*. Praises American contributions in all areas of artistic endeavor. Laments the place of the arts in American general education, noting that the emphasis on education in the United States has "been to enable the young to develop skills necessary for economic security." Argues that this lack of concern for the arts has devitalized the education of our youth in general. Shows that "there is the unalterable fact that we must, in the performing arts, operate at a deficit." Addresses through lengthy discussion the difficulty that composers have in earning a living from their compositions. Calls for symphony orchestras to regularly program contemporary music by American composers. Gives the following as Schuman's Law and Postulates: "Nonprofit institutions in the performing arts compromise their reason for being in direct proportion to programs and policies which are adopted for fiscal reasons extrinsic to artistic purpose." Two postulates accompany this law in the text. Concludes with this statement: "Success or failure in art cannot be measured in the plusses and minuses of ledgers, but in philosophy and mission, and in the clarity and conviction with which they are given life in our theaters, in our concert halls, and in our classrooms."

S68   _____. "Presentation to Samuel Barber of the Gold Medal for Music." *Proceedings of the American Academy and Institute of Arts and Letters*, 2nd series, No. 29 (1979).

S69   _____. "The Purpose of a Symphony Orchestra." *Symphony Magazine* (August 1980): 11-17.

Originally presented at the thirty-fifth National Conference of the American Symphony Orchestra League held in New York City from June 16 to 20, 1980. Begins with a tongue-in-cheek account of committee reports at a meeting of the American Symphony Orchestra League ten years in the future (1990) as predicted by a computer. Argues that symphony orchestras must devote more performance to contemporary music. Notes the dearth of American music on orchestral programs and observes the paucity of American-born conductors. Proposes the following philosophy of orchestral programming: "1) the systematic and continuing exploration of the great literature of the past on a rotating basis over a period of years, 2) the systematic and purposeful effort to develop a repertory of contemporary works which have already found favor, and 3) the introduction of new works, both by established composers and newer ones."

S70   _____. "Roy Harris Remembered." *High Fidelity/Musical America* 30 (August 1980): MA 18.

First presented as a speech to the American Academy and Institute of Arts and Letters, this affectionately written tribute to the late composer extols Harris "as a major figure in the history of art in the United States." Furnishes insight into Harris's musical style, declaring that he "was, above everything, a classicist." Discloses Schuman's devotion for Harris's music and suggests that "The time has now come to reexamine the total output of this prolific creator."

S71   _____. "Aaron Copland." *Perspectives of New Music* 19 (1980-81): 52-53.

This tribute was initially written for an occasion honoring Copland at the Kennedy Center. The genuine respect and affection by Schuman for his fellow composer is perhaps best demonstrated in the opening paragraph, where Schuman refers to Copland as the "Dean of American Composers." Also published under the title "More Comments on Copland" in the *American Record Guide* 44 (November 1980): 6-7.

S72   _____. "Foreword." *American Music Recordings: A Discography of 20th-Century U.S. Composers*, edited by Carol J. Oja. Institute for Studies in American Music. Brooklyn College of the City University of New York, 1982, pp. vii-viii. ISBN 0 914 67819 1 ML 156.4 N3U3

Advocates the role of the commercial recording in making contemporary music available to the general public. Praises the Koussevitzky Music Foundation for its support of this publication.

S73 _____. "An Advance Bequest Certified Deposit Is Simple as ABCD." *Philanthropy Monthly* (May 1983): 28-29.

Recognizes the Advance Bequest Certified Deposit as an appealing way for individuals to contribute to the charity of their choice.

S74 _____. "New York in the Eighties." *The New Criterion* 4 (Special Issue 1986): 59-62.

Contends that, for the arts, "New York is the place to be." Based on a May 13 interview with the composer by *The New Criterion*.

S75 _____. "Reiner in Memoriam." *The Podium: Magazine of the Fritz Reiner Society* (Spring-Summer 1988): 35-36.

A reprint of the eulogy delivered by Schuman at the 18 November 1963 funeral of Fritz Reiner. Originally intended for inclusion in the Fall-Winter 1987 *Podium* article.

S76 _____. "Introduction" to Aaron Copland's *What to Listen for in Music*. New York: McGraw-Hill, 1988, pp. vii-xvi. ISBN 0 070 13091 4 MT6 C78 W4 1989

Schuman's new introduction to the third edition of Copland's book offers an important evaluation of Copland and gives some of Schuman's own thoughts about listening to music. Schuman maintains that "the music of Aaron Copland is recognized as part of our heritage," and he calls Copland "the quintessential artist in a democratic society."

S77 _____. "A Populist with Classic Roots." *The New York Times*, October 21, 1990, section 2, p. 45.

Schuman, Ned Rorem, Jerome Robbins, Adolph Green, and Midori each wrote a concise essay for a tribute to Leonard Bernstein called "Leonard Bernstein Remembered by His Friends." Schuman's contribution describes Bernstein's career as "without parallel in the history of music."

S78 _____. "For Wiley H." *A Celebration of American Music: Words and Music in Honor of H. Wiley Hitchcock*, edited by Richard Crawford, R. Allen Lott, and Carol J. Oja. Ann Arbor: The University of Michigan Press, 1990, pp. 12-13. ISBN 0 472 09400 9 ML200 C44 1989

A collection of essays and original compositions presented as a Festschrift to Hitchcock. Schuman's contribution is a *jeu d'esprit* eight measures in length entitled "For Wiley H.," which uses only C's and E's, the two musical letters found in Hitchcock's name, and is modeled on the famous four-note motive of Beethoven's Fifth Symphony. Associated with the piece is a letter to Hitchcock from Schuman dated 1 September 1987.

S79 _____, and Rosenbaum, Samuel R. "The Status of the Composer." *The American Symphony Orchestra*, edited by Henry Swoboda. New York: Basic Books, 1967, pp. 177-89. ML1211 S9 1967

Published as part of an outstanding collection of seventeen essays devoted to an overview of the symphony orchestra in America, the article by Schuman and Rosenbaum, presented in the form of an interview, examines the position of the contemporary American composer of art music.

Author Index

Adam, Claus, B710
Anderson, E. Ruth, B47
Anderson, Owen, B415
Anderson, W.R., B48
Apple, R.W., Jr., B49
Archer, Eugene, B50, B51
Archibald, Bruce, B416
Armstrong, Donald Jan, B747
Artner, Alan G., B417, B418
Ayres, Alfred, B54

B., J., B420
Bals, Karen Elizabeth, B421
Bargreen, Melinda, B422, B423, B424,
    B711
Baron, John H., B4
Barry, Malcolm, B425
Bassett, Leslie, B712
Battisti, Frank L., B426
Becker, Warren, B17
Belfy, Jeanne Marie, B792, B793
Bellows, George Kent, B181
Bendheim, Anne, B427
Benjamin, Philip, B55
Berger, Arthur, B794
Berges, Ruth, B826
Bergsma, William, B795
Bernstein, Leonard, B428, B429
Berrett, Joshua, B430
Bialosky, Marshall, B748
Birkhead, Carole C., B796
Blechner, Mark, B713
Block, Maxine, B56

Blois, Louis, B431
Bloom, Julius, B57
Boelzner, Gordon, B15
Borroff, Edith, B5, B60
Boyer, D. Royce, B749
Breuer, Robert, B433
Brillhart, Jerome Bellamy, B434
Broder, Nathan, B63, B64, B435, B436
Bronston, Levering, B437
Brown, Michael R., B65, B438, B439,
    B440
Brown, Royal S., B441, B442, B443
Brown, Steven, B444, B445
Brozen, Michael, B446
Brussel, James A., B66
Burkat, Leonard, B67
Burnsworth, Charles C., B6
Butler, Stanley, B7
Butterworth, Neil, B68

C., D.C., B447
Canby, Edward Tatnall, B448, B449,
    B797
Canby, Vincent, B70
Carrington, Mark, B750
Carter, Elliott, B450, B451
Chapin, Louis, B73, B74
Chase, Gilbert, B75, B76
Chase, William W., B714
Chertok, Pearl, B715
Clark, John W., B77, B452
Cohn, Arthur, B9, B10

Index of Compositions by Schuman

General Index

Abraham Kaplan Camerata Singers, W75b, W75c, B609
Abravanel, Maurice, W32a, D91, B442, B528, B679, B681
Adams, John, B189
Adelphi College, B263
Adler, Samuel, p. 23, W56, W93, D123, B850, B851, B855
Akiyama, Kazuyoshi, W14k
Albany Symphony Orchestra, W95
Alcantara, Theo, W23c
Alice Busch Theater, p. 23, W98, B834
Alice Tully Hall, p. 17, p. 22, p. 23, W45f, B544, B736, B738, B841
American Academy and Institute of Arts and Letters, B249, B268, S70
American Ballet Theatre, W37, W37a, B806, B824
American Bandmaster's Association, p. 22, W88
American Brass Quintet, W87
American Choral Directors Association, B265
American Composer Series, B199
American Composers' Concerts and Festivals, B1
American Composers Orchestra, W29j, W41i, B544, B611, B651
American Music Awards, B359
American National Theatre and Academy, B45
American Symphony Orchestra, W39f

American Symphony Orchestra League, B312, B360, B534, S69
André Kostelanetz and His Orchestra, D115
Antheil, George, D109
Archibald, Bruce, p. 18, B416
Artner, Alan G., B418
Arts Council of America, S46
Artymiw, Lydia, B694
ASCAP, B3
ASCAP's Festival of American Music, W14
Asen, Simon, W59b
Aspen Festival Orchestra, W39c
Aspen Music Festival, p. 13, W29i, B69, B178
Association for Supervision and Curriculum Development of the NEA, S52
Atlanta Symphony Orchestra, W14p, W14q, W75d, W95, B531, B643
Atlantic Sinfonietta, D60
Avery Fisher Hall, p. 16, p. 23, B169, B396, B760, B790

Bacharach, A.L., B48
Bacon, Ernst, B159
Balada, Leonardo, D92, B600, B641
Balassa, Sándor, B486
Ballet Theatre Orchestra, D108, D109, D110, B800
Bals, Karen Elizabeth, B23
Barber, Samuel, p. 16, D4, D5, D10, D24,

D35, D47, D48, D58, D72, D85,
D93, D121, B97, B120, B237,
B320, B365, B530, B547, B568,
B677, B741
Barlow, Howard, p. 7, W13b, W14c
Barnett, Vincent, W61
Bartholomew, Marshall, W38a
Bartók, Béla, B237, B471, B493
Beach, Amy, D24
Becker, John J., D65, D66, D84, B698
Beckhard, Robert, B266
Beethoven, Ludwig van, B360, S11, S78
Belmont, Eleanor Robson, p. 22, W84
Benjamin Franklin Lectures, S20
Bennett, Robert Russell, D35, D36, D53
Berg, Alban, B493
Berger, Arthur, S22
Bergsma, William, p. 11, p. 13, D16, D30,
D45, B511, B711, B741
Berkshire Music Center Orchestra, W23b,
B486
Berlin Philharmonic Quartet, W44b
Bernat, Robert, D83
Bernstein, Leonard, p. 5, p. 7, p. 9, p. 16,
p. 19, p. 20, p. 24, W14h, W22h,
W22i, W22j, W22k, W22l, W22m,
W22n, W22o, W22s, W22w,
W22y, W29d, W29e, W29f, W41f,
W41g, W41h, W60a, W69a,
W71a, W75b, W75c, W101, D4,
D5, D8, D14, D22, D26, D28,
D37, D38, D58, D81, D82, D87,
D93, D94, D106, D109, B39, B98,
B189, B210, B234, B295, B415,
B429, B430, B437, B441, B446,
B447, B458, B472, B474, B475,
B497, B498, B499, B520, B522,
B524, B541, B551, B552, B553,
B554, B559, B572, B586, B597,
B603, B609, B612, B646, B660,
B661, B663, B668, B678, B688,
S77
Bicentennial Horizons of American Music
and the Performing Arts, S64
Biggs, John, D30
Bilik, Jerry, D17
Billings, William, p. 15, p. 24, D53, B420,
B443, B510, B637, B696
Billy Schuman and his Alamo Society

Orchestra, p. 3
Bing, Rudolf, B186
Blitzstein, Marc, D47, D121, B310
Bloch, Ernest, D86, B237
Blossom Music Center, W63f, W81d,
B515, B757
Blume, Friedrich, B64
Boettcher Hall, B659
Boghosian, Varujan, B248
Bohle, Bruce, B280
Bolcom, William, B492, B627
Borroff, Edith, B5
Boston Composer's Orchestra, W89c
Boston Pops Orchestra, W63d, D49, D116
Boston Post, B477
Boston Symphony Orchestra, p. 7, p. 8, p.
9, p. 10, p. 13, p. 15, p. 21,
p. 25, W13c, W14a, W14d, W14e,
W14g, W22a, W22b, W22d,
W22e, W22f, W22g, W22v,
W22cc, W25a, W25b, W28d,
W29a, W29b, W39a, W49h, W53f,
W58a, W58b, W75a, W101,
W101a, D25, D27, B67, B232,
B237, B317, B344, B372, B409,
B428, B429, B432, B477, B480,
B484, B485, B487, B492, B496,
B588, B608, B616, B639, B642,
B675, B708, B784, S4
Boston University, B109
Bowles, Paul, D121
Brahms, Johannes, D119
Brandeis University, B61, B62, B112,
B341, S45
Broadcast Music, Inc., p. 18, W63, B136,
B278
Broder, Nathan, p. 5, p. 10, B63, B140
Broiles, Melvin, W84a
Brooklyn Ethical Culture School, p. 5
Brooks, William, B76
Broward Center for the Performing Arts,
B630
Brown, Elaine, W25e, B762
Brown, Steven, B445
Bruckner, Anton, D16, B395
Buckley, Emerson, W53p, B628
Burgin, Richard, W14g, W22d
Burgos, Rafael Frühbeck de, W53l, W53o,
B589, B693

Handel, George Frideric, p. 3, B694
Hanson, George, W14q, B531
Hanson, Howard, D9, D20, D50, D54,
    D76, B565, B665, B706, B765
Harbach, Barbara, D123, B850, B851,
    B855
Harp, Herbert, D17
Harris, Roy, p. 5, p. 6, p. 7, p. 8, D2, D3,
    D66, D82, D84, D121, B63, B74,
    B103, B107, B120, B139, B152,
    B173, B189, B242, B362, B428,
    B447, B450, B451, B499, B568,
    B570, B583, B586, B597, B625,
    B641, B663, B672, B678, B687,
    B689, B698, B706, B741, B751,
    B765, B780, S4, S70
Harrison, Jay S., p. 18, B45
Harrison, Lou, D45
Harrison, Max, B528
Hartford Symposium of Musical
    Criticism, S14
Hartt College of Music, p. 14, W45a
Hartt Opera Guild, B843
Harvard Glee Club, p. 9, W25a, W25b,
    W35a
Harvard University, p. 7, p. 12
Harwood, C. William, W32e, W53j
Haubiel, Charles, p. 4
Haydn, Franz Joseph, B605
Haydn-Mozart Concerts, p. 18
Heatherington, Alan, W29k, B690
Helfman, Max, S6
Hendl, Walter, W32c, D2, D3
Hennagin, Michael, D45
Henze, Hans Werner, D12
Herrmann, Bernard, D56, B483, B563,
    B564
Heyman, Barbara, B171
High School of Performing Arts, B244,
    B326
Hilsberg, Alexander, p. 19, W68
Hilton, John, p. 19
Hindemith, Paul, D60, B74, B103, B168,
    B319, B807
Hirshhorn Museum and Sculpture Garden
    of the Smithsonian Institution,
    p. 21, W77
Hirsu, Valentin, W59h
Hitchcock, H. Wiley, p. 9, B172, B322,

S78
Hobart, Max, W53k, B481
Hofmann Theater, B455
Holland, Bernard, B827
Holst, Gustav, D17, D122, B753
Honegger, Arthur, B558
Horblit Award Concert, W82c, W83b,
    W86b
Horst, Louis, W40a
Houston Symphony Orchestra, p. 23,
    W22r, W32e, W53j, W53cc,
    W63h, W97, W97a, B264, B453,
    B465, B466
Howard, George S., W21a
Hughes, Edwin, B45
Hughes, Langston, p. 15, p. 24, W52,
    W103
Humphrey, Hubert, B224
Hungarian Quartet, W44a
Hutcheson, Ernest, p. 11, B163

I Cantori, p. 23, W92
Imbrie, Andrew, D29, D45
Indianapolis Symphony Orchestra, p. 16,
    W59a, B209, B495, B516
Institute of Musical Art, p. 11, B197,
    B392, S13
International Choral Festival Choruses,
    p. 20, W72a
International Festival of the Arts, p. 23,
    W99
Iowa State University Singers, p. 20, W73,
    W73a
Iowa State University Department of
    Music, W73
Irving, Robert, p. 19, W66a
Israel, Brian, D9
Ithaca College, p. 22, W91
Ithaca College Choir, p. 22, p. 23, W91a
Ives, Charles, p. 18, W63, D14, D23, D36,
    D51, D54, D58, D76, D112, B10,
    B95, B178, B361, B365, B491,
    B514, B515, B526, B556, B574,
    B700, B704

J.W. Fisher Foundation, W73
Jacksonville Symphony Orchestra,
    W53dd, B445
Jacobi, Peter, B190

Järvi, Neeme, W63e, B514
Jekowsky, Barry, W53y, B455, B510
Jerald Lepinski's Classic Chorale, W54b, B777
John F. Kennedy Center for the Performing Arts, B54, B143, B200, B222, B233, B257, B286, B301, B305, B338, B376, B576, B580, B599, B626, B773, S50, S62, S71
Johnson, Bret, B759
Johnson, Harriett, B458, B649
Johnson, Thor, p. 11, p. 14, W49a
Jolles, Susan, W83c, B815
Jones Hall, B466
Jordan Hall, B481
Juilliard Division of Dance, p. 12, B315
Juilliard Graduate School, p. 11, B197
Juilliard Opera Center, D46, D71
Juilliard Orchestra, W39b, W53w, W59c, W75e, W79b, D39, D46, D71, B338, B469, B493, B598, B624, B672
Juilliard School, p. 4, p. 5, p. 6, p. 11, p. 12, p. 13, p. 16, p. 17, W45i, W81c, W100b, B19, B55, B80, B83, B115, B116, B131, B136, B163, B190, B191, B192, B193, B194, B195, B196, B197, B216, B227, B235, B239, B245, B259, B260, B307, B311, B315, B317, B323, B324, B340, B346, B347, B361, B366, B367, B379, B389, B393, B401, B408, B469, B493, B506, B674, B826, S16, S24, S34, S56
Juilliard String Quartet, p. 11, W44c, D75, D78, B136, B146, B194, B710, B735

Kalish, Gilbert, D31
Kapell, William, B548
Kastendieck, Miles, p. 20, B542, B649
Katims, Milton, p. 11, B194
Kay, Ulysses, D111
Keats, Sheila, p. 5, p. 10, p. 18
Kendall, Christopher, W59k, B423
Kennedy, Robert F., p. 19, B176, B458
Kenyon, Nicholas, B543

Kerner, Leighton, B546, B547
Kimmelman, Michael, B548
Kindler, Hans, D1
King, Martin Luther, p. 19, B458
Kirchner, Leon, D29
Klein, Howard, B203, B549
Klein, Kenneth, B128
Klotzman, Dorothy, W53s, B626
Knitzer, Jack, D70
Kocmieroski, Matthew, D30, B711
Kodály, Zoltán, p. 4
Kohon Quartet, D76
Kolodin, Irving, p. 20, B551, B552, B612, B649
Kosman, Joshua, B557, B808
Kostelanetz, André, p. 14, p. 17, W53, W53a, W53b, W53e, W53h, W53i, W62a, W62b, W63a, W80a, W80b, D48, D115, B468, B476, B549, B571, B590, B682
Koussevitzky, Mme Natalie, W29
Koussevitzky, Serge, p. 7, p. 8, p. 9, p. 10, p. 11, W13c, W14a, W14d, W14e, W22a, W22b, W22e, W25a, W25b, W28d, W29a, B67, B107, B217, B312, B428, B429, B496, B498, B520, B642, B675, S4
Koussevitzky Music Foundation, p. 10, p. 15, W29, W58, B642, S72
Krawitz, Herman, B117, B119, B186
Krips, Josef, W22p, W49g, B467
Kroeger, Karl, B560
Kupferberg, Herbert, B562
Kutzing, Erika, D70

La Farge, Christopher, B89
Labunski, Felix, D65
LaClede Band, W67a
Lane, Louis, W63f, B515
Lang, David, D12
Lang, Paul Henry, B45
Larsen, Libby, D14
Latham, William, D17
Laurentian Singers, W54, W54a
Layton, Robert, B255
League of Composers, p. 8, W19, B298, B351, B410, B716
Lehwalder, Heidi, D40
Lenox Quartet, W44d, B732

Shaw, Robert, p. 9, p. 11, p. 20, W14p, W26a, W72a, W75d, B128, B194, B419, B643
Sheldon, Gary, W53x, B454
Sherman, Robert, B411
Shewan, Robert, D11, D64, D99, B759
Shewan, Stephen, D11, D64, D99, B748
Shields, Roger, D104
Shupp, E.E., Jr., B660
Sibelius, Jean, B625
Sidlin, Murry, W53v, B659
Siebert, F. Mark, B779
Siegmeister, Elie, S10
Sigma Alpha Iota, p. 14, W47, B72, B359, S23
Sill, Andrews, W14u, B14, B444
Simmons, Walter, B742
Singing City, W25e, B762
Skelton, William, W61a
Skrowaczewski, Stanislaw, W59g, W59j, B530, B532
Slatkin, Leonard, p. 22, W14r, W14s, W14t, W22x, W22z, W22aa, W39f, W49h, W49i, W49k, W53r, W53u, W53w, W63c, W63d, W79d, W81d, W89a, W95c, D6, D7, D26, D57, D97, D118, B189, B204, B279, B417, B430, B489, B490, B491, B523, B529, B580, B585, B616, B630, B644, B645, B652, B653, B655, B664, B666, B696, B697, B703, B704, B705, B706, B757
Slonimsky, Nicolas, p. 8, B363, B743, S1
Smallens, Alexander, p. 8, W20a, W21b, B780, B782
Smith, Cecil, B744
Smith, Gregg, D10, D13, D15, D32, D33, D45, D47, D62, D63, D68, D69, B840
Smith, Lawrence Leighton, W53dd, B445
Smith, Moses, p. 7
Smith, William, W53n, W60c, B694
Snook, Paul A., B671
Solomon, Izler, p. 16, W39c, W59a
Sousa, John Philip, D9, S62
Sowerby, Leo, D11, D64, D99, B748
Speyer Experimental Junior High School for Boys, p. 3

Spivacke, Harold, W64
St. Lawrence University, W54
St. Louis Symphony Orchestra, p. 22, W14r, W14s, W14t, W22x, W54d, W63c, W79d, W89, W89a, W95, D6, D7, D26, D57, D97, D118
St. Paul Chamber Orchestra, W29n, B503
Starobin, David, D61
State University of New York College at Fredonia Concert Band, D17
Statue of Liberty, p. 23, B760, B768, B770, B771, B774, B786
Steigerwalt, Gary, W47b, W86c, D24, B846
Stein, Stephen, W53cc, B465
Steinberg, William, W29c, W65a, D86, B596
Steinway, Mrs. Theodore, p. 8
Stern, Isaac, p. 13, W39a, W39b, B237, B484, B493, B588, B708
Sternfeld, Frederick W., B854
Steuber, Lillian, p. 14, W47a
Stevens, Denis, p. 14, B674
Stith, Marice, D9, D15, D20, D122
Stokowski, Leopold, p. 8, W14f, W28c, B189
Stravinsky, Igor, B471, B493, S15
Stutsman, Grace May, B675
Stuttgart Symphony, W32d
Suderberg, Robert, D94
Sullivan, Dan, B370
Switten, Henry, p. 7, W10a
Symphony of the Air, W59b
Symphony Orchestra of the National Taiwan Academy of Arts, W53s, B626
Symposium on Music Criticism (Harvard University), p. 12
Szell, George, W59e, D72

Taft, William Howard, p. 3
Taggard, Genevieve, W17, W20, W26
Tanglewood Festival, W22cc, W23b, W49h, B486, B492, B608, B616, B627
Taylor, Deems, S5
Tchaikovsky, Peter Ilyich, D17
Teacher's Convocation on the Performing Arts, B370

About the Author

K. GARY ADAMS is a Professor of Music at Bridgewater College in Virginia.